The Rise of the Tea Party

THE RISE OF THE TEA PARTY

*Political Discontent and Corporate Media
in the Age of Obama*

by ANTHONY DiMAGGIO

MONTHLY REVIEW PRESS
New York

Library of Congress Cataloging-in-Publication Data
Dimaggio, Anthony R., 1980–
  The rise of the Tea Party : political discontent and corporate media in
the age of Obama / by Anthony Dimaggio.
     p. cm.
  Includes bibliographical references and index.
  ISBN 978-1-58367-247-1 (pbk. : alk. paper) — ISBN 978-1-58367-248-8
(cloth : alk. paper) 1. Tea Party movement. 2. Tea Party movement—Press
coverage. 3. Mass media—Political aspects—United States—History—21st
century. I. Title.
 JK2391.T43D56 2011
 320.520973—dc23
                        2011040870

Monthly Review Press
146 West 29th Street, Suite 6W
New York, NY 10001
www.monthlyreview.org

5 4 3 2 1

Contents

To Mary, Frankie, and my family,
for all your love and support over the years

Acknowledgments

I want to thank all my friends and family for helping me along the way in finishing this book and in pursuing my academic and intellectual endeavors. At Illinois State University, I thank Carlos Parodi, Jamal Nassar, and Ali Riaz for all their help over the years and for their mentoring. Journalistically, I thank those who've helped me along the way, including Paul Street, Jeffrey St. Clair, Alexander Cockburn, Chris Spannos, Michael Albert, and Leslie Thatcher. In my graduate studies at University of Illinois, Chicago, I thank Doris Graber, Andrew McFarland, Andrew Rojecki, and Evan McKenzie. Special thanks to everyone at the Open University of the Left as well, especially Robert Hughes.

I am indebted to a number of scholars and intellectuals who have helped review my media research over the years. Many thanks go out to Bob McChesney, Michael Parenti, Yahya Kamalipour, Lee Artz, Danny Schechter, Deepa Kumar, Peter Phillips, Henry Giroux, Mickey Huff, and all the people at Monthly Review Press who helped me prepare this book and my last. My thanks go out especially to Michael Yates, who was instrumental in streamlining this book and making it readable for general and scholarly audiences. Thanks also go out to Noam Chomsky and Edward Herman for their work in the area of propaganda. Your research has influenced my own thinking and research in so many ways. Professionally, Paul Street deserves praise, as our long conversations over the last year and a half were vital in helping me flesh out the thesis for this book. Paul, your inspiration and intellect are invaluable, and I am indebted to you for everything you've done on this project.

Finally, I want to thank my friends and family for all their assistance over the years. Thanks to Mom, Dad, Kelly, Alissa, Sam, Marty, Jon, Paul and Erin, Kevin, Dan, Tony, Grant, Amentahru, Jake, Zach G., Wael, Erik and Stef Abderhalden, and Erik Lisauskas for being there for me. Most important, I want to thank my wife, Mary, and my son Frankie for being by my side. I could not have gotten through this project without your patience, love, and support.

Manufacturing Dissent in a Time of Public Distrust

This book is not simply about the Tea Party. Rather, it is an exploration of the ways in which business interests dominate society through the power of ideas and the pull of material affluence. The Tea Party plays an important role in the dissemination of pro-business ideology, but it is merely one of many forces to do so. Furthermore, the Tea Party is largely a mass-mediated force. Contrary to popular depictions, the Tea Party relies upon elite, top-down organizing for its success as the group serves the interests of the Republican Party and business power. The power of the Tea Party to influence the public mind, then, is a product of corporate America and Republican institutional forces.

The Tea Party exercises tremendous power over the public in the realm of ideas. Ideas can be extremely effective in influencing the public policy attitudes of the masses. They do not, however, operate in a vacuum or independent of the material forces that are at work in a capitalist society. Sociologists and public relations scholars David Miller and William Dinan argue that "ideas are produced and fight their fight only in the context of the material circumstances in which all—economy, polity, ideology—operate . . . it is just as wrong to imagine that the market runs the game by itself as it is to assume, as some have, that ideas can float free."[1] Miller and Dinan are right. In a political culture dominated by capital, ideas rarely emerge independently of material interests. Although many Americans like to believe they formulate their opinions independently of pro-business doctrinal constraints, such thoughts are unwarranted. Materialist explanations that acknowledge business interests as the most powerful political faction cannot be ignored by those examining American politics and culture.

The forces of corporate capitalism and the Tea Party are intertwined. The ideas promoted by the Tea Party, including rhetorical distrust of government, opposition to healthcare reform, and supposed rebellion against the politics-as-usual status quo in Washington, draw on a romanticism of "free market" capitalism disseminated across American political culture. These messages grew in popularity among the American people during 2009 and 2010. The Tea Party has a number of institutional forces to thank for its victory in the war of ideas, including the mass media, the Republican Party, and business interests. It may seem paradoxical to claim that the Tea Party has gathered prominence by rebelling against government while at the same time benefiting from government support. A closer examination of the group, however, finds that there is no contradiction. Tea Partiers may be effective in projecting the impression that they are against "big government" and Wall Street corruption, but a review of the group's politics demonstrates they are situated within the bipartisan system and reliant on corporate funding to survive.

The Tea Party's dependence on institutional forces guarantees it a privileged political position. In the war of ideas, not all participants are equal. Business interests are the most privileged interests operating within the political system.[2] Scholars have long concluded that business is the most privileged force in American politics, and that understanding is explored at greater length at the beginning of chapter 1. Business power extends beyond their ability to invest in or withdraw investment dollars from specific localities. Business dominance also reaches past the powers corporations exercise through the electoral system and via campaign contributions. There are many paths through which corporate power is exercised in the United States, but one of the most important is through the power of ideas, as seen in the dominance of "free market" capitalist propaganda in the United States. This book is most concerned with the powers of propaganda, a concept that is regularly misunderstood in the American political and economic mainstream. Many Americans associate propaganda with the rhetoric accompanying the genocidal violence of Nazi Germany or the fascism of Mussolini or Stalin. All too often, however, Americans ignore the ways in which U.S. officials use propaganda to further their own ends. The Tea Party's use of propaganda has also been marginalized in public discourse.

Propaganda is an important tool of political and economic elites. The Bush administration's public relations campaign designed to sell the public on the (nonexistent) Weapons of Mass Destruction (WMD) threat from Iraq was the most brazen propaganda campaign in recent years, but not the only one. Propaganda initiatives undertaken by the business community may be difficult to spot, but that does not mean they are any less common than those initiated by government. As with the case of WMD, the rise of the Tea Party and the right-wing backlash against healthcare reform were marked by staggering levels of propaganda.

Most Americans are unaware of the relationship between the Tea Party and propaganda. The selective application of the concept of propaganda restricts the public's understanding of the term, and obscures its relevance to the study of this "movement" and, as we shall see, its relationship to healthcare reform. In official and media discourse, propaganda is understood as something engaged in by "other countries and their leaders." We must move beyond this parochial "understanding" of propaganda if we expect to understand how manipulation operates in a democratic society.

Many intellectuals, officials, and media pundits will respond uncomfortably when confronted with the claim that U.S. politics is propagandistic. Polls do not question the public about whether they believe political and business officials practice propaganda. The "average" American, however, may very well feel this way, considering that most Americans distrust their leaders and view them as unrepresentative of the public at large. For one stark example, one can look to a majority of Americans who have consistently believed since the early 1970s that government is "run by a few big interests looking out for themselves."[3]

PROPAGANDA DEFINED

In order to understand propaganda, we must begin with a concrete definition. Psychologists Anthony Pratkanis and Elliot Aronson define propaganda as "the communication of a point of view with the ultimate goal of having the recipient of the appeal come to 'voluntarily' accept this position as if it were his or her own." This definition goes back to early twentieth-century foundations of American propaganda, as Pratkanis and

Aronson note that it "was used to describe the persuasion tactics employed during World War I and those later used by totalitarian regimes."[4] At that time, early pioneers of propaganda such as Edward Bernays and Walter Lippmann played a vital role in promoting the government's pro-war messages. They spoke favorably of propaganda as driving "the conscious and intelligent manipulation of the organized habits and opinions of the masses," and as necessary in light of the public's alleged inability to form coherent political opinions.[5]

As Bernays explained, the dissemination of propaganda is motivated by efforts "to capture our minds in the interest of some policy or commodity or idea" to benefit those "who manipulate this unseen mechanism of society." Those who utilize propaganda against the public "constitute an invisible government, which is the true ruling power of our country."[6] As the philosophical founder of public relations and modern advertising, Bernays envisioned "the public as a malleable mass of protoplasm, plastic raw material that—in the hands of a skilled manipulator—could be manufactured at will."[7] Bernays felt that the public was unable to serve as anything more than a passive vessel for the acceptance of business and political propaganda. As he concluded in the years following his propagandizing on behalf of the U.S. entrance into the First World War, "no serious sociologist any longer believes that the voice of the people expresses any divine or especially wise and lofty idea."[8]

The public's definition of propaganda has changed over time. Bernays's early definition framed propaganda as neutral in connotation: it could be used for positive or negative purposes. Bernays also saw propaganda more generically—as an attempt to persuade the public through the dissemination of one point of view at the expense of another. Others now define propaganda as the restriction of views expressed in political discourse to those views accepted by political officials and business leaders.[9] Many associate propaganda with the manipulation of public emotion and fears in the pursuit of specific political and economic objectives.[10] In this book, I define propaganda as including all of the components described above, although I stress some parts more than others. On the most generic level, propaganda includes the promotion of one point of view at the expense of another. This definition is limited, however, in terms of promoting a critical understanding of the role of propaganda in manipulating the public. In line with Chomsky and Herman, I argue that propaganda is also practiced through restricting views to those expressed by political and economic elites.

Propaganda campaigns rely on the blatant manipulation of fear and emotion, which I document at length throughout this book. However, propaganda at its core is driven by the tailoring of "acceptable" viewpoints to those expressed in the bipartisan American political spectrum, and to views that are supported by business interests. The Tea Party's messages reside within this propaganda system, as seen in its support for pro-business dogma that constitutes the core of Republican politics.

CORPORATE HEGEMONY

The study of propaganda encompasses the manipulation of the public in favor of market fundamentalism. By market fundamentalism, I am referring to an ideology that eschews costly regulation of corporate America, stresses the minimization of public services and common goods, and frames business elites and the public as beholden to no higher social purpose than the pursuit of profits and the consumption of material goods. The rise of the Tea Party is merely the most recent chapter in a process whereby public discourse is dominated by market fundamentalist voices. Tea Partiers claim they oppose Wall Street corruption, but in reality these same individuals refuse to blame business for causing the 2008 economic crisis, and they are all too willing to embrace propagandistic claims related to Obama "socialism" and the Democratic Party's supposed destruction of the U.S. economy and way of life.[11] Such demagoguery is a necessary part of any propaganda campaign dedicated to preventing progressive reforms. This particular campaign demonstrates the strong rightward drift of American politics, with the Tea Party's successes pushing the Democratic Party even further away from promoting working-class interests.

Consumerist ideology is a central component of the rightward drift in American culture. This topic has been the subject of extensive scholarly attention. The public's embrace of business and consumerist propaganda is explored at length by those who study modern advertising and public relations. The emergence of the public relations (PR) industry in the 1920s and its subsequent ascendancy in later decades are seen as key moments in the development of the public's pro-business sentiment. The public relations industry serves as the "cutting edge" of business power, targeting the hearts and minds of the American public.[12] Public relations scholar Stuart Ewen concludes that the public relations industry "offered itself as a means of efficiently creating consumers and as a way of homogeneously 'controlling the consumption of a product.'"[13] But modern advertising performs a more vital function. Business leaders understood by the early twentieth century, Ewen explains, that "the mere selling of products was no longer an adequate goal of advertising." Rather, the ultimate end of advertising became the marketing of an entire consumerist "way of life determined by a profit-seeking, mass productive [capitalist] machinery." So began a comprehensive project of "social planning," one that was designed "to create a national unified culture around the social bond of the consumer market."[14]

Instrumental in creating a mass consumer market is the concept of hegemony. Hegemony, simply defined, refers to the ability of business entrepreneurs and political officials to exercise "leadership" over the public by cultivating public support for capitalist values.[15] The concept of hegemony was originally developed by the Italian Marxist Antonio Gramsci as an explanation for why individuals fail to rebel against business privilege and power. He saw the "active and practical involvement of hegemonized groups" in embracing pro-business propaganda and ideology as the major reason for the failure of the public to rebel.[16] Gramsci's insights into the study of hegemony remain relevant to the study of mass media, politics, and propaganda.

Hegemony involves "the process of moral, philosophical, and political leadership that a social group attains only with the active consent of other important social groups."[17] Business elites engage in "conscious ideological warfare," imposing a pro-business agenda within the public policy process and limiting government responsiveness to the masses.[18] The perceived benevolence and virtue of the capitalist ideology is not produced by coercion but rather is seen as common sense by the general public, with alternative socialistic and other leftist ideologies deemed unworthy of consideration.[19] Under free market capitalism, the welfare state is consistently under assault by business interests. Political and business elites propagandize the public in favor of pro-business dogmas and against social welfare programs benefitting the masses, working class, and poor. By opposing mass-based welfare policies, Americans are embracing policies that work directly against their own self-interest.[20] As this book will show, the Tea Party is instrumental in intensifying the false consciousness that arises from its attacks on progressive healthcare reforms such as universal healthcare. However, the dominant pro-business, anti-welfare ideology is not universally accepted. Gramsci's theory of hegemony also encompasses active resistance on the part of subordinate social groups. As critical theorist Daniel Little explains, Gramsci argued that the proletariat has the ability to influence the terms of its consciousness, so there is an extended struggle between the bourgeoisie and the proletariat over the terms of the representation of the existing social reality. The bourgeoisie generally exercises "hegemony" over the terms of ideology, through its control of the instruments of consciousness; but the proletariat can exert influence through its own cultural institutions. This perspective introduces a major change into the classical theory of ideology, in that it denies that the subordinate class is simply the passive tool of the dominant ideology.[21]

This book explores in detail the ways in which the subordinate class rejects hegemonic messages, while at the same time it falls prey to these messages in relation to the debate over national healthcare reform.

MANUFACTURING DISSENT

Manufacturing public opinion extends beyond advertising and public relations. In my previous book, *When Media Goes to War*, I documented the distrust of the public that is shared by corporate media executives and political elites.[22] Government officials view progressive public attitudes, in addition to left-leaning dissidents, with suspicion. Discussion of such distrust traces back to the seminal work of scholars such as Noam Chomsky and Edward Herman, both of whom document officialdom's efforts to "manufacture consent" by restricting public dialogue to the opinions expressed by political and business elites. The concept of "manufacturing consent" was not developed by Chomsky or Herman, but rather by the journalist and philosopher Walter Lippmann.[23] Lippmann served under the U.S. Committee on Public Information, the vast government propaganda agency dedicated to convincing the public of the need to enter the First World War. He coordinated the formation of a "publicity bureau" with President Woodrow Wilson, which one historian described as a "clearinghouse for information on government activities that would mobilize the propagandistic skills of artists, intellectuals, journalists, and other media professionals from around the country."[24] Lippmann saw technocratic "social engineers" and "social scientists," among other planners and intellectuals, as the rightful heirs of decision making in a "democratic" society.[25] Extensive public deliberation on political issues was seen as counterproductive and harmful, since the public was allegedly incapable of understanding the nuances inherent in any policy debate, due primarily to time constraints and other logical problems.[26]

Lippmann was contemptuous of the idea that the public could (or should) play an active role in politics. Putting the scholarly romanticism of Lippmann aside,[27] he was open in his distrust of the American people, as this review of his ideas demonstrates:

- Lippmann described the "popular will" of the people as "erratic" in its "working." He derided those advocating more direct forms of democracy, instead declaring that "we must abandon the notion that democratic government can be the direct expression of the will of the people. We must abandon the notion that the people govern."[28]

- He advocated the "manipulation of the masses through symbols," which "may be the only quick way of having a critical thing done." Symbols were deemed necessary for manipulation in such circumstances that "cannot wait for a referendum or endure publicity," such as "during war," "when a nation" is forced to "trust strategy to a very few minds." Lippmann felt that these individuals (of whom he was one) would altruistically look out for the interests of the broader public.[29]

- Lippmann candidly admitted that "every leader" can be seen "in some degree [as] a propagandist . . . the official finds himself deciding more and more consciously what facts, in what setting, in what guise he shall permit the public to know" about the political and social issues around them.[30]

- He spoke with disdain of the "oligarchical tendencies" of "collective action," while dismissing the "dogma of democracy" that receives *rhetorical* support from political officialdom. The American people, he concluded, constituted a "bewildered public," due to their lack of "coherent political training." Basing policy making on majority rule, he felt, was an "absurdity," since the public is "uninformed, irrelevant, and meddlesome"—ensuring a "congenital difference between the masterful few and the ignorant many."[31]

- Lippmann felt that the "common interests very largely elude public opinion entirely, and can be managed only by a specialized class whose personal interests reach beyond the locality." While admitting that this specialized class can at times behave in an "irresponsible" fashion, this did not prevent Lippmann from participating in such manipulation. In the name of promoting the public good and "making the world safe for democracy," Lippmann's Committee for Public Information operated independently of the allegedly ignorant masses, who were seen as unable to comprehend their own best interests.[32]

- Stripped of any direct participatory role in governing, Lippmann saw the public's only role as one of a passive advocate of the agendas promoted by political and business elites. "The intrinsic merits of a [policy] question are not for the public . . . the analysis and the solution of a question are not for the public . . . the specific, technical, intimate criteria required in the handling of a question are not for the public . . . what is left for the public is a judgment as to whether the actors in the controversy are following a settled rule of behavior or their own arbitrary desires."[33]

Lippmann's blatant paternalism toward the public is clear when evaluating the above excerpts. More important than his many conclusions with regard to the public, however, is whether those opinions were embraced by political and business leaders in subsequent years. I spent a significant amount time in my book *When Media Goes to War* documenting the ways in which political elites resist the public's will in the area of foreign policy formulation. This opposition to public opinion on foreign policy issues is also documented at length in other studies.[34] Left unexamined in those works, however, is whether the same pattern holds with regard to domestic politics.

Domestically, public policy works according to the same principles of official contempt and paternalism described above. In *Politicians Don't Pander* political scientists Lawrence Jacobs and Robert Shapiro find through their surveys of political officials and public policy case studies that "politicians manipulate public opinion by tracking public thinking to select the actions and words that resonate with the public." Politicians do not identify what the public thinks so that they can implement the popular will; rather, they try to change public opinion to fit a preexisting policy. Jacobs and Shapiro quote Republican and Democratic pollsters who represent leaders in Congress and the White House, admitting that they "don't use a poll to reshape a [public] program, but to reshape your argumentation for the program so that the public supports it."[35]

Analysis throughout this book confirms Jacobs and Shapiro's findings, which demonstrated that public opinion extended well to the left of the views expressed by both parties and the mass media during the Clinton era. In the 2009–10 period, majority support for a public option or universal healthcare was disregarded by political officials. Most saw these preferences as irrelevant in light of the ascendancy of Tea Party–Republican propaganda during 2009 and 2010 as well as the potential encroachment upon the profits of the healthcare industry.

THE PROPAGANDA MODEL DEFINED

Critical studies of media focus on the propagandistic nature of "mainstream" reporting. In his work *Triumph of the Market* Edward Herman depicts journalists as hegemonic actors, as "members of the economic elite," working "with associated class biases." Subsequent analyses reinforce the role of reporters as hegemonic, establishment-oriented actors.[36] Pro-business reporting manifests itself through the "biases of corporate advertisers, whose ideological assumptions and fondness for the status quo is similar to that of the media's owners," and "reinforce[s] establishment positions" and "marginalize[s] dissent."[37] The "final factor" listed by Herman in "media control by market forces is the ideological premises of the system, which reflect a culture centered in private property." Included within this corporate culture are the perceived "merits of free enterprise" and the "threat of state ownership and intervention" against the power, prestige, and privilege of the private economy.[38]

Business pressures represent one of a number of media "filters" established by Chomsky and Herman. In their analysis of U.S. media, they establish a propaganda model for describing reporting of American foreign policy that contains five filters. In *Manufacturing Consent*, the authors describe these as including: 1) "concentrated [business] ownership, owner wealth, and profit orientation of the dominant mass media firms"; 2) "advertising as the primary income source of the mass media"; 3) "the reliance of the media on information provided by government, business, and 'experts' funded and approved by these primary sources and agents of power"; 4) the use of official and elite-based 'flak' as a means of disciplining the media"; and 5) "anti-communism as a national religion and control mechanism."[39] Operating together, these forces play an instrumental role in molding media content in favor of business interests, and in reinforcing corporate power. The explanatory power of these filters is validated in a number of studies that followed *Manufacturing Consent*, although the propaganda model is still ignored by most "mainstream" scholars.[40]

THE PROPAGANDA MODEL RECONCEPTUALIZED

Any theory of power should consider the primary roles of material and idea-based forces (the latter firmly rooted within the capitalist system) in determining political attitudes and in promoting business power. In this book I establish a propaganda model as applied not only to the mass media but to the broader area of public opinion. Whereas the traditional propaganda model draws upon the filters established by Chomsky and Herman, my propaganda model as applied to public opinion is more encompassing in that it seeks to identify a wide range of societal factors that play a role in influencing *public opinion* in favor of business power. The list I provide should not be seen as exhaustive, however, since it is limited by the questions surveyed in standard public opinion polling questionnaires.

A propaganda model for public opinion posits that material as well as intangible forces work upon the minds of the public in order to reinforce business power and class rule. These forces operate through the processes of socialization and indoctrination. Simply stated, those who grow up benefiting from more affluent, privileged backgrounds, and those who are more likely to be exposed to pro-business dogmas are increasingly likely to form opinions that fall within a "market fundamentalist" hegemonic framework. The filters that drive this process are potentially many, and this book examines many of the most important ones.

In establishing a new propaganda model I argue that the power of affluence and pro-business dogma in molding the public mind is a product of the American class structure and the privileging of pro-business perspectives within that structure. Pro-business positions are driven by intangible forces such as corporate propaganda, as well as by the material advantages conferred by income and wealth. I provide ample evidence that privilege, and the ideas of the privileged, are vital in strengthening and reinforcing public support for ruling-class values. Hegemonic forces are most successful when socializing more affluent social groups, though they are also effective to a lesser extent in molding the minds of the less privileged.

My propaganda model is based upon hegemonic powers of two types: the material and the intangible. These two forces include at least nine independent filters which, when combined, play a powerful role in molding the public's political attitudes. I assess the predictive power of these filters by undertaking a statistical analysis—also known as multivariate regression analysis—that allows me to examine the power of each variable while also controlling for all the others. It is through this process that I can measure the causational powers of each variable, since all of the other variables are controlled for. By "controlling for," I am referring to the statistical procedure referred to as "multivariate regression analysis" whereby I measure the relationship between individual variables on the one hand and opinions of the Tea Party and other public policy issues on the other, while holding other variables constant. Through this process, one is able to isolate the individual effects of each variable, when compared to the other variables in question.

Before proceeding, some definitions are in order. Materialist filters are those that relate to the tangible lifetime advantages that individuals possess because of their personal backgrounds. These variables are expected to play a role in the public's formation of political attitudes. All of these variables are statistically differentiated by income to show how their impact might be affected by the fact that some individuals within each group are richer and others are poorer. Included among these filters are: race (distinguishing between whites versus non-whites), sex (men versus women), income (higher versus lower income), education (higher versus lower education), political efficacy (voters versus non-voters), and class and race-based religious fundamentalism (higher- versus lower-income "born again" Evangelicals, and white versus non-white Evangelicals).[41] In chapter 6, I include a seventh material variable—individual health insurance coverage (the insured versus uninsured)—in my analysis of healthcare reform. As already mentioned, all of these variables are characterized by marked differentiation in affluence, with the former of each pair being more affluent in that they earn higher incomes, and the latter being less affluent and earning lower incomes.[42]

The choice of the above variables is based upon the expectation that the privileged within each group benefit from many years (in many cases a lifetime) of material advantage, in addition to socialization that is reinforced by peer groups, family, and friends in favor of hegemonic pro-business views. One could call the privileged within these groups the "haves." These individuals should favor business power for a number of reasons, including the following:

- The highly educated should be more indoctrinated in favor of business-friendly dogmas than the less educated as a result of their materially privileged position as higher-income earners and as a result of the pro-business, neoliberal propaganda that increasingly drives the educational process.[43]

- Men and whites should be more likely to support conservative business propaganda due to their privileged position in society with regard to occupational earnings, occupational prestige, and their freedom from race- and gender-based discrimination.

- Higher-income earners should be more likely to oppose progressive policies and support pro-business ones by the sheer fact that they stand to lose more as a result of progressive taxation and redistribution of wealth from the wealthier to the disadvantaged.

- Voters should be expected to be more establishment-oriented in their economic views by nature of their greater participation in the political-economic system—which is likely a reflection of their material affluence. Previous examination also shows that voters are generally more privileged, from an economic point of view.[44]

- In light of their generally high levels of privilege and material affluence, well-off (white and higher earning) Evangelicals should take more business-friendly positions than non-Protestants and poorer, non-white Evangelicals.

- Finally, those with health insurance—as a product of their good fortune—should be less concerned with progressive policy initiatives such as those extending healthcare to the disadvantaged and poor. In a neoliberal society, people are taught that their occupational success (to which healthcare is tied) is a product of their own hard work, and that those who are less fortunate (without a job or health insurance) have their own personal laziness to blame.

Also included in my filters are four intangible forces: political ideology, partisanship, media consumption, and political attentiveness. These four variables influence the public mind in less direct materialist ways. They are not differentiated by income, but instead by stronger and weaker levels of support for pro-business, hegemonic *ideas*.[45] Among those that are more likely to reinforce business power are self-identified conservatives, self-identified Republicans, Fox News viewers, the politically attentive (who follow politics closely in the mass media). Among those less likely to reinforce business dogmas are self-identified independents and liberals, self-identified Democrats, non–Fox News viewers, and those less attentive to politics (and to media reporting of politics).

It is true that most if not all the variables I describe as materialist can also be seen as intangible. An individual who grows up male, for example, not only benefits from a higher income when compared to women, he also benefits from preferential treatment on a cultural level, in light of the rampant sexism and discrimination directed against women. The intangible nature of the materialist factors included above should not be ignored. However, I am forced to draw some line between the two types of forces in light of the fact that some of these variables are based almost entirely on the power of ideas (in the case of media consumption, partisanship, political attentiveness, and ideology), whereas the others are dramatically less so. Fox News viewers, for example, are no more likely to earn higher incomes when compared to non-Fox viewers. Fox News viewers should be expected to support hegemonic business views primarily due to the indoctrinating power of this media outlet, rather than because of the nonexistent affluence conferred upon them as Fox viewers. Along the same lines, forces that seem intangible are, in reality, heavily grounded in materialism and affluence. For example, Republicans, conservatives, the politically attentive, and Fox News viewers may not statistically be more affluent in terms of their income, but they are part of institutions that are—at their core—concerned with promoting the interests of business elites and corporate capitalism. I continue to refer to these variables as intangible throughout this book, however, because they are more directly based upon the power of ideas *relative to* the other variables described above, which are differentiated more directly by income.

Central to this study is the prediction that intangible forces play *the most important role* in influencing public opinion, even more so than those variables marked by material affluence. I expect this to be the case, for one, because partisanship, ideology, political attentiveness, and media consumption are more explicitly political in their orientation, compared to factors such as race, sex, and income, which linger more in the background with regard to their political relevance. Women may be more likely to sympathize with progressive opinions because of their disadvantaged material position, but this does not mean something is programmed into women mandating that they be progressive.

Secondly, and more important, intangible forces are expected to play the dominant role in molding opinions because of their significance in a democratic society. In a democracy, the primary means of persuasion is based upon the building of consent, rather than through the blunt instrument of military force. The most effective way to build such consent is through the power of ideas, as reflected in variables such as partisanship, ideology, political attentiveness, and media consumption. Other variables may also be effective in driving opinions (such as sex and race), although their influence on political attitudes can also vary according to other factors such as geography. The intangible forces above, in contrast, do not vary geographically. You see the same messages from Republican officials and conservative media pundits regardless of where you live. Washington-based political debates remain the same whether you are following them in Illinois or Texas.

MEDIA POWER IN POLITICS

Mass media outlets across-the-board, rather than simply individual outlets like Fox News, influence public attitudes in favor of hegemonic, business-friendly attitudes. I use political attentiveness in this study as a proxy measurement for attention to the mass media. This choice is warranted in light of data I present in chapters 4 and 6, which demonstrates that those who paid close attention to the Tea Party and healthcare reform were overwhelmingly reliant upon the mass media as the primary mechanism through which they gain their political knowledge. Throughout the rest of this study, greater and weaker "political attentiveness" should be understood as referring to greater and lesser attention to mass media reporting on political issues. In a society in which most knowledge of politics is obtained not through direct experiences but through secondhand sources, the media play the central role in promoting hegemonic messages.

The role of the mass media in imposing hegemonic views increases dramatically during times of extended public policy debate, when the need to manufacture opinions is most vital. It is during these periods of public discussion that hegemonic messages are the most likely to break through to the general public and reach less privileged demographic groups. These disadvantaged groups are typically less in tune with the dominant political and economic rhetoric driving Washington–based policy debates. Those hailing from more affluent demographic backgrounds are more attentive to politics, and more often exposed to elitist messages throughout their lives. Such behavioral patterns help explain why these groups are more likely to hold hegemonic, pro-business views, even at the onset of national public policy debates.

THE LIMITS OF CONSENT

This book presents evidence that hegemonic material and intangible powers exercise great control over the public mind. These powers, however, are not without their limits. As Gramsci argued, many people *do* reject the conventional wisdom disseminated by business and political elites. These people more often than not hail from less privileged demographic groups. A number of less privileged demographic groups are more likely to reject the *entire* capitalist political-economic system upon which the United States is based. Similarly, those who are less regularly exposed to intangible hegemonic forces are less susceptible to market fundamentalist views. Table 1 presents the results from a Pew Research Center poll from early 2010 that questioned the public about their support for capitalism and socialism. The poll revealed high levels of skepticism of the capitalist status quo, and significant minority support for alternative political and economic models. Table 1 simultaneously demonstrates the power of pro-business hegemony among privileged and disadvantaged demographic groups, while also shedding light upon the limits of that hegemony, as seen in the resistance to capitalism and openness to socialism among the less privileged. In confirming business power, material and intangible hegemonic forces encourage pro-business views in all the groups documented in Table 1.

The weaknesses of hegemony, however, are also apparent in national survey data. Estimates from the Gallup and Pew polling organizations demonstrate that total positive perceptions of socialism among the public are surprisingly high, reaching as much as 29 to 36 percent of the population.[46] Of course, neither poll examined what Americans meant when they said they supported "socialism," but such initial results are encouraging for those on the left in light of decades of political and media propaganda dedicated to demonizing socialistic ideologies and the very notion of common goods. The weaknesses of hegemony are also seen among the

TABLE 1: Opinions of Capitalism and Socialism as a Function
of Material and Intangible Forces

Demographic Group	Percent with Positive Perceptions of Capitalism	Percent with Positive Perceptions of Socialism
Men	68%	23%
Women	55%	30%
Higher Education (college)	67%	23%
Lower Education (no college)	50%	33%
Higher Income (greater than $75k)	75%	19%
Middle Income ($50–75k)	56%	18%
Lower Income (less than $50k)	53%	36%
Registered Voters	64%	25%
Non-voters	46%	39%
Whites	63%	23%
Non-Whites	53%	47%
Republicans	71%	12%
Independents	61%	25%
Democrats	53%	43%
White Evangelicals	59%	19%
Non-White Evangelicals	54%	48%
Higher-Income Evangelicals (greater than $75k)	71%	13%
Middle-Income Evangelicals ($50–$75k)	61%	19%
Lower-Income Evangelicals (less than $50k)	53%	33%
Conservatives	68%	17%
Moderates	59%	27%
Liberals	51%	51%

Note: No media variables are included here because individuals were not serveyed about media consumption for the April 2010 Pew Research Center survey.

Source: Pew Research Center, 2010

disadvantaged. Of those who responded to the Pew survey, sympathy toward socialism was strongest among less privileged groups and those less exposed to intangible hegemonic forces. Employing statistical analysis that controls for all the variables listed in Table 1, I find that nearly all the material and intangible variables, including race, income, party, ideology, sex, education, and Evangelism (as based on race), are statistically significant predictors of opinions with regard to socialism and capitalism.[47] Only Evangelism (based on income) and political efficacy (based

FIGURE 1: Support for Capitalism and Socialism by Income

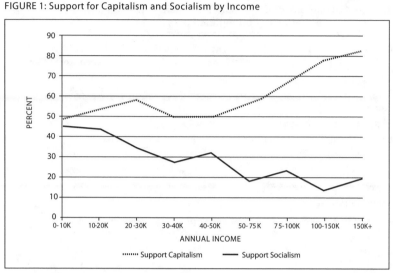

Source: Pew Research Center, 2010

on voting) are not statistically significant, although Table 1 suggests that
the differences within these two groups are rather large, ranging from 14
to 20 percentage points greater support for capitalism and opposition to
socialism among voters and higher-income Evangelicals.

The differences between demographic groups in Table 1 are stark.
Nearly half of non-whites and non-white Evangelicals share a positive perception of socialism, compared to whites and white Evangelicals, who are
strongly opposed to socialism and supportive of capitalism. Other less
privileged groups are stronger in their sympathies for socialism. For
example, nearly one-third of women and lower-income Evangelicals, and
approximately four in ten of non-voters, are sympathetic to socialism.
Men and higher-income Evangelicals express a stronger commitment to
capitalism and opposition to socialism. The intangible forces of partisanship and ideology play a major role, as Republicans and conservatives are
among the strongest supporters of capitalism and opponents of socialism.

Education and income play key roles in the indoctrination process.
Unfortunately, public opinion surveys fail to measure the wealth of individuals as reflected in total personal assets, since these surveys only question
people about their yearly incomes. Even these measurements are limited,
as they fail to separate out individuals earning over $150,000 a year. The
differences are drastic. Take one example: a married couple working as
public school teachers may earn $150,000 a year, although they would not

FIGURE 2: Support for Capitalism and Socialism by Education

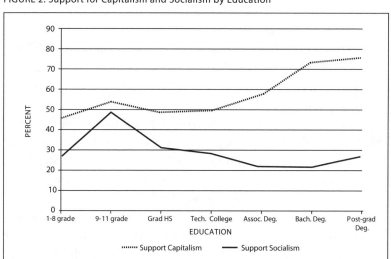

Source: Pew Research Center, 2010

be differentiated in surveys from the corporate CEO who earns tens of millions a year, and holds tens or hundreds of millions (or more) in personal assets. Such blunt survey measurements make it impossible to distinguish between the relatively affluent middle- and upper-middle-income earners, and the extremely rich that constitute the corporate owner and investor class. Although limited, the personal income question in public opinion surveys is still valuable in documenting the differences between the poor, working and middle class, and middle- to upper-income earners with regard to their political attitudes. A hegemonic system, after all, is not worth much if it fails to influence the masses of Americans.

Figures 1 and 2 document the roles of income and education in influencing public attitudes toward socialism and capitalism. Figure 1 provides evidence of the gulf between high- and low-income earners with regard to these competing ideologies. The difference in support for capitalism and socialism is greatest for those earning more than $100,000 a year, among whom less than 20 percent support socialism and more than 80 percent support capitalism. The gap between support for socialism and capitalism is nearly nonexistent for those at the bottom of the income scale, with support for both ideologies among the lowest income earners being nearly equal. Figure 2 uncovers similar indoctrinating effects for education. A significant gap is found between those with the most prestigious post-graduate degrees, as compared to those with a high school degree or less.

Most starkly, those without a high school degree (with between nine and eleven years of education) are nearly as likely to support socialism as they are to support capitalism.

This finding stands in dramatic contrast to those with college degrees, with support for socialism within this group reaching as low as 20 percent, and support for capitalism ranging between 60 and 80 percent.

These preliminary empirical findings are relevant in the study of public policy debates. Unfortunately, most pollsters fail to poll the public with the types of questions that gauge whether Americans reject the foundations upon which the political-economic system is built. Rarely are questions asked about whether Americans think that officials lie to or deceive the public, or about whether the United States is an imperial power, or probe whether capitalism is a fundamentally sound economic system. Most questions are concerned more with the minutiae of specific public policy debates, measuring, for example, whether the public supports for-profit health insurance exchanges or a public option. The limits of public opinion polling notwithstanding, there is still reason to suspect that the variables discussed in this introduction are relevant in predicting respondents' attitudes on policy issues along a left–right continuum. Such issues may not question the soundness of the U.S. political system, but they do provide a measurement for whether material and intangible hegemonic forces play a role in influencing public policy attitudes in more liberal or conservative directions. In chapters 4 and 6, I analyze polls that survey the public on a number of these types of issues, measuring the effects of material and intangible hegemonic forces with regard to opinions of the Tea Party and healthcare reform. Both issues are strongly delineated by liberal-left and conservative-right perspectives, with those supporting the Tea Party siding with a group that is strongly pro-business. Similarly, those opposing even minimally liberal healthcare reforms allied themselves with corporate healthcare interests that were intent on derailing progressive changes to the healthcare system.

MASS MEDIA HEGEMONY, THE TEA PARTY, AND HEALTHCARE REFORM

Reading this book, you may naturally wonder about its relevance once the Tea Party phenomenon begins to fade from the news and from public discourse. My answer to such concerns is to emphasize the numerous ways in which this study's relevance extends beyond simply studying the Tea Party. In terms of larger themes, I add a number of insights with regard to our understanding of U.S. politics. I provide a grand theory of public opinion and the larger social forces that influence it, using the Tea Party and healthcare as case studies. This theory alone will be worth examining in more detail in the future for those who seek to test its relevance for other domestic case studies. Other insights include the following:

- In the short term, I predict that the Tea Party movement will likely remain in the public eye at least into the 2012 elections. I present evidence that the Tea Party is not in fact a genuine social movement but a highly mediated, top-down constructed phenomenon. The Tea Party is largely a fiction, constructed by Republican and business interests in order to return the party to power in the 2010 and 2012 elections. In light of this mission, the group will likely remain a strong part of public policy debate through the 2012 presidential election, upon which it will no doubt be celebrated by journalists and conservatives as the means through which Tea Party activists and "insurgents" will seek to "overthrow" the Washington status quo.

- In terms of its broader significance beyond the Tea Party, I document the power of the mass media to disseminate pro-business propaganda and influence public policy attitudes. This power is exercised against the material interests of much of the public, which run counter to conservative opposition to healthcare reform and expansion of the social welfare state. Previous academic studies naively suggest that the mass media is only influential in shaping the issues people think about, rather than influencing their actual public policy attitudes. I highlight the tremendous power of corporate media to manufacture opposition to progressive policy proposals.

- Most important, I illustrate the lengths to which officials are willing to go to manipulate the public during times of economic and political crisis. In an age of widespread public distrust of officialdom, government officials have lost the ability to govern. The public is no longer confident in its political leaders, who are seen as corrupt, unrepresentative, and illegitimate. The public's crisis of political confidence has reached unprecedented levels, and conservative officials and business forces are responding by constructing a top-down social "movement," as seen in the Tea Party. In reinforcing ruling-class interests, the Tea Party presents identical policy positions to those of dominant business interests, although it appears at first glance to be a manifestation of public outrage at the political-economic system.

Government-promoted false populism is becoming the norm among conservative officialdom at a time when the parties cannot get reelected based on their widely discredited, market fundamentalist policy platforms. These policies—such as the bipartisan effort to cut and privatize Social Security and Medicare—are highly unpopular, and viewed by most Americans as toxic to Americans' well-being. Manufactured populism benefits the parties by reinforcing public distrust of government. The manufacture of dissent in favor of conservative/Tea Party narratives emboldens both parties to intensify their attacks on the social welfare state. This is clearly the lesson to take from the 2009–10 healthcare debate, in which Democrats abandoned progressive reform in favor of expanding market-based care. At a time when the public sees government as unable to promote the common good, the poison pill of the Tea Party reinforces public cynicism and reduces prospects for progressive solutions to social problems.

THE TEA PARTY AS "RANCID POPULISM"

This is not the first study to highlight the manipulation of populism by elitist forces. In his much-cited work *Who Will Tell the People*, William Greider warned of a "rancid populism" that permeates the political system, while identifying the market fundamentalist forces that have "perfected the art of maintaining political power in the midst of democratic decay." Although the Democratic Party is reliant on corporate-friendly public relations to retain power, as seen in the historic election of Barack Obama in 2008, the Republican Party has long been understood as the *most* effective in employing PR tactics in the pursuit of electoral and business power.[48] As Greider explains, Americans are witnesses to "a most improbable marriage of power—a hegemony of monied interests based on the alienation of powerless citizens."[49] Although these insights were expressed prior to the economic crisis, they remain relevant today. As a marketing strategy, and as a rebranding of the Republican Party, the Tea Party is a "rancid populist" force. It has succeeded in "uniting alienated voters into political coalition with the most powerful economic interests." This "populist" strategy, Greider argues, "requires the [Republican] Party to agitate the latent emotional resentments and turn them into marketable political traits. The raw materials for this are drawn from enduring social aggravations—wounds of race, class, and religion, even sex."[50] Charting the divisions in public opinion as based upon these "enduring social aggravations" is the goal of much of the rest of this book.

The pro-business, Republican-supported Tea Party is succeeding as a false populist force, thanks heavily to its marketable "grassroots" image as constructed in the mass media. However, one should also recognize that the group would be nowhere near as successful if it were not for the legitimate grievances and anger of a general public, which is seeing its income and wealth stagnate after three decades of outsourcing, deregulation, deindustrialization, attacks on the social welfare state, and toxic speculation on Wall Street.[51] Widespread public disillusionment and unhappiness with the political-economic status quo will likely continue into the indefinite future, making Americans further susceptible to manipulation by false populist forces funded and organized by political and business elites.

PLAN OF THE BOOK

This book consists of six chapters. In chapter 1, I describe the results from my national study of the Tea Party, which finds that it is not a social movement but a small conglomeration of elitist interest groups operating across the country. It includes a review of the literature related to interest groups and social movements, followed by predictions of what one would expect to find if the Tea Party represents a social movement. Chapter 1 contains a review of the six major Tea Party institutions that compose the group. I examine these groups and their activities to assess whether the Tea Party is a social movement. I also review the national figures driving the Tea Party, in addition to the Tea Party Caucus in Congress. These figures are examined to assess how their backgrounds and ideologies fit within the larger Tea Party phenomenon. Finally, I analyze more than 150 local chapters and their levels of organization and activism, buttressed by a review of national Tea Party organizing, as reflected in conferences and other events.

In chapter 2, I undertake a case study of the Tea Party throughout the Midwest, specifically in the city of Chicago and its suburbs. These locations are vital as a sample of Tea Party chapters, since rapidly growing "boom town" suburbs, which are plentiful in Chicago, represent the most organized geographical area of the Tea Party. Additionally, the Tea Party claims the Midwest as one of its two most organized regions of the country (following the South). Chicago also remains the home of the famous "origin" of the Tea Party, the Rick Santelli "rant" heard round the world, which is widely credited with having helped spark the Tea Party in 2009. In short, if there is evidence that the Tea Party is a social movement, it should be apparent in the Chicago metropolitan area.

Chapter 2 adds a layer of nuance to the findings presented in chapter 1 regarding the Tea Party's alleged status as a social movement. I examine the Tea Party as it relates to partisan electioneering and report upon its level of organization in terms of active local chapters and local turnouts. I assess the politics of the Tea Party at local meetings and rallies, evaluating its activities in accord with the scholarly literature on interest groups and social movements. The findings supplement those of chapter 1, as I provide further evidence that the Tea Party is not a mass movement.

If the Tea Party is not a movement, why has it become so popular with the public? Chapter 3 answers this question by directing readers' attention to how the Tea Party is covered in conservative news outlets such as Fox News and right-wing radio, and in "objective" newspapers and other news organizations. This chapter provides some evidence of differentiated coverage between both conservative outlets and more mainstream ones, while also identifying the overarching similarities in coverage across different mediums. Simply put, the Tea Party is a heavily mediated phenomenon, receiving sympathetic coverage across *all* major American mass media outlets.

Chapter 4 assesses the changes in public opinion that took place as a result of the media's sympathetic coverage of the Tea Party. I undertake an empirical analysis of national public opinion polling and track how the Tea Party is perceived among those paying close attention to the group. I present evidence that the mass media played a vital role in encouraging growing support for the Tea Party. This chapter also demonstrates that the Tea Party's appeal, at least initially, was restricted to more privileged demographic groups. The group also expanded its influence among the less affluent as it benefited from heightened, sympathetic coverage from the mass media during the fall of 2009 and throughout 2010.

Chapter 5 is an empirical analysis of media coverage of the Tea Party's most focused-on policy issue: healthcare reform. The chapter examines healthcare coverage across different mainstream, liberal, and conservative media outlets. It highlights differences in coverage in terms of varied support and opposition for Democratic healthcare reform, while also tracking the similarities in coverage across outlets. Chapter 5 finds that conservative narratives dominated media coverage during the debate over healthcare reform, in great part due to the rise of the Republican Party and Tea Party in the fall of 2009 and early 2010, and during the run-up to the midterm elections.

In chapter 6, I review the evidence of the media's effects on public opinion on healthcare reform. Journalists played a dominant role in manufacturing dissent against progressive, and then Democratic, healthcare proposals, in line with the rhetoric promoted by Republicans and the Tea Party. The chapter empirically documents the relationship between increased media consumption and opposition to healthcare reform. As with public support for the Tea Party, opposition to healthcare reform was concentrated most strongly among more privileged demographic groups. Less privileged groups were more likely to support reforms aimed at expansion of the social welfare state, although anti-healthcare messages did gain footing among the disadvantaged due to increasingly critical media coverage throughout mid to late 2009 and early 2010.

The conclusion includes a discussion of the seeming decline of the Tea Party throughout early 2011, as seen in growing public opposition and in its deteriorating protest turnouts compared to radically larger public revolts against market fundamentalism, as seen in the United States and in the rest of the world. The conclusion also includes a short wrap-up for the book's most important findings: that the media's manufacture of dissent is a direct product of the growing inability of U.S. political and business elites to govern during a time when the public exhibits contempt for officialdom and distrust of privileged political and economic actors; and that material and intangible hegemonic forces play the dominant role in filtering public opinion in favor of business interests.

ONE

Don't Call It a Movement:
The Tea Party as a Mass Uprising

Before understanding the role of the Tea Party in manufacturing public dissent, one must first understand what drives the phenomenon. This and the next chapter are devoted to explaining precisely what the Tea Party is. I explore in detail the ways in which it has been misperceived by the American public. Most important, I analyze the ways in which the Tea Party does not constitute a mass movement.

Reporting the "Revolution" in 2010

Late 2010 witnessed a divergence in media coverage of the Tea Party, with two trends evident in news and editorializing. The first trend defined the Tea Party as a bottom-up social movement that influenced the midterm elections on a massive level and was being co-opted by the Republican Party. The second trend asked whether the Tea Party was a false social movement, in the sense that its members were being manipulated by wealthy corporate interests. The first trend was personified by reporting in the *Los Angeles Times*, which stated that "surprise primary election returns in Florida and Alaska [in addition to earlier primary elections] underscored" the Tea Party's "outsider status" and the "movement['s] . . . strength and resilience."[1] The *New York Times* chronicled the efforts of

Tea Party activists who traveled to Washington and joined forces with Dick Armey's *Freedom Works* organization to "take over the country, voter by voter." As the paper reported, "The goal is to turn local Tea Party groups into a standing get-out-the-vote operation in Congressional districts across the country," by encouraging public "turnout [of] hundreds or thousands to the streets to protest and wave signs and yell and make an impact on public policy debate."[2]

In September 2010, the *New York Times* framed the Tea Party–Republican alliance as having only recently emerged, reflecting a tension between party-based and movement interests. "As much as Tea Party fervor is expected to help Republicans in November, it may also create problems for them. The Tea Party has brought a huge amount of *unexpected* energy into the campaign, and it could drive sufficient Republican turnout to become a major and perhaps decisive factor in many races."[3] The Associated Press (AP) wondered if the Tea Party was "becoming the GOP?" The AP reported that the Tea Party had "taken hold in the Grand Old Party, unseating lawmakers, capturing nominations for open seats, and forcing Republicans to recalibrate both their campaign strategy and issues agenda."[4] The *Washington Post* updated readers on Tea Partier Christine O'Donnell's "big [primary] win in Delaware," which sent a "message to the Republican establishment" that "you are not in charge."[5] Endemic within such reporting were two assumptions: that the Tea Party is an independent social movement but that by the fall of 2010 it was actively becoming intertwined with the Republican Party; and that the Tea Party was pulling the Republican Party further to the right, against the wishes of the more "moderate" core members.

The second, more critical trend in reporting on the Tea Party was evident in a news report from Jane Mayer of *The New Yorker*, which alleged that the group was being centrally directed and manipulated by right-wing billionaire activists. More specifically, Mayer highlighted the political activism of David and Charles Koch, wealthy industrialists who donated nearly $200 million to conservative groups from 1998 to 2008, and founded the Americans for Prosperity Foundation, which trained local Tea Party activists to oppose the initiatives of President Obama and Democrats in Congress.[6] Conservative Americans seized on *The New Yorker*'s critical reporting as evidence of liberal media bias, while liberals in the mass media countered that they felt this critical line of inquiry into the Tea Party was largely unreported.[7]

What both of the above perspectives neglect are the long-standing *institutional* ties among the Tea Party local chapters, broader corporate interests, and the Republican Party. The reporting from *The New Yorker*, while at times discussing Republican politics and corporate support for the Tea Party, was characterized by an almost conspiratorial framework, depicting Tea Party activists as being manipulated by a few wealthy businessmen working through shadowy networks. The reporting on the Tea Party as a "social movement" ignored the consistent findings that the group exhibits little to no sustained activism at the grassroots level, and was an extension of Republican Party politics from the beginning of my analysis in early 2010. Ignored in national media coverage is the insight of left-journalist and *Nation* writer Jeremy Scahill, who warned of the "astroturf" origins of the Tea Party, a group he saw as "run by the lobby of big corporations" and as "fake grassroots" in its politics and identity.[8]

A classic study of social movements, Sidney Tarrow's *Power in Movement*, finds that a movement's success is dependent upon "expanding opportunities," defined through increased government openness to movement demands. As Tarrow explains, "For brief periods the power in movement seems irresistible; but it disperses rapidly and passes inexorably into more institutional forms. Clever power holders exploit these opportunities by selectively facilitating some movements and repressing and ignoring others."[9] Tarrow's description of movement co-optation was clearly adopted by the Associated Press, which described the Tea Party as "becoming the GOP" in the fall of 2010. However, as I demonstrate through extensive on-the-ground and national analysis, the Tea Party was always a direct outgrowth of Republican, pro-business politics. This does not mean, however, that the Republican Party was free of tensions during the rise of Tea Party candidates throughout the 2010 national primaries.

In many cases, Tea Party victors in the midterm primaries were more conservative than the incumbents they defeated. Many of the Tea Party victors advocated the elimination of broad-based popular programs such as Medicare and Social Security, in addition to the end of government regulation of business. "Establishment" Republicans largely feel the same, but are far less cavalier or brazen in their rhetoric. Such radicalism has been a staple of Republican politics for years, but it was never expressed quite so lucidly or consistently within an electoral season before the 2010 midterm elections. The blunt attack of Tea Partiers created some limited fractures within the party among its more and less conservative members. Tea Partiers who were victorious in the primaries appeared to be increasingly successful in pulling the Republican Party even further to the right in its rhetoric and policies. This process, however, hardly represents a revolution or monumental departure from Republican Party politics, as has been erroneously suggested by those stressing the potential of the Tea Party to "unhinge" the Republican "establishment."[10] Rather, the growing conservatism of the party is an ongoing process documented in empirical studies for the last several decades.[11] The Tea Party is significant primarily in that it represents the *most recent* chapter in the radicalization of the Republican Party.

The image of radical Tea Party candidates pushing the Republican Party toward greater conservative extremes is borne out in some of the empirical data in this chapter. However, one must be careful in examining what social forces were most responsible for the growth of intra-party conflict among Republicans. The rightward movement of the Republican Party appears not to be the result of bottom-up citizen pressures but of the successes of a small number of well-connected, media-savvy Republican activists affiliated with the Tea Party. Rather than building a mass movement of activists, these elite actors make up a conglomeration of interest groups that have "gone public" by cultivating popular opinion in favor of Tea Party narratives.

THE TEA PARTY:
A FRONT FOR PRO-BUSINESS GROUPS

Government systems and wealthy individuals have long served as patrons for interest groups, and as a major driving force behind political organizing.[12] The available evidence suggests that the main patrons and supporters fueling the Tea Party include the business community, far-right Republican activists and party officials, and the mass media.

Political organizing has been historically dominated by business and corporate professional (occupational) groups.[13] Highlighting the "privileged position of business" does not mean that all such interests operate with a single voice.[14] Competition among individual sectors of the capitalist economy does exist, although corporate interests generally agree across-the-board that business should be the most privileged political actor when compared to other types of interest groups. Nowhere is this reality more apparent than in historical analysis demonstrating that corporate interests unite in opposing "unwarranted" government regulation, progressive taxation, and an expansive social welfare state, and are more likely to favor deregulation and massive government-to-business subsidies.[15] Past investigation finds that comprehensive, unified coordination of business interests across each economic sector does not exist, but this should not be taken as evidence that conflicting corporate interests fail to occupy the most prominent spot in the lobbying food chain.[16] None of the findings about the diverse interests of competing business interests raise serious doubt that the Tea Party's primary role is to reestablish Republican power, in addition to furthering business power and rolling back attempts at regulation of business and shrinking the welfare state. In years past, intellectuals stressed the prominence of "pluralistic" competition among a variety of interest groups and concerned citizens, or at least suggested that business actors did not consistently dominate every segment of the public policy process.[17] Critics later challenged the idea of pluralistic competition, finding either that business interests dominated policymaking or that participation during the mid- to late twentieth century was not as pluralistic as commonly assumed.[18] A "power elite" was found to stand at the top of the policymaking hierarchy, although this elite was often broken down into specific business interests that dominated particular public policy areas.[19] Private money—overwhelmingly supplied by competing business interests and capitalist-oriented professional groups—plays *the* defining role in the interest group system and in influencing the nature of politics and law.[20] Those individuals of higher socioeconomic status are more likely to dominate policymaking.[21] The power of corporate economic interests may be reduced during reform eras (such as the New Deal of the 1930s and the Great Society of the 1960s), when democratic interests break through and exert greater influence over public policy, but "cyclical" trends in public policy mean that business interests often succeed in rolling back progressive victories, as is the case today.[22]

Privileged business elites share a strong distaste for the liberal welfare state.[23] The Republican Party—strongly supported by business pressures and a sympathetic media system—remains the primary patron that organizes and sustains the Tea Party. The mass media play a secondary but crucial role as patrons granting sustained attention and support to the Tea Party, primarily through reporters' reliance on an increasingly conservative political system.[24]

Even though the interest group system is dominated by business interests, this does not mean that citizen-based activism is absent from politics.

Indeed, one of the great recent contributions to the study of interest groups was finding that social movements, citizens groups, and other forces can, and do, play an instrumental role in gaining significant media attention, in influencing the political process, and in breaking up policy areas dominated by business elites.[25] The question to be answered here, however, is whether the Tea Party represents an independent social movement that is succeeding in changing the national political scene and the dominant business political-economic structure. Are Tea Partiers transforming politics on their own terms and creating genuine pressure against the establishment while at the same time reflecting widespread public distrust of Wall Street and Washington?[26] I dedicate the rest of this chapter to answering this question.

Defining a Social Movement

I assumed, upon beginning my examination of the Tea Party, that it was a grassroots social movement. There was little reason to think otherwise in light of media reporting that consistently presented the group as a bottom-up, populist uprising. In studying the group closely at the local and national level, however, it became clear that the popular media narrative was without merit.

Conservative activism is often seen as sorely lacking in participatory elements. Political scientists Jacob Hacker and Paul Pierson document the long-standing top-down organization of anti-tax groups such as Americans for Tax Reform and the Club for Growth, which lack any sort of mass organization and are primarily interested in electioneering.[27] Political-communication scholar Matthew Kerbel finds that activist conservative media outlets such as RedState, The Drudge Report, Powerline, and InstaPundit are largely venues for "pipelin[ing] information from Republican Party operatives." Those who coordinate these sites are "conservative figures with access to an existing idea and media infrastructure, including well-funded think tanks, talk radio, news outlets like Fox News, and until they lost it, control of all three branches of the national government. This infrastructure has permitted the conservative blogosphere to participate in broader institutional structure already engaged in messaging, public relations, campaigning, and governing." Kerbel sees these conservative outlets as "astroturf" media—"fake grassroots blogs designed to appear bottom-up when in fact they're supported by monied interests," and defined through a hierarchical centralized structure.[28] In his seminal work, *Social Movements*, Charles Tilly established a number of preconditions needed for a social movement to emerge. These include "a sustained, organized public effort, making collective claims on target authorities"; reliance upon "special-purpose associations and coalitions, public meetings, solemn processions, vigils, rallies, demonstrations, petition drives, statements to and in public media, and pamphleteering"; and "participants' concerted public representations of worthiness, unity, numbers and commitment on the part of themselves and their constituencies."[29] In their work, *Social Movements*, Donatella Della Porta and Mario Diani establish that movements rely upon "dense, informal networks" characterized by collective identity and action.[30] They elaborate that "a social movement process is in place only when collective identities develop which go beyond specific events and initiatives. Collective identity is strongly associated with recognition and the creation of connectedness."[31] According to these definitions, the Tea Party falls short of being a social movement in *every* area.

PHILOSOPHICAL CONTEMPT
FOR COLLECTIVE ACTION

A primary reason the Tea Party is not a social movement is its contempt for collective identity and action. Porta and Diana establish common identity and action as fundamental to social movements, but the entire idea of collectivity is rejected on an ideological level by Tea Partiers, who subscribe to an ideology of neoliberalism. When I refer to Tea Party "activists," however, I am referring to the small core of activists that attend Tea Party rallies. This group is quite different in their contempt for collective action than the public as a whole, which opinion polls demonstrate remain sympathetic to collective action and social movements.[32]

As a concept, neoliberalism remains deeply antagonistic to the building of social movements. Neoliberalism is defined by critics as "a more virulent and brutal form of capitalism" that is dedicated to "obliterate[ing] public concerns and make[ing] politics everywhere an exclusively driven market project." Neoliberalism is characterized by the "ascendancy of" a "corporate culture into every aspect of American life," and by "efforts to deteriorate union power, disassociate income levels from intensity and duration of work, dismantle public services and public goods in the name of establishing private ones, and foment a general distrust among the public in the notion that the government can promote the needs and well-being of the masses."[33] The neoliberal, "free market" agenda includes attacks on public goods and services such as public housing, public spaces, food stamps, public healthcare, and any other program that is funded through progressive taxation and redistribution of wealth from the rich to the masses and poor.[34] Critics equate neoliberalism with the growth of poverty, inequality, and mass desperation.[35]

Individualistic worship of "free markets" is antithetical to the very idea of a social movement. Nowhere is this more clearly seen than in the tremendous popularity of conservative philosopher Ayn Rand among Tea Partiers. Rand had contempt for social movements and supported the neoliberal mindset well before the term came into vogue in contemporary U.S. politics. Rand was fixated on the virtues of individualism, as opposed to the virtues accompanying collective identity. She despised the social movements that emerged in the 1960s. In her essay, "The Cashing-In: The Student Rebellion," Rand dismissed the 1960s student movement as "anti-ideology" in orientation, ignoring the fact that the movement was clearly driven by vigorous opposition to the war in Vietnam. Rand refused to consider this motivation as a legitimate factor for organizing, rejecting the protesters and groups like SDS as "extremists."[36]

Rand maintained that "mass disobedience is an assault on the concept of rights; it is a mob's defiance of legality as such." The specific point of illegality of this disobedience included, she argued, the "obstruction of a public thoroughfare [referring here to student sit-ins in public buildings on the U.C. Berkeley campus]," which was "so blatant a violation of rights that an attempt to justify it becomes an abrogation of morality. An individual has no right to do a 'sit-in' in the home or office of a person he disagrees with—and he does not acquire such a right by joining a gang." Rand felt collective action, as expressed by student groups in the 1960s, represented "intimidation" of the highest order. The nonviolent occupation of university buildings was deemed "violence," as directed by the "collectivists" against the morally virtuous capitalist system.[37]

Rand's opposition to social movements also included distrust of civil rights activism. In her book, *The Virtue of Selfishness*, Rand subscribed to a worldview in which individuals looked to their own personal fulfillment rather than collective fulfillment as a sign of social progress. Rand argued that "the proper method of judging when or whether one should help another person is by reference to one's own hierarchy of values: the time, money, or effort one gives or the risk one takes should be proportionate to the value of the person in relation to one's own happiness." She did not believe that any collective entity known as "the public" existed, "since the public is merely a number of individuals." Rand viewed "collectivism" as "amoral" and found the notion of "collective rights" of oppressed groups to be "a contradiction in terms."[38]

Rand displayed her own contempt for the civil rights movement and the Civil and Voting Rights Acts when she framed these legal initiatives as "a gross infringement on individual rights" to engage in racism, and argued that "private racism is not a legal, but a moral issue—and can be fought only by private means, such as boycott or ostracism." In her support for the "right" of individuals to decide whether or not to engage in racism and discrimination, Rand succumbed to the notion that racism is a problem to be dealt with only on the individual level. Though she viewed racism as merely "the lowest, most crudely primitive form of collectivism," the only "solution" was individual boycotts of business, rather than all-encompassing government protections against discrimination.[39] Such opposition to collective action in promoting racial equality remains incredibly relevant to modern-day politics, as it was echoed by self-designated Tea Partier and congressional candidate Rand Paul in the 2010 primaries. Paul, an avowed fan of Ayn Rand (although not named after her), publicly opposed the Civil Rights Act as an unwarranted intrusion on the "right" of individuals to privately decide whether they should be allowed to engage in racial discrimination and prejudice.[40]

Like the Tea Partiers, Ayn Rand had contempt for programs that redistributed wealth from the rich to the poor. In her much-read novel *The Fountainhead*, Rand expounded upon what she saw as the evils of Robin Hood. Rand's hero, rather, was the individual "who robs the poor and gives to the rich, or to be more exact, the man who robs the thieving poor and gives back to the productive rich."[41] This opposition to social welfare is clearly seen in Tea Party protests that oppose Democratic proposals for a public option or for the expansion of Medicaid. Amid the rise of the Tea Party, Rand was fiercely attacked for advocating a version of libertarian capitalism in which "no other nexus between man and man" exists other than man's "naked self-interest." Most important in the case of Tea Party supporters, Rand was criticized for the notion that "civilization is the progress toward a society of privacy. The savage's whole existence is public, ruled by the laws of his tribe. Civilization is the process of setting man free from men."[42]

I have witnessed Tea Partiers' disdain for collectivity at Tea Party rallies and meetings firsthand. Ayn Rand placards, for one, are extremely
common at Tea Party protests. Messages expressed by Tea Party adher-
ents at events across the country include: "Ayn Rand Was Right," "Atlas
Is Shrugging" (referring to Rand's famous novel), "We Are John Galt"
(referring to the heroically portrayed capitalist character in *Atlas
Shrugged*), "John Galt Was Right," "Read *Atlas Shrugged*," and "Your Life
Belongs to You" (a line from *Atlas Shrugged*). Rand placards coexist comfortably alongside other protest signs that warn of the "socialist" threat
from healthcare reform and the dangers of "rewarding" the undeserving
poor with increased welfare spending.

Progressive scholar Carl Boggs frames the social movements of yester-
year as being driven by a commitment to challenging free market capitalism and unrepresentative government in general. "Since the 1960s popular movements in the U.S." sought to "broaden a public sphere that has
all too often been distorted by market priorities, electoral spectacles, and
bureaucratic machinations."[43] Boggs's understanding of social movements as reliant upon a public sphere and public goods is roundly rejected by Tea Partiers, who oppose the expansion of the welfare state for the
disadvantaged. Whatever one thinks of Ayn Rand's version of libertarian
capitalism, it is clear that it is incompatible with social movements based
upon collective identity, collective action, and public goods. Some might
challenge this conclusion, noting that Tea Partiers appear to engage in
collective action, but there is little to take seriously in this challenge. The
Tea Party is composed of members who share little to no commitment to
social solidarity and group identity. Detractors might also cite Tea
Partiers' alleged embrace of collective programs such as Medicare and
Social Security—supported by 62 percent of Tea Partiers. Such support
is belied, however, by Tea Partiers' support for candidates set on dismantling these programs, and advocacy—expressed among 53 percent of Tea
Partiers—for privatizing Medicare and Social Security.[44]

NATIONAL AND LOCAL EVIDENCE

In her book *Boiling Mad: Inside Tea Party America*, Kate Zernike, a
reporter for *New York Times*, argues that the Tea Party is a leaderless,
"authentic popular movement" and that it cannot be explained as driven
"simply as partisan politics."[45] Similarly, the *New York Times* depicted the

Tea Party's power as potentially massive in the run-up to the 2010 midterm elections: "Of the 18 Senate races that the *New York Times* considers competitive, there are 11 where the Tea Party stands to be a significant factor. While it is harder to predict the Tea Party's influence in the House races ... there are at least 48 out of 104 competitive seats where it could have a major impact."[46] This promise of power was repeated following the election, with various news outlets discussing the rise of the Tea Party "movement" in light of more than three dozen Tea Party upstarts winning office in the House and Senate.

The central problem with the literature on the Tea Party is the lack of empirical rigor. Zernike's book is largely based on anecdotal observational evidence. Among Zernike's conclusions are the assumptions that the Tea Party is authentic, decentralized, fluid, and leaderless.[47] Zernike clearly engaged in a wide-ranging observation of the Tea Party, attending protests, rallies, and meetings for the group across the country. However, her analysis appears random, reflecting her discussions with Tea Partiers during her beat reporting for the *New York Times*, and neglecting a systematic analysis of individual case studies across an extended period of time. Zernike accepts at face value Tea Partier claims that they represent an expansive, bottom-up social movement without engaging in critical investigation or prodding. In light of these limitations, Zernike's book lacks a critical understanding of the Tea Party. Rather than simply assuming the Tea Party is grassroots, it would have been more appropriate for Zernike to begin her investigation by asking: *Is* the Tea Party a mass movement?

Will Bunch's *The Backlash: Right-Wing Radicals, High-Def Hucksters, and Paranoid Politics in the Age of Obama* discusses the Tea Party, but it is also anecdotal. It assumes without critical evaluation that the Tea Party is a social movement that is being driven by conservative media rather than by "objective" news outlets.[48] Bunch's analysis ranges from blatantly inaccurate to overly simplistic. A closer examination of the Tea Party exposes its lack of participatory dimensions. Furthermore, criticisms of the conservative media that exonerate the "mainstream" press in the rightward drift of American politics are without merit.

Perhaps the most high-profile, empirically problematic work on the Tea Party is Scott Rasmussen and Douglas Schoen's *Mad as Hell: How the Tea Party Movement Is Fundamentally Remaking Our Two-Party System*. This book claims to rely upon original interviews and survey data but disseminates a variety of distortions regarding the Tea Party that border on propaganda. The work assumes, without comparative analysis of other social movements, that the Tea Party is an "unprecedented" movement in its size and scope. It also uncritically accepts claims that the mass media is liberally biased against the Tea Party. It simply reproduces discredited media studies without bothering to present any original media research, relying instead on trivial, anecdotal examples.[49] Finally, Rasmussen and Schoen's book accepts without critical investigation Tea Party claims that it is driven by mass participation at the local level.[50]

The Tea Party is lacking in *all* of the requirements for a social movement. For a movement to undertake sustained collective action, it must include regular meetings throughout a large number of localities. Wide levels of participation must be maintained, with an empowerment of local members, rather than a top-down dominance of organizing by elitist actors. The Tea Party is fundamentally lacking in such participatory aspects. The April 15, 2010, tax day rallies across the country appeared at first glance to represent a vibrant, growing social movement, as it boasted turnouts from 150 different cities, and estimates of more than 100,000 people having turned out across the country.[51] My survey of local Tea Party organizing, however, finds that participation in the Tea Party is restricted to infrequent demonstrations. A review of local activism across the 150 towns claiming an April 2010 turnout finds that a majority—56 percent—had no website at the time of the demonstrations with which to coordinate local meetings. This finding is problematic for a movement claiming a strong local presence, considering that online communication is now the primary means of organizing protests and providing information for organizing meetings and dates.

A closer look at the 150 cities where the Tea Party Patriots organization claimed turnouts in the April 2010 rallies finds that 92 percent exhibited *no evidence*—either through their own local site or through the larger Tea Party Patriots national umbrella site—of any sort of regular meetings that were taking place, "regular" defined as at least one meeting taking place per month for two consecutive months during the spring of 2010, in the run-up to the tax day rallies.[52] A small minority of local Tea Party chapters—just 8 percent—provided any evidence about regular meetings. In the Chicago metropolitan area, which I surveyed most closely, a majority (65 percent) of the chapters that allegedly existed according to the national umbrella website Tea Party Patriots had their own website.[53] Of all the metropolitan groups, however, less than 15 percent posted any information about regular meetings. There were only twenty local

Tea Party groups listed on the national Tea Party Patriots website for a metropolitan area claiming more than 250 jurisdictions. This presence is incredibly meager, translating into only 7.5 percent of all municipalities with a visible Tea Party presence. The percent of cities and towns with regular meetings is even smaller, representing a minuscule one percent of all municipalities.

In 2010, CNN polling revealed that 5 percent of Americans claimed to have attended a Tea Party rally.[54] Such numbers suggested a mass movement of working Americans rebelling against the Democratic Party; 5 percent of the adult public is more than 11.5 million people. In reality, however, national turnout was far smaller. My estimates suggest that no more than 100,000 to 200,000 people (or at most .0008 percent of the adult public) turned out for the April 15 rallies, which represented up until that point the biggest in the Tea Party's short history.[55] Local turnouts for April 15 were incredibly small when contrasted with the large number of people who claimed to be attending rallies. In Chicago, approximately 2,000 demonstrated at the Daley Center, although 5 percent of the city's adult population would have required a minimum turnout of 105,000.[56] New York City estimated 2,000 protesters, although the 5 percent participation level would suggest a turnout of 315,000.[57] In Atlanta, Des Moines, and Washington, estimated turnouts were a few hundred, 1,200, and 4,000 respectively. A 5 percent turnout for these cities would have required 20,000 for Atlanta, 7,500 for Des Moines, and 22,500 for Washington.[58] Other Tea Party rallies I observed in Chicago, such as the 9–12 Tea Party rally or meeting in Morton Grove, was similarly small at approximately 150 people.[59]

Expecting a full turnout at the April 15 rallies of the full 5 percent of Americans who claimed to attend a rally in 2010 is somewhat unrealistic. Conceding this point, turnouts still should have been much larger than they were for what was by far the largest Tea Party protest to date. Attendance at April protests, when examining the sample cities above, was as little as .6 percent to as much as 17 percent of the full turnouts one would expect if the entire 5 percent of Americans claiming to attend a rally were present. This finding suggests that the "mass" level of participation claimed by Tea Party supporters is radically exaggerated.

Other measurements of national Tea Party participation further reinforce the low levels of public involvement in this group. A comprehensive study by the *Christian Science Monitor* and Patchwork Nation in 2010 found that local participation in the Tea Party was "hardly a groundswell." The study concluded that "the Tea Party movement, despite the large amount of coverage it has received, is probably not the force that media outlets have portrayed it as." Searching through online directories of local Tea Party organizations, Patchwork Nation analyzed records for "the overwhelming majority of registered members." The group's study concluded that the Tea Party consisted (as of April 2010) of "roughly 67,000 members in counties across America." When broken down, this total translated into less than three Tea Party members per 10,000 people in cities across the country, or just .03 percent of the adult population. These numbers are a far cry from the 4 to 5 percent of adults who claimed in 2010 to be attending Tea Party rallies or meetings.[60]

An assessment of the national Tea Party in the run-up to the midterm elections also raises important questions regarding the power of "movement" participation. September witnessed meager turnouts for Tea Party-sponsored events. LibertyXPO, a national organization seeking to cultivate and organize Tea Partiers, suffered the collapse of its September 10 D.C. convention, which was deliberately scheduled to overlap with the 2010 9–12 D.C. rally, itself equally poorly attended. LibertyXPO's meeting was an abysmal failure in attracting participants, and failed to garner even the $40,000 it needed to recoup the conference costs, despite its organizers having spent an entire year in contact with local Tea Party chapters.[61] Similarly, the 2010 9–12 D.C. rally held two days after LibertyXPO benefited from a turnout of only a few thousand protesters.[62] At a time when broad-based participation at national conventions and protests was most necessary, Tea Partiers failed to engage in the mass organizing.

Most devastating for the Tea Party's movement potential was the collapse of its convention in the month prior to the midterm elections. The October 2010 National Tea Party convention in Las Vegas, originally scheduled for July of that year, was pushed back, supposedly due to punishing summer temperatures. Activists spearheading the convention announced it was rescheduled for mid-October, but they cancelled the event in light of weak planned turnout.[63] The February 2010 Nashville convention also saw low attendance, with only 600 Tea Partiers appearing from across the United States.[64] Some might argue that the Nashville attendance was so low because of the high entry cost, although this claim is negated by the fact that the LibertyXPO 2010 Tea Party conference was free, and advertised well in advance of the meeting date.[65]

The inability of the Tea Party to coordinate local chapters as a national movement is markedly different from those Tea Party rallies that did attract wide participation, but were manufactured from the top down. One important case in point is the fall 2010 Glenn Beck rally in Washington aimed at "restoring [America's] honor" and coinciding with Martin Luther King's "I Have a Dream" anniversary speech. That rally, heavily promoted by Fox News and other conservative media, succeeded in attracting at least 100,000 people.[66] Revealingly, it took the "star" power of a Fox News national media pundit to draw mass numbers of "Tea Partiers," while the Tea Parties' own organizing failed to see similar turnouts. The Las Vegas fall 2010 Tea Party convention and LibertyXPO failures, and the underattended early 2010 Nashville Tea Party rally needed systematic, massive participation on the local level to succeed, while the Beck–Fox News rally merely needed to take advantage of Fox's millions of viewers to garner mass turnouts. The collapse of Tea Party rallies, then, represents strong evidence that the group is not a mass movement.

Evaluating National Tea Party Groups

A comprehensive examination of the six major national Tea Party-affiliated groups suggests that involvement in the group is wildly overestimated. The most important Tea Party–affiliated national group, FreedomWorks, coordinates Tea Party rallies. It is highly centralized and a creature of Republican and business interests. The group is led by former Republican majority leader Dick Armey of the House of Representatives. Armey has a long history of lobbying for corporate America and promoting Republican politics. A second national group, Tea Party Nation, is a closed "participatory" network, as it will not allow the general public to find out information about its activities and events without signing up and waiting for approval from its website's coordinators. Furthermore, Tea Party Nation is more of an umbrella group than a grassroots organization because it merely links to local Tea Party groups operating in the states. The group is quite elitist due to its for-profit status and that it charge $549 (in addition to other hotel, transportation costs, and other fees) for Tea Partiers to attend its February 2010 national convention in Nashville.

The third national group is the Tea Party Patriots, which, as noted above, has an extremely weak local support base in the 150 cities examined. A fourth group, Our Country Deserves Better, is a formally registered political action committee, rather than a grassroots social movement. Though it did help organize the Tea Party Express bus tour, that project was organized from the top down in alliance with Republican speakers and by Republican operatives who funneled most of the revenues back to a Republican consulting firm—more than $1 million in 2009 alone.[67] The fifth group, the 1776 Tea Party Patriots, claims many local contacts in cities across the country, but little information is publicly available about the group and it posts no updates on regular local meetings.[68] The limited information available about the 1776 Tea Party Patriots suggests that it is dominated by the obscure, extremist Minuteman Project, which is a group of vigilantes concerned with "protecting" the U.S. border from Mexican immigrants.[69]

The sixth and final national group, Resistnet (later renamed the Patriot Action Network), has sponsored the national Tea Party Express bus tour. The Tea Party Express, however, is not even formally a part of the Tea Party movement. It was expelled from the larger national Tea Party federation due to the racially inflammatory comments of one of the group's members, who embraced the Obama "birther" conspiracy theory.[70] Resistnet claims to be "grassroots" and mass based, but its local activists are few and far between. Resistnet has virtually no local support, and the meager support it does receive calls for subatomic measurements. The group is largely concerned with electoral politics rather than organizing to influence local and national politics. It is composed of various congressional district groups throughout the country. The number of members in each district chapter, however, is minuscule. As of my late September 2010 national survey of Resistnet, the organization boasted just 546 committee members for the entire country. Such small numbers represent just .00005 percent of the adult population of the United States.[71]

Local examples put the meager size of Resistnet into better perspective. The First Congressional District of Illinois (made up of the Chicago suburbs I surveyed in my local case study of the Tea Party) includes the cities of Evergreen Park, Alsip, Blue Island, Oak Forest, and Tinley Park. The overall population for these cities was estimated in 2010 at over 150,000, although there were only nine members of Resistnet registered for this area, or just .00006 percent of the local population. The Fourth Congressional District in Illinois includes the cities of Chicago, Cicero, and Stone Park. These cities comprise more than 2.8 million people, but retain a total of nine Resistnet members, or just .000003 percent of the area's adult population. The larger national membership of Resistnet comprises just .00005 percent of the U.S. adult population.[72] In short, Resistnet is far from a mass-based organization.

UNIFORMITY OF RHETORIC

The central tenets driving local Tea Party meetings were so uniformly consistent across all the events I observed that it is difficult to conclude they are manifestations of a bottom-up, decentralized, and diverse movement. It is unlikely that a decentralized movement could have such dramatically consistent framing in terms of the language used and ideology expressed across its chapters. Such uniformity is strongly promoted in the few local meetings that do take place and is a function of top-down communication strategies from Tea Party leaders and media pundits. In my observation of the Tea Party in the city of Chicago, members were instructed in terms of the precise language to use when it came to canvassing neighborhoods in seeking support for Tea Party themes and Republican candidates. Attending Tea Party events and meetings in Chicago and the suburbs of Naperville, Schaumburg, and Palatine, I heard the same catchphrases and slogans employed across those chapters.[73] Such uniformity is unlikely to emerge in an organic, decentralized movement, but rather through top-down coordination via elite Republican and media actors. An examination of right-wing media coverage confirms this point, with the most prominent themes of the Tea Party emanating from pundits in right-wing media.[74]

Uniform Tea Party rhetoric predictably focuses on Republican partisan themes. These attacks warn of economic doomsday in regard to Democratic Party policies—most specifically against mild extensions of the social welfare state. Obama and his efforts at healthcare reform were routinely condemned as "socialist," despite the fact that they were private market plans, with a modest extension of Medicaid. Obama was demonized for "reckless spending" and for "bankrupting our children's futures" with "unsustainable debt." Obama's union support base was consistently lambasted for being composed of "union thugs." Tea Partiers continually spoke of the importance of linking support for the trio of "free markets," the Founding Fathers, and Constitutional originalism. The claim that healthcare reform is unconstitutional was consistently repeated. That these three, very specific points covering the Founding Fathers, Constitutionalism, and "free markets" regularly appeared together suggests that the ideology driv-

ing the Tea Party is a direct manifestation of the conservative political apparatus, originating from Republican Party members and trickling down to
right-wing media, and finally to the public itself. The uniformity of rhetoric is also a product of the Republican dominance of Chicago-area rallies
and other events I observed. The only officials running for public office
invited to speak at these events were local Republicans, repeating the same
warnings about debt, socialism, and unconstitutionality. The claims that
the Tea Party is "mainstream" and "nonpartisan" also regularly permeated
Chicago area meetings, despite the fact that the vast majority of Tea Party
members in attendance conceded that they ritually watched Fox News, distrusted the "liberal media," loathed the "destruction" of the country at the
hands of Obama, and desperately wanted to see the Republican Party
return to power in the fall.

TEA PARTY BUSINESS ELITES
AND THE MANIPULATION OF THE MASSES

Directing the Tea Party are the prominent national figures who attracted
media coverage in the first place. These leaders are plugged into the
national corporate and political power structure; they are not part of any
sort of grassroots, bottom-up group of Tea Partiers who grew to national
prominence as a result of many years of activism, agitation, and sacrifice.
In contrast, the most prominent leaders of the left's antiwar movement
were not insider political officials with close ties to corporate America,
but people who spent decades engaging in grassroots activism, to rise to
national prominence only after challenging the political-economic status
quo. Such figures on the left included dissidents such as Noam Chomsky,
the late Howard Zinn, Ralph Nader, and Cindy Sheehan, among others.
     Top-down organizing of the Tea Party reaches back to the mid- to late
2009 "Town Hall" rallies, in which Tea Partiers disrupted public forums
set up to discuss the merits and drawbacks of healthcare reform. Elitist,
Republican-oriented groups such as Freedom Works and the billionaire
Koch brothers' Americans for Prosperity were implicated in organizing
the events. Americans for Prosperity spent millions on television advertising against healthcare reform, and was a major factor in organizing the
Republican-allied Tea Party Express bus tour.[75] Cross-national events
organized by the Tea Party Express were instrumental in garnering media
attention toward the Republican cause.

In sharp contrast to the grassroots origins of left-wing antiwar figures, the most visible national Tea Party members include former vice-
presidential candidate Sarah Palin, former Republican House majority
leader Dick Armey, and Republican House Representative Michele
Bachmann. These officials serve as the most visible public faces for a
heavily mediated "movement." All three occupied, or continue to occupy, key political positions at the state and congressional levels, have
extensive ties with corporate America, and violate their own rhetorical
support for "free markets" by granting massive welfare subsidies to corporate America. These violations highlight the inherent contradictions
within a "movement" whose most prominent members reject the core
values espoused by that "movement." Hegemonic propaganda, however, does not need to be internally consistent. It merely needs to convince
the public to support pro-business policies that run contrary to the
material interests of the masses. In the sections below, I explore Tea
Party leaders' contradictions in the context of their rhetorical support
for "free markets" and their actual contempt for such principles. These
discrepancies were never conceded by any Tea Partiers with whom I
had direct interaction.

Dick Armey

As the former Republican House Majority Leader, Dick Armey supported legislation that would have subsidized energy corporations with taxpayer money by funding the transport of more than 77 million tons of
nuclear waste to the Yucca Mountain repository, to be stored there indef-
initely. Armey authorized massive corporate welfare subsidies, such as
appropriations that greatly benefited corporate military contractors. He
enthusiastically supported agribusiness subsidies, voted against a bipartisan campaign finance reform bill that would have imposed limits on the
amount of money corporations can contribute to political campaigns, and
sided with health insurance providers over consumers by attacking a
Senate bill attempting to establish a "patient's bill of rights."[76] All of these
actions are examples of official contempt for "free markets."

After leaving Congress, Armey became the head of Freedom Works.[77]
As Armey's Tea Party allies publicly rallied against the bailout, Armey
quietly lobbied on behalf of corporations like CarMax for loan subsidies
from the Troubled Assets Relief Program. Armey now lobbies for feder-

al corporate welfare even as he continues to condemn social welfare programs like Medicare as "tyranny."[78] Most problematically for Tea Partiers
is Armey's role in creating the conditions necessary for the economic crisis. Armey voted for both the Gramm-Leach-Bliley and Commodities
Futures Modernization Acts, which re-regulated the banks to become
"too big to fail" and removed the toxic derivatives associated with the
2008 housing and financial collapse from public regulation.

Michele Bachmann

As a House Republican from Minnesota, a prominent speaker for the Tea
Party, and founder of the Tea Party Congressional Caucus, Michele
Bachmann has amassed a record of collaborating with corporate
America. Her top campaign contributors in 2008 included the securities
and investment industry, insurance corporations, pharmaceutical interests, real estate firms, and other healthcare interests.[79] The tension
between Bachmann's rhetoric and actions has not stopped her from
attacking the 2008 economic bailout, which rescued the finance industry
upon which she is reliant for political contributions. Bachmann has
received contributions from healthcare interests that directly profited
from the pro-market 2010 Democratic healthcare reforms. These reforms
were greatly influenced by Republican efforts to ensure that progressive
options such as Medicare-for-all and the public option were removed
from consideration.

Bachmann has established a record of decrying social welfare spending
while supporting taxpayer subsidies for agribusiness. Bachmann's family
farm received $250,000 in government handouts as a part of Congress's
agribusiness subsidy program. Bachmann lists her investment in the farm
at $250,000 and posted a $50,000 income from the property in 2008.[80]
Such profits represent a relatively small amount of the agribusiness subsidies directed by the national government toward corporate agricultural
interests, but they are evidence nonetheless of Bachmann's contempt for
the free market principles she claims to embrace.

As one of the most prominent leaders of the Tea Party, Bachmann is
explicit about her desire to remove the mysticism regarding the under-
the-surface links between the Tea Party and Republican politics. She
explained in the run-up to the midterms that "unity is what we're all looking forward to this fall. But I think the patience of the American people is

very thin. They are looking to the GOP right now for leadership, quite frankly. . . . We'd be foolish not to adopt the Tea Party mainstream America agenda."[81] Such comments reveal the fundamental and long-standing links between the Republican Party and Tea Party that existed since the beginning of this so-called national movement.

Sarah Palin

Sarah Palin is embraced as one of the leading proponents of the Tea Party, speaking regularly at the group's rallies, and receiving favorable ratings from most Tea Partiers in opinion surveys.[82] She has built a career on corporate welfare, despite her rhetoric declaring the importance of "free markets." She ran on a ticket in 2008 that received $2.4 million from oil and gas contributions, with these industries ranking as the eleventh-largest contributor to the McCain campaign. Palin is an enthusiastic supporter of handing over public lands for corporate resource extraction and profit. She endorsed a corporate campaign to drill for oil in as much as one-tenth of the Arctic National Wildlife Reserve when she was governor of Alaska.[83] Most important with regard to Palin's lack of consistency was her support for the Troubled Assets Relief Program (TARP) – also known as the "bailout" – which she expressed during the 2008 election.[84]

OTHER REPUBLICAN–TEA PARTY TIES

The links between the Tea Party and Republicans are further buttressed by evidence of the group's partisan origins. The Tea Party Express tour reportedly funnels most of its money back to a consulting firm—Russo, Marsh, and Rogers—with strong ties to the Republican Party and a history of supporting Republican political candidates.[85] The Tea Party Patriots, the umbrella group coordinating various Tea Party groups across the country, also has a history of working with Armey's Republican-affiliated Freedom Works.[86] Even the Tea Party Patriots' mission statement, titled a "Contract from America," is inextricably linked to the Republican initiative introduced in Congress during Newt Gingrich's tenure as speaker of the House, which was named the "Contract with America." The Contract from America is largely a repetition of Republican talking points. The document's policy proposals coincide with those of the Republican Party, as it opposes the introduction of cap-and-trade legislation, opposes efforts at healthcare reform, increased taxes, and "runaway spending."[87]

Tea Party leadership is heavily linked to the Republican Party. One example is Matt Kibbe, the president and CEO of Freedom Works. Kibbe's history in Republican political consulting spans more than two decades.[88] Another example is Mark Meckler, a national Tea Party leader who has a history of political consulting work promoting GOP candidates. Meckler himself complains about his frustration with "other Tea Party groups [that] are being run by Republican political consultants forking over lots of cash for recruitment."[89]

There is clearly more to the Tea Party phenomenon than simply the elite sponsors and wealthy patrons who have helped organize "movement" events. Business elites, however, are still incredibly important in driving Tea Party politics. The major beneficiaries of the Tea Party ideology are corporate elites and their Republican allies. Wealthy patrons have long served as sponsors of conservative activism and Republican politics, and they are the direct beneficiaries (and architects of) the Tea Party's neoliberal agenda. Koch Industries is a strong example of the intimate links between Tea Party politics, the Republican Party, and corporate America. The Koch brothers' corporate conglomerate benefited from close ties to the George W. Bush administration, which dropped nearly ninety criminal charges against the company related to falsifying internal documents and other transgressions. Koch Industries contributed $800,000 to the Bush administration and other Republicans running for Congress.[90] The Koch brothers have devoted millions in resources to funding Tea Party and other Republican-related events in their battle to prevent progressive public policy reforms. Other business groups can also be included as driving the so-called movement, particularly through the campaign contribution process.

TEA PARTY VERSUS "ESTABLISHMENT" REPUBLICANS IN THE MIDTERM ELECTIONS

In the September 27, 2010, issue of *Time*, reporter Michael Scherer discussed the "conservative revolt" that was "rattling the Republican establishment" during the midterm elections season. The Tea Party, Scherer argued, "upended the elite of the Republican Party," having "created a crisis of legitimacy among the GOP establishment" that was initially too focused on "retaining their power" to notice the alleged revolution unfolding in front of them.[91] The *Time* narrative symbolizes much of what is wrong with the distorted coverage in the U.S. media, which exaggerates differences between Tea Party and "establishment" Republicans. This chapter's findings so far do *not* suggest that the phenomenon known as the Tea Party was ineffective in pulling the Republican Party to the right throughout 2010. The party's limited rightward shift, however, should be seen more as the product of the opportunistic political organizing of far-right conservative Tea Party candidates—aided by the mass media—than as a result of mass-based pressure. A number of underdog Tea Party candidates were successful in winning primary upsets over well-entrenched, much less conservative Republicans. However, it was the success of Tea Party candidates that helped push the party in a more radical direction.

Congressional primary Tea Party victors such as Kristi Noem of South Dakota, Anna Little of New Jersey, Christine O'Donnell of Delaware, Joe Miller of Alaska, and Mike Lee of Utah were all successful, despite raising far less than their competitors or less than the congressional incumbent average during the primary season. In South Dakota, Noem raised more than $577,000 in contributions by late September (when this analysis was undertaken), representing less than 60 percent of the national average raised by House Republican incumbents running in 2010.[92] In New Jersey, Little raised only $68,000 by late September, compared to her House competitor Diane Gooch, who raised more than $544,000.[93] In Delaware, O'Donnell raised $376,000, compared to Republican Senate incumbent Mike Castle, who raised more than $3.2 million.[94] In Utah, Mike Lee raised just over $962,000, compared to his incumbent Senate competitor Robert Bennett, who raised nearly $5 million.[95] Finally, in Alaska, Miller raised more than $288,000, compared to incumbent Senator Lisa Murkowski, who raised more than $3.75 million.[96]

A systematic examination of those House members holding power prior to the 2010 midterms but claiming the Tea Party mantle demonstrates that Tea Party officials are indeed more conservative than the average Republican, although the differences are modest at best. The House of Representatives–based "Tea Party Caucus" in mid-2010 was composed of 52 conservative Republicans, including Michele Bachmann, Joe Wilson, and Pete Sessions. Any indication that the Tea Party Caucus is thoroughly establishment-oriented would raise serious questions about the prospects of the Tea Party becoming a force for change outside of the "politics-as-usual" of Washington.

The politics of the Tea Party Caucus are strongly supportive of Republican interests. Ideological scores covering members of Congress (as determined by their voting record on major legislation) are provided by interest groups such as Americans for Democratic Action. ADA's ideology scores range from 0 points (meaning very conservative) to 100 points (meaning very liberal), and "moderate" resides between the two poles. Based on an analysis of Tea Partiers' 2009 voting records, I aggregated ADA data, and found that those in the House Tea Party Caucus in late 2010 averaged a score of 2.35 points as indicated by their 2009 voting record, an extremely conservative ranking. In comparison, the average House Republican scored 7 points—still extremely conservative, though slightly less so than those in the Tea Party Caucus. The average Senate score for Republicans was even less conservative at 14 points, translating into a more than 11-point difference with those in the House Tea Party Caucus.[97] In short, Tea Party Caucus members are somewhat more conservative than "average" Republicans, although the difference is more one of degree than of substance.

The above results simultaneously overestimate and underestimate the difference that the Tea Party appears to make in pulling the Republican Party to the right. The average ideological scores of the Tea Party House members represent a somewhat significant divergence from past scores of the party. The average ADA score of 2.35 points for Tea Party Caucus members should be compared not only to the average Republican score for 2009 voting of 7 percent, but also to the average 2008 Republican voting score, which stood at 22 points. In other words, the Tea Partiers of 2009 were nearly 20 points more conservative than House Republican counterparts from just one year earlier. Similarly, Senate Republicans' ADA voter scores in 2008 averaged 20 points, a more than 17-point difference with Tea Party Caucus members' scores a year later.[98] Of course, the rightward shift of the party from 2008 to 2009 not only affected Tea Partiers but was evident among all Republicans. This finding suggests that polarization of the party is about far more than just the "Tea Party" phenomenon, despite journalists' single-minded focus on the group.

Tea Party supporters in the general public also appear to be somewhat more conservative when compared to Republican supporters in general. Table 1.1 documents these differences in detail. Such differences, how-

TABLE 1.1: The Tea Party–Public Chasm on Public Policy Issues

Policy Opinion	Tea Party Supporters	Republicans	General Public
Think immigration is a very serious problem	82%	72%	60%
Think global warming will have no impact	66%	51%	29%
Think Obama has increased taxes	64%	48%	34%
Think *Roe v. Wade* was a bad thing	53%	45%	34%
Oppose same-sex marriage and civil unions	40%	41%	30%
Want gun control laws eased	30%	22%	16%

Source: CBS–*New York Times* poll, April 2010

ever, are more profound when comparing Tea Partiers to the general public, rather than with rank-and-file Republicans.

Across the policy issues above, Tea Partiers are between 8 to 16 percentage points more conservative than Republicans as a whole, except with the issue of gay marriage, in which there appears to be no significant difference between Tea Partiers and other Republicans. A mid-2010 Gallup poll—reproduced in Table 1.2—found that in nine of ten policy questions related to the size of government, the economy, and domestic and foreign policy, Tea Party supporters were more conservative than rank-and-file Republicans.[99] One begins to see how far out of line the Tea Party is with the rest of the public when examining those who are neutral toward and opposed to the Tea Party. As seen in Table 1.2, Tea Partiers are more likely to take conservative and (more) alarmed positions than those neutral toward and opposed to the Tea Party, in relation to various social and policy issues in nine of the ten questions surveyed by Gallup.

One should be careful not to draw the conclusion from Tables 1.1 and 1.2 that there are substantive disagreements between Tea Partiers and Republicans. Both groups lie far to the right of the general public on the policy issues in question, with Tea Partiers ranging from 10 to 37 percentage points to the right of Americans as a whole in the CBS–*New York Times* poll. Tea Partiers have far more in common with the Republican Party than they do with Tea Party opponents, those neutral toward the Tea Party, and the general public. Indeed they *are* the Republican Party— albeit representative of its most extreme elements. Those extreme elements have come to represent the core of Republican politics as the party has consistently moved to the right over the last three-and-a-half decades. Few moderate Republicans remain today, as the far-right faction of the party now dominates policymaking. With regard to their partisan origins, Tea Partiers were aptly described in a fall 2010 Bloomberg poll as "super Republicans."[100] This finding, supported by the evidence above, debunks the claims of Tea Partiers that the group "transcends partisan politics," that it represents "a rejection of radicalism," that "the ideas that the Tea Party stands for are close to the national consensus," and that "the issues that the Tea Party stands for are arguably even more popular than the movement itself."[101]

Conceding that Tea Party electoral candidates pushed the Republican Party slightly to the right is quite different, however, from suggesting that the Tea Party is a social movement. The recent incremental rightward shift of the Republican Party could just as easily be a product of behind-the-scenes organizing of a small number of local Republican candidates and other activists. Tea Party candidates did not need a mass movement to win elections in which Democratic candidates were unpopular with the general public. Victories in many localities were far easier to achieve at a time when the public was looking for fresh alternative candidates—those who were widely reported by journalists as political "outsiders." Under such circumstances, and considering the generally poor state of the American economy, significant losses for Democratic incumbents were hardly a surprise and were predicted in academic studies.[102]

THE TEA PARTIERS AS THE POLITICAL ESTABLISHMENT: THE ROLE OF CAMPAIGN CONTRIBUTIONS

There should be no exaggeration of the differences between "establishment" Republicans and Tea Party candidates, with the latter inaccurately depicted as creating a revolution from within the Republican Party.[103] The difference between Tea Party Republicans and average Republicans is one of degree, not one of substance. Although it was impossible to

TABLE 1.2: The Tea Party, Policy Threats, and the Public

Issues Seen as "Extremely Serious Threats"	Tea Party Supporters	Republicans	Tea Party Neutral	Tea Party Opponents
Federal Government Debt	61%	55%	44%	29%
Size & Power of Federal Gov't	49%	43%	30%	45%
Healthcare Costs	41%	37%	37%	33%
Discrimination against Minority Groups	13%	9%	17%	17%
Illegal Immigration	41%	38%	32%	14%
The Environment and Global Warming	13%	10%	27%	30%
Unemployment	35%	33%	34%	32%
Situations in Iraq and Afghanistan	24%	22%	31%	22%
The Size & Power of Large Corporations	16%	14%	21%	32%
Terrorism	51%	51%	43%	29%

Source: Gallup Poll, July 2010

measure the ideology of Tea Party upstart candidates prior to their taking office, data were available for Tea Partiers already in Congress, and an emerging body of data was also available demonstrating that the forces driving upstart candidates were thoroughly elitist and pro-business. According to ADA voting scores, those within the Tea Party Caucus in late 2010 were only 4.65 points more conservative than the average House Republican in 2009. Similarly, their financial support base and ability to raise campaign contributions was not substantively different from that of other House Republicans.

Table 1.3 shows that Tea Party Caucus members and new Tea Partiers or "upstarts" (who had not held office prior to the 2010 midterms) in the House and Senate were remarkably similar to Democratic and Republican incumbents in terms of average campaign contributions raised. When viewed in the aggregate, all Tea Partiers who ran in the House were very similar when compared to all Democrats and

Republicans who ran in that chamber, at least in terms of their average campaign contributions. When examined together, all Tea Partiers in the Senate were even more privileged than all Democratic and all Republican actors, as the former raised on average more than three to four times as much as the Democratic and Republican Senate averages for all the candidates from each party.

Tea Party upstarts were able to garner large campaign contributions, in no small part because of the massive media attention directed toward them and the increased legitimacy coverage conferred upon their campaigns. In this sense, Tea Party Caucus members and new Tea Partiers share more in common with other "politics-as-usual" incumbents in Washington, in terms of their massive campaign contributions and high levels of visibility, than they do with political "outsiders."

When examining campaign contributions and reliance on corporate funding, Tea Party Caucus members are as entrenched, and at times even more entrenched, than other members of Congress. The average House Tea Party Caucus member raised $1.47 million by the midterm elections, compared to the average House incumbent who raised $1.42 million.[104] When examining House candidates' contributions from political action committees, the overwhelming majority of contributions to members of Congress (75 percent) are provided by business interests.[105] Whereas 83 percent of the political action committee (PAC) contributions to Republican members of Congress originated from business interests, the figure stood at 88 percent for those members of the House Tea Party Caucus.[106] The number is far smaller for new Tea Partiers, since just 46 percent of their PAC money came from business interests, and a far larger share came from single-issue groups. However, this comparatively smaller reliance on corporate funding is likely the result of new Tea Partiers' lack of success in attracting corporate PAC money, which is due to corporate America's choice to be conservative in donating funds to new Tea Partiers, rather than the result of any sort of moral rejection of corporate funding.

Mass media reporting after the 2010 midterms ignored the elitism of entrenched House Tea Party Caucus members, preferring the narrative of the "insurgent" new Tea Partier who allegedly stood outside the boundaries of Republican "establishment" politics. There was no way to assess this claim on the voting level, as new Tea Partiers had not yet had a chance to vote on any legislation. However, other data strongly suggests that the standard media narrative was flawed. For one, the average House

TABLE 1.3: The Tea Party, Incumbents and Other Challengers
in the 2010 Midterms

House of Representatives	Average Campaign Contributions	Senate	Average Campaign Contribution
Tea Party Caucus	$1,474,172	Tea Party Caucus	N/A
New Tea Partiers (Winners)	$1,432.266	New Tea Partiers (Winners)	$7,331,806
Incumbent Democrats	$1,421,034	Incumbent Democrats	$9,633,236
Incumbent Republicans	$1,319,802	Incumbent Republicans	$7,834,286
All Incumbents	$1,421,034	All Incumbents	$8,633,053
All Tea Partiers (Winners & Losers)	$805,583	All Tea Partiers (Winners & Losers)	$9,603,091
All Democrats	$755,949	All Democrats	$2,800,022
All Republicans	$449,952	All Republicans	$2,295,262

Source: Center for Responsible Politics and Opensecrets.org

Republican already scored near the extreme conservative end of the political spectrum, at 7 percent, according to the ADA voting records. Additionally, Tea Party Caucus members scored 2.35 in the ADA voting records. Such extreme and conservative polarization ensured that there was little room for new Tea Partiers to move much further to the right. This point is also reinforced at the policy level. Republicans have been promoting a radical vision for policy change for more than three decades, supporting the privatization of Social Security, draconian cuts in Medicare and Medicaid, and the further deregulation of business. Tea Party upstarts running in 2010 offered little difference in the substance of their rhetoric, although they were more openly brazen in pushing for a greater national commitment to free market–based neoliberal policies.

The "Tea Party upstarts as outsiders" argument ignores the ways in which new Tea Partiers are astoundingly similar to older establishment Tea Partiers. The best way to demonstrate this point is by examining Tea Partiers' ties to the very business forces that were leading the conservative drive against progressive healthcare reform (the healthcare and insurance

TABLE 1.4: Tea Party Caucus vs. Upstarts in the Economic
            Establishment (2010 Midterms)

Tea Party Groups	Campaign Contributions from Healthcare and Insurance Interests	Campaign Contributions from Banks, Finance, and Real Estate Interests
Tea Party Caucus Total	$5,882,257	$4,183,394
New Tea Partier Total	$1,998,858	$2,355,397
Tea Party Caucus Average	$125,154	$89,008
New Tea partier Average	$52,601	$61,984
All Tea Partier Total	$7,881,115	$6,538,791
All Tea Partier Average	$88,878	$75,496

Source: Center for Responsible Politics and Opensecrets.org

industries) and were primarily responsible for causing the 2008 economic collapse and subsequent bailout (the real estate, finance, and banking
industries). By examining the extensive ties of Tea Partiers (old and new)
to these business interests, one will see that Tea Party officials are conventional and establishment oriented and do not represent a break in any way
from the past.

Tea Party Caucus members are more privileged in their campaign
contributions than other members of Congress, including fellow
Republicans. A 2010 study by the Center for Responsive Politics found
that "the top contributors to the 50 members of a newly established congressional Tea Party Caucus" included "health professionals," the "real
estate industry," and "oil and gas interests." Furthermore, donations from
health professionals, oil and gas interests, and Republican and conservative groups were, on average, higher for Tea Party Caucus members than
for members of the House of Representatives in general and even their fellow House Republicans.[107] These findings should not be surprising, considering that nearly half of the caucus (as of fall 2010) served in Congress
for at least a decade, with many candidates serving even longer terms.

At first glance, campaign contribution data in Table 1.4 suggests that
new Tea Partiers were significantly less reliant on contributions from the
above-mentioned industries. New Tea Partiers were less likely to raise
money from business interests, when compared to those in the Tea Party

TABLE 1.5: Tea Partiers, Healthcare Reform, and the Economic
Economic Establishment (2010 Midterms)

Campaign Contributions by Industry	Tea Party Caucus (% w/Each Industry as a Top Ten Contributor)	New Tea Partiers (% w/Each Industry as a Top Ten Contributor)	Non-Tea Party, Non-Incumbent Winners (% w/Each Industry as a Top Ten Contributor)
Health and Insurance	94%	95%	77%
Banks	30%	16%	29%
Real Estate	70%	74%	81%
Finance	32%	39%	40%
Securities and Investment	30%	29%	23%

Source: Center for Responsible Politics and Opensecrets.org

Caucus, who received a significant $7.88 million from healthcare and insurance interests and $6.5 million from banking, finance, and real estate interests, for a grand total of $14.4 million. New Tea Partiers received on average 58 percent less from healthcare and insurance interests and 30 percent less from banking, finance, and real estate interests.

These numbers, however, are misleading. They reflect the relative *inability* of Tea Party upstarts to raise contributions from business PACS, when compared to Tea Party Caucus members. This point is driven home in Table 1.5, which demonstrates that new Tea Partiers were just as likely, and at times more likely, to rely on business interests as their top donors when compared to caucus members. New Tea Partiers were more likely to rely on business interests in three of the five categories in Table 1.5. New Tea Partiers were about as likely to rely on corporate contributions when compared to Tea Party Caucus members. Whereas the total dollars Tea Party upstarts received from business interests was lower than the sum raised by Tea Party Caucus members, these contributions will in all likelihood grow significantly in the future, as suggested by upstarts' strong reliance on corporate funds. Tea Party upstarts were not seen as a sure thing in light of their underdog status as non-incumbents in 2010. As a result, business contributors were relatively less likely to take a chance on them, at least until they had proven themselves to be electable. Such apprehension will likely decline as the 2012 elections approach.

House Tea Party Caucus members and Tea Party upstarts appear to share far more in common with those already in Congress than they do with some mythical "insurgent" candidates. Equally problematic for a "grassroots" Tea Party are the close links between the Tea Party Caucus and the forces responsible for the economic crisis. The economic crisis is understood by political economy experts to be the direct result of the housing bubble and the deregulation of complex financial instruments tied to the housing market, as well as other larger systemic forces and structural flaws undergirding the capitalist system.[108] The collapse is intimately linked to the finance, banking, investment, and real estate industries, all of which had a strong incentive to promote weaker home-loan standards and borrowing, in addition to the weakening of regulations for the banking and mortgage industries.

A GRAIN OF TRUTH?
THE TEA PARTY AS A POLITICAL "OUTSIDER"

The above statistics should not be taken as a sign that *all* Tea Partiers are establishment-oriented. The comparatively disadvantaged Tea Party victors in the 2010 primaries were generally more conservative than their competitors, and this increased conservatism, aided by public perceptions of their relative freshness compared to other Republicans, likely played an important role in Tea Party electoral successes. In Delaware, for example, Tea Partier Christine O'Donnell was much more conservative than her competitor Mike Castle, who supported the bank bailout, and was widely considered to be one of the most liberal-to-moderate of all Republicans.[109] In Alaska, Tea Partier Joe Miller was widely seen as more conservative than his more moderate competitor Lisa Murkowski, who was liberal on social issues such as abortion and stem cell research and supported the 2009 bank bailout.[110] In Utah, Tea Party primary victor Mike Lee was more conservative than competitor Robert Bennett. Bennett was attacked by conservatives for supporting the 2008 bank bailout and for working toward bipartisan healthcare reform with Democrats in Congress.[111]

The relative "freshness" of new Tea Party candidates, however, seemed to fade quickly by the time of the midterm elections. By November, Tea

Party upstarts who won their respective races had greatly distanced themselves from less elitist Tea Partiers who lost their elections. Nowhere was this trend more apparent than in polling data immediately prior to the elections, which conclusively demonstrated that those Tea Partiers most likely to be leading in their respective races were those who had raised large amounts of money in campaign contributions.[112] My statistical analysis of the 2010 midterms found that being a Tea Party candidate in and of itself conferred no statistical advantage for those running for office. What accounted for the "electability" of certain Tea Partiers was their greater ability to raise campaign contributions.[113] On average, Republicans running for House offices in 2010 raised $375,163. Of those Tea Party upstarts who received more than the Republican average, most of them (55 percent) won their respective races. Although money itself did not guarantee victory, it was instrumental in distinguishing between electable and unelectable candidates. This trend was clearly seen among Tea Party upstarts who raised less than the House Republican average, of whom not a single one won in their respective races. In an electoral age where greater financial resources allow candidates to saturate audiences with campaign ads, Tea Partiers who raised the largest amounts of money disproportionately benefited from greater name recognition among the voting public.

RUNNING THE ECONOMY INTO THE GROUND:
TAKING THE TEA PARTY CAUCUS TO TASK
FOR THE ECONOMIC CRISIS

The Tea Party presents itself as thoroughly anti-establishment. Its activists and officials claim to oppose the 2009 economic bailout, to detest Democratic healthcare reform and the alleged assault on private sector care. They claim to be against the corruption-as-usual of the two-party system and an entrenched business elite. It is certainly true that the vast majority of Tea Party Caucus members—75 percent—opposed the Troubled Assets Relief Program. But suggestions that Tea Party officials are part of a movement that is rebelling against corporate elitism and government corruption should be evaluated skeptically. A sizable number of those in the Tea Party Caucus were involved in creating the economic crisis they now criticize.

Nineteen of the 29 Republicans in the Tea Party Caucus as of late 2010 were in power during the 1999 to 2000 session of Congress. Most of them played an instrumental role in creating the economic crisis Americans face today by allowing national banks to become too big to fail, and in deregulating the toxic derivatives that were intimately linked to the 2008 economic collapse. Eighteen of the 19 Tea Party Caucus members who were in power in Congress from 1999 to 2000 voted in favor of the 2000 Commodity Futures Modernization Act, which exempted derivatives from regulation by the Securities and Exchange Commission and the Commodity Futures Trading Commission.[114] As a form of insurance on other financial investments and assets, derivatives are regularly used to underwrite home loans and corporate investments in the housing market, and contributed greatly to the economic crisis as the housing bubble was collapsing. Tea Party Caucus members, alongside other Republicans and a Democratic president, supported the deregulation of derivatives with the understanding that markets operate most efficiently when *not* subject to government regulation. This assumption was shown to be flagrantly inaccurate in the wake of the 2008 economic collapse—something known by progressive regulators for nearly eight decades, ever since such regulations were established to reduce investor speculation during the New Deal.

Similarly, the vast majority of the Tea Party Caucus members in 1999—18 of the 19 in power at the time—voted in favor of the bipartisan Gramm-Leach-Bliley Act. This bill regulated the national banking industry in order to allow risky investment–oriented banks and traditional commercial banks to engage in massive mergers and buyouts.[115] The act repealed long-standing legal protections that required the separation of investment banks and other banking interests—protections that dated back to the Glass-Steagall Act passed during the New Deal and Great Depression period. Glass-Steagall was originally established to prohibit banks from becoming too big to fail and was meant to prevent an economic crisis resulting from unchecked financial and investment-based speculation. The law's repeal, and the further financialization of the economy during the 1970s and 1980s, underlines much of the economic trouble the United States faces today, with much of the investing on Wall Street now driven by speculation and the casino-style derivatives—the real value of which remains obscure even to investors.

The Tea Party Caucus in power in late 2010 was celebrated for leading a "grassroots rebellion" against an economic crisis, though one it played an intimate role in creating. These Tea Party leaders were effective in obscuring their role in creating the economic collapse, as mass media outlets, pundits, and political officials spared them from embarrassing revelations. Though rank-and-file Tea Partiers claim to publicly oppose corporate welfare and bailouts, they are at a loss to explain how a legitimate social movement can exist when its most prominent members created the economic crisis they now lament. Tea Party supporters are also put in a difficult spot by the Tea Party Caucus's incestuous relationship with the healthcare industry. Tea Party Republicans in Congress played an instrumental role in opposing the creation of a public option or universal healthcare, thereby setting the stage for the passage of the pro-market healthcare reforms supported by Democrats. This major intervention in favor of directing taxpayer subsidies to corporate America represents a major violation of the free market rhetoric embraced by Tea Partiers. That Tea Partiers at the local level appear to be largely unaware of, or unconcerned with, the role their leaders played in the economic collapse and in expanding market-based healthcare is not an encouraging sign for those depicting the group as an informed grassroots uprising against the status quo politics in Washington and against Wall Street's greed. Furthermore, the widespread failure of local Tea Party activists to form a broad-based mass movement is deeply troubling in light of the massive amount of reporting that suggests the Tea Party is a grassroots uprising. Such rhetoric about the "Tea Party insurgency" helped propel the Republican Party to victory in the 2010 midterms, but is largely fictional.

TWO

The Tea Party Does Not Exist:
Observations on the Ground in Chicago

With Paul Street

Our findings with regard to Tea Party activism in Chicago supplement those of the last chapter, where we found that Tea Party organizing was lacking at the local level. In this chapter we present a summary of more than six months of local observation, documenting the widespread confusion, lack of participation, extreme secrecy, and lack of movement building of the midwestern Tea Party.

The extensive ties between the Tea Party and the Republican Party do not in and of themselves mean that the group fails as a social movement. When considering strong Republican ties *alongside* the lack of participation in the chapters across the country, the Tea Party fails to meet the basic requisites of a social movement. We have already demonstrated the lack of participation in the Tea Party across national chapters. Our experiences with chapters of the Tea Party in the Midwest further reinforce our national findings.

Because of everything we had read in national and local media, we began this study by assuming the Tea Party was a social movement. The evidence gathered from a nationwide survey raised serious questions about this conventional wisdom. Observation of Tea Party organizing in the Chicago area allowed us to strengthen our conclusions by adding another layer of detail and nuance to the national findings. The observations took place during the spring, summer, and fall of 2010, at the time when national attention to the Tea Party had reached its highest point yet. Analysis of Tea Party activism covered five cities in the metropolitan area, including the city of Chicago and the suburbs of Schaumburg, Palatine, Naperville, and Morton Grove.

Chicago is an ideal location for a case study of the Tea Party for a number of reasons. First, it is the city where the Tea Party was allegedly founded, with CNBC host Rick Santelli's "rant heard round the world" in February 2009 calling for a Tea Party following the inauguration of President Barack Obama. Second, Chicago is one of the largest cities in the country, in one of the most active regions of the Tea Party—the Midwest, where many Tea Party upstarts won in the midterm elections. Illinois saw the election of five upstart Tea Party candidates to the House of Representatives, *more than any other single state in the country*, with four of the five Tea Party victories in the state coming from the Chicago metropolitan area. Finally, the Chicago area shares a relatively large concentration of "boom town" cities, characterized by large levels of growth in relation to the emerging housing bubble in the post-2000 period. It is in these boom towns that the Tea Party saw its strongest levels of activism.[1] If there is evidence that the Tea Party is a social movement, it should be found in the Chicago metropolitan area.

In assessing whether Chicago Tea Party chapters represent a social movement, we looked for certain indicators. We expected to find evidence of the following: 1) relatively large turnouts at meetings; 2) a plethora of local groups that were openly organized and represented at rallies; 3) regular meetings in many towns and cities throughout the metropolitan region; 4) the existence of an open meeting format characterized by active participation and discussion among members; 5) regular volunteering among meeting attendees to engage in future activities; and 6) traditional social movement activities at rallies, including pamphleteering and leafleting. Such activities, if associated with evidence of flourishing individual Tea Party–based community organizations, would indicate serious participation at the local level.

These expectations are based upon our experiences participating in various social movements over the last decade. Our involvement in the women's rights, antiwar, anti-sweatshop, anti-corporate globalization, and environmental movements informed us of what to look for in Tea Party meetings and demonstrations.[2] The meetings and rallies we attended within left-leaning social movements *were* defined by the criteria listed above, so it was reasonable to expect that any social movement on the right would also conform to such standards. Local organizing within left social movements was accompanied by regular (weekly or monthly) meetings, an open-discussion format, sustained participation in local and national initiatives, and participation in demonstrations attracting tens to hundreds of thousands of participants. Attendance of local and national left-oriented protests was also regularly accompanied by a massive amount of leafleting and pamphleteering, with those who were demonstrating representing a diversity of political organizations in their home communities. Our expectations are also based indirectly on the scholarly prerequisites for a social movement discussed at the beginning of the last chapter.

WIDESPREAD IGNORANCE AND CONFUSION

One major obstacle to the formation of a coherent, unified Tea Party movement is the mass confusion exhibited by its members, which is largely the product of misinformation disseminated by conservative officials, business elites, and reactionary media pundits. These figures—as seen in the likes of the Kochs and Limbaughs of the right—are willing to rely on falsehoods, manipulation, and propaganda in communicating with their right-wing base. Some of the major points of ignorance that were evident in local meetings we observed are:

- An obsession with the notion that the United States, although the richest nation in the world, can no longer "afford" to engage in deficit spending during a time of economic crisis. This attitude endured among Tea Partiers with whom we engaged, despite the fact that the national debt as a percent of GDP is far from its historical height, and despite the well-established Keynesian understanding among economists that governments need to run deficits in the short term during times of economic crisis to promote economic recovery and create demand at a time when businesses are shedding jobs and hoarding cash. Tea Partiers we observed were more than willing to repeat the blatant falsehood that national debt had reached "unprecedented" levels, despite statistical evidence indicating this was not true.[3] Tea Partiers' obsession with national spending and debt may not reflect an actually existing debt crisis, but it is incredibly valuable to business elites and Republicans who frame any sort of government spending on public goods as a threat to national "prosperity."

- A false impression that taxes in the United States reached crushingly high, unsustainable levels under Obama, despite his administration pushing a pro-tax-cut agenda, as seen in the Democrats' stimulus package and Obama's support for further tax cuts during the 2010 midterm elections, which were directed overwhelmingly at the wealthy. National polling reinforced this false conclusion, with 64 percent of Tea Partiers thinking that Obama "has increased taxes for most Americans."[4] Furthermore, Tea Partiers we observed were oblivious to the fact that the United States already has among the lowest taxes in the first world. This reality did not comport with group members' mythical feelings of persecution by Obama "socialists" intent on encroaching upon their property rights. Their attitudes did, however, fit comfortably within a business-dominated framework that seeks never-ending tax cuts for the wealthy and continuous cuts in public goods and services.

- Confusion about what socialism is and a distortion of the concept as it is understood by those on the left and by socialist intellectuals.[5] Modest increases in taxes for those making over $250,000 a year were framed in alarmist ways as evidence of a "socialist takeover," as were Democrats' mildly progressive attempts to reform the excesses of the private healthcare system. For example, the prohibition of exclusions based on preexisting conditions and the legal requirements that all Americans purchase private health insurance through private state insurance exchanges were all market-based "solutions" to America's healthcare problems, and were originally promoted by Republicans themselves. Republican congressman Paul Ryan, for example, proposed just such an expansion of private insurance care in early 2011, which would have forced those under 55 onto private insurance, while formally ending Medicare as Americans know the program today. Ryan's and Democratic expansions of the private health insurance market are the polar opposite of socialism, although one would not know this after observing local Tea Party meetings. Such depictions are divorced from reality, but extraordinarily useful to business elites intent on skirting progressive reforms.

- Ignorance about social welfare programs that Tea Partiers claim to support, yet undermine in their personal statements and political actions. It was common for Tea Partiers to claim that they were "moderate" in their support for traditional welfare programs benefiting the masses, including Social Security and Medicare and that they wanted to see these programs continue into the future. However, their support for right-wing Republicans directly contradicted such statements, considering that those officials directed considerable energies over the last three decades to pursuing major cuts to and privatization of these programs. Confusion among Tea Partiers was reinforced in national polls, with 62 percent of group members explaining that programs such as Medicare and Social Security are "worth the cost," but with a majority (53 percent) also supporting the privatization of these programs in the name of running them more efficiently.[6] Such a position reveals a staggering ignorance, as the entire concept of "social security" is based on the notion of *collective* rather than privatized responsibility for providing for retirement payments to the elderly. The commitment to "security" in retirement is ensured specifically through setting aside Social Security payments and ensuring that they are independent from the potentially massive fluctuations of the stock market, which were so effective in devastating personal retirement (401-k) funds. The privatization of Social Security is tantamount to the effective repeal of the entire program, although this reality appears to be beyond the grasp of most Tea Partiers. Such ignorance is again of great value to the political and business elites who are intent on dismantling these programs and redirecting their resources toward the private sector, while still promising to fulfill the goals of maintaining income security and providing adequate healthcare.

- Finally, there is a contradictory "understanding" of the causes of the current economic crisis, which makes it difficult, perhaps impossible, to engage in a productive dialogue. Tea Party activists we observed believed that the activities of Obama and the Democratic Congress were the most direct reason for America's continued economic problems. Many Tea Partiers are seriously concerned with Obama's status as an "exotic," "socialist," "other," which is reflected at rallies and in national data indicating that 59 percent of Tea Partiers either think Obama was born in another country or cannot be sure that he is really a citizen.[7]

None of the Tea Partiers with whom we spoke indicated any understanding of the bipartisan nature of current economic troubles.
Nationally, 57 percent of Tea Partiers expressed a favorable view of
Bush, with just 27 percent sharing an unfavorable view. Just 5 percent
felt that the Bush administration was "mostly to blame for the current
state of the nation's economy," and only 15 percent said Wall Street
was to blame. In contrast, Obama was twice as likely to be blamed
(compared to Bush), and the most common response among Tea
Partiers (expressed by 28 percent) was to blame the Democratic-con-
trolled Congress. Ninety-two percent explained that national problems were the result of Obama's policies, which were "moving the
country toward socialism," not from bipartisan neoliberal policies of
deregulation, outsourcing, and downsizing, which have been a main
staple of U.S. policy for decades and are eviscerating America's middle class and poor.[8] It is true that a majority of Tea Partiers (61 percent) say that "free trade" has hurt the public.[9] Such feelings are
directly contradicted by their support for a renewed commitment to
free market economics at the domestic level (as advocated by most Tea
Partiers with whom we spoke). Nonetheless, Tea Party ignorance with
regard to the causes of the economic crisis remains extremely valuable
to those advocating a version of capitalism that is most sympathetic to
the needs of investors and the corporate agenda while granting the
fewest concessions possible to the masses of Americans.

At the most general level, the rage expressed by Tea Partiers is under-
standable, even predictable. Their most common concern is congruent
with national polling figures, which demonstrate that Tea Partiers (as well
as the general public) feel that the largest problems facing the country are
the economy and the lack of jobs.[10] These common concerns help
account for the strong appeal of the Tea Party among a sizable minority of
Americans. An overarching concern with a bad economy and job loss
marks the beginning and end of their rational anger, however. When
asked to articulate their rage on a policy-specific level, their explanations
degenerate into a hysteria clearly fueled by the manipulation of national
political elites and pundits. Our observation of local Tea Partiers consistently uncovered an anger driven by issues such as healthcare reform, "big
government," and the perceived lack of representation in Washington.
Such concerns were also cited nationally in opinion polling, which found
that the most common reasons cited by Tea Partiers for their anger

included: "government spending," "healthcare reform," and government "not representing the people."[11]

These concerns appear rational on the surface, but the ways they are manifested among Tea Party activists are not. Fear over nonexistent "socialist" healthcare, a mythical "unprecedented spending" in Washington, and Obama's alleged non-citizenship are a far cry from informed understandings of the problems facing the country. The structural causes of the United States' economic decline include the growth of outsourcing, the long-standing assault on popular social welfare programs and unions, deindustrialization, the growth of speculation, the crisis of overproduction and saturation with material goods, and the continued decline in the value of middle-class and working-poor wages. Most of these developments are classic manifestations of class warfare as promoted by business, but one would be hard-pressed to identify them in the rhetoric of Tea Partiers.

Tea Partiers are an integral part of an American right that has spent decades brushing off warnings about a system of class warfare as "conspiratorial," despite the extensive damage done to the country's working class. It seems unlikely that the same right that has long denied these problems is now going to change direction and embrace progressive ideas. One can hope that the general public, including many who merely express sympathy for the Tea Party in opinion polls, will eventually become open to working toward progressive policy goals, but expecting the small cadre of Tea Party activists to do the same is unrealistic.

WEAK LOCAL INFRASTRUCTURE AND CHAPTER ORGANIZING

The Tea Party's failures in Chicago are instructive because they mirror larger failures across the country. Chicago metropolitan area Tea Party chapters are few and far between. This much was admitted by a lead organizer of the suburban Palatine Tea Party chapter, who complained that participation in the northwestern suburbs of the city was meager to nonexistent. This organizer conceded that he was aware of no serious activism in northwest suburbs except in Elgin and Palatine. This was a dramatic admission, considering that the northwest suburbs account for more than one-third of the entire suburban population of Chicago. National polling figures from the *New York Times* suggest that, as of early 2010, 21 percent of the public reported knowing of a local Tea Party chapter that was "politically active."[12] Our assessment of the Chicago metropolitan area suggests that *active* local chapters are more difficult to find. Just 1 percent of municipal jurisdictions throughout the Chicago area in early to mid-2010 showed evidence of monthly Tea Party meetings.

A common complaint among Tea Party activists with whom we spoke was that many of their friends, family, and acquaintances were ideologically sympathetic with the "movement," but that none had bothered to become involved. One protester complained of the "lethargy" problem, where individuals they knew seemed interested but did not become actively involved. In the few chapters that did organize local meetings, at least half (often much more) of those attending the events indicated that they were not even from the city hosting the meeting, but had to travel there due to the failure of their own city to organize a Tea Party chapter. Closer inspection of the few chapters that did exist demonstrated continued participation problems even for those who attended meetings.

Turnout, Volunteerism, and Civic Dialogue

Observation of Tea Party meetings was possible in only a small number of cities and towns in the Chicago metropolitan region because of a systematic failure of groups to organize. The lack of organization across the region was accompanied by extremely weak organization within individual chapters. Weak participation was evidenced in three areas: small turnouts for meetings; a lack of concrete proposed actions within those meetings; and an unwillingness to become involved beyond passively attending meetings. Attendance at Tea Party "organizing" events never averaged more than a few dozen people at the meetings we attended. Numbers were often much smaller. These figures are meager in light of the minuscule number of local chapters that existed. Attendance was larger, however, at other types of events. For example, a "Town Hall Health Care" forum that took place in the suburb of Schaumburg averaged approximately 65 people, and a Town Hall in Naperville in which Tea Partiers advocated term limits for city board members included more than 80 attendees. These figures, however, deeply exaggerate the Tea Party's numbers. The Schaumburg Town Hall, though advertised by the Palatine Tea Party on its website and organized by a Schaumburg Tea Partier, was also promoted in public places throughout Schaumburg as a venue to promote the candidacy of Republican Tea Party congressional candidate Joe Walsh. In light of these facts, it would be unwise to conclude that most who turned out were active "members" of the Tea Party. Many likely attended as a result of seeing the advertisements. Additionally, the event was intended to promote Joe Walsh's campaign, rather than serve as a real Tea Party planning meeting. Massive turnout at this single event, then, did little to buttress claims that the Tea Party is an empowering, community-based movement. No time was set aside at the meeting for coordinating and planning Tea Party activism from rank-and-file members.

In the Naperville Town Hall, the vast majority of people who attended (90 percent) were not there in relation to the Tea Party's agenda item (term limits), but for other town-related public matters. Only one person was identified as a Tea Partier, though most of the time spent at the meeting was spent on non–Tea Party community matters. In short, major turnouts at town halls are not necessarily evidence of Tea Party empowerment.

THE MOVEMENT OF FOUR

The small average turnouts for meetings might not have been as devastating in terms of the prospects for a Tea Party movement if there were a larger number of local chapters, and if those who did attend were highly committed, enthusiastic, and active. This, however, was not the case. Seldom did more than four or five active participants (that is, those who spoke regularly) attend meetings, far short of what one would deem a vibrant local movement. Participation at meetings came from a small vocal minority, whereas most who attended were reluctant to vocalize their opinions. In the case of the Naperville Town Hall rally, nine of the more than 80 individuals who attended spoke up in regard to the term limit proposal. Of those nine, Tea Party speakers were nearly nonexistent, despite being given ample time to come forward. While only one Tea Partier spoke, the other eight community members who spoke regarding term limits identified with other civic-related groups—including representatives from a homeowners organization, a voter education league, and a citizen action alliance. All of these groups were working throughout the Chicago suburbs and presented the idea of term limits as a "good government" issue, rather than as a Tea Party issue. In the case of the Schaumburg Town Hall, a handful of the approximately 65 who attended contributed to public discussion, despite the event's allotment of two hours for speaking and questions.

In all the suburban meetings observed in this study, typical participation was less than a quarter of those at each meeting. In the meetings in the city of Palatine, the town organizer boasted of having upward of 1,000 members, claiming this Tea Party chapter was "one of the largest in Chicagoland." Average attendance at meetings, however, was between 20 to 25 for the meetings by early to mid-2010, a revealing figure if one is to believe that the Palatine chapter is "one of the largest" in the area. When discussion did take place in the meetings, it was typically unaccompanied by decisive plans for action. In one Palatine meeting, the first half to two-thirds of the meeting was taken up with pontificating about the Tea Party's importance and the dangers of Obama "socialism" and "big government," and few concrete campaigns materialized for audience consideration. At that meeting, it took nearly an hour and a half before a few attendees volunteered to organize a booth for an upcoming town festival to hand out information about the Tea Party. Even the booth issue was not decided that day, but postponed for another date. Those organizing the meeting felt it was not fair to those who indicated interest in attending the meeting but did not bother to show up to be denied input on the decision. This issue of action was left to be decided only after online Tea Party "members" had a chance to provide their input. Participation, in the case of the Palatine meeting, was more forced than voluntary, as the requests of the meeting organizer to recruit participants to coordinate the booth event were initially met by long periods of silence by the meeting attendees.

Attendance problems were also apparent in the Chicago chapter. Attendance at Chicago planning meetings was meager, despite this chapter organizing the largest April 15 rally in the metropolitan area. The planning session dedicated to making signs for this rally saw no more than a half-dozen people turn out for a rally that was reported to have drawn a few thousand. The preparation meeting took place at a single table in an empty downtown bar. There was no groundswell of enthusiastic conservatives. In another meeting, dedicated to "activist training," just four people attended, and three of the four were not even from the city of Chicago. Some might excuse the poor in-person attendance if most of the organizing was taking place among a large number of people online. This, however, was not the case. By tracking the Chicago Tea Party listserv during the spring, summer, and fall of 2010, one could see that it was lightly trafficked. Comments throughout the spring averaged approximately three per day at the height of the planning for the April 15 rally, but fell to just over one per day from the summer through fall of that year. By the fall, online comments had reached an all-time low of just one comment for every three days. Such low levels of participation were confirmed by the number of participants, which was restrictively small. Though as many as 14 members were posting comments in April of 2010, that number had fallen to less than five a month by early fall.

Little of substance was discussed in these listserv postings; in fact, the main topic of discussion was the slow disintegration of the city's Tea Party chapter. Those emailing the list complained of poor leadership, divisiveness, and incendiary attacks emanating from organizers and members. A few indicated that they were leaving the group altogether because of leadership problems; they situated their exodus within a broader framework that acknowledged that the group was rapidly deteriorating. Those who attended Chicago organizing meetings in person admitted to not following the online communications, as these were seen as counterproductive.

Tea Partiers in the chapters observed for this case study lacked the political will to engage in direct action. Most of the few individuals who did attend meetings could accurately be characterized as weekend warriors in that they felt they were part of a social movement, but that this movement did not require them to do anything outside of showing up at a Tea Party meeting and nodding their heads regarding organizers' warnings about Democratic "socialism" and "tyranny." In short, it was clear across all the meetings attended that most attendees had no commitment to participatory politics. If this was a social movement, then the term itself had no meaning.

Organized Authoritarianism, Apathy, and Stifled Participation

Another obstacle to bottom-up participation was the contempt local organizers held for open-dialogue meetings. Rather than viewing Tea Party meetings as a place for members to discuss their ideas and proposals for action, organizers regularly presided over long-winded "presentations" about the importance of the Tea Party that were designed more to sell the idea of the organization than to effectively organize its members. Meetings proceeded to their halfway to three-quarters point without any active audience discussion of what was needed to be done to promote a Tea Party movement. Organizers monopolized these forums, informing audience members about what the Tea Party was and about future plans, rather than dialoguing with attendees about what the Tea Party *should* be about and what the future plans *might* entail. This environment was toxic for spontaneous grassroots activism.

Tea Party organizers were conscious of their curtailment of audience dialogue. At one Palatine meeting, the presenter proceeded to lecture his audience for more than an hour and a half about the all-encompassing "dangers" Islam poses to Americans, while ignoring individuals who raised their hands. Those seeking to talk eventually gave up after realizing the presenter was not going to allow them a chance.

Organizers at times displayed their contempt for meetings. The two main presenters at one Palatine meeting openly admitted that they no longer wanted to host regular meetings, because they did not "have a lot of time" for them. One of those presenters informed the audience that she was "not really an activist," presumably in defense of her announcement that she could not be expected to coordinate monthly meetings. In the case of Chicago, those who claimed to be organizers via discussions on the online listserv did not bother to attend the "activist training," preferring the comfort of what were increasingly hostile online communications to direct engagement with others. Such highly personalized, privatized "activism" conforms to the Randian politics of individualism and is directly at odds with traditional definitions of a social movement.

Elitist Ignorance on Social Movements

Ignorance regarding what constitutes a social movement is a major factor in stifling a grassroots Tea Party uprising. The major figures involved in leading the Tea Party nationally share little understanding of or interest in the prerequisites of a social movement. In her keynote speech at the 2010 Nashville Tea Party meeting, Sarah Palin pandered to the audience by announcing: "I'm a big supporter in this movement. I believe in this movement. . . . America is ready for another revolution and you are part of this. . . . It's inspiring to see real people, not politicos, not inside-the-Beltway professionals come out and speak for commonsense conservative principles." Palin did not miss the opportunity to promote Republican Party interests, providing a "shoutout" to Scott Brown, the Republican who had recently won the late Edward Kennedy's Massachusetts Senate seat. Melding the interests of Republicans and Tea Partiers, Palin celebrated the "Massachusetts chowda revolution": "In many ways Scott Brown represents what this beautiful movement is all about. He was just a guy with a truck and a passion to serve our country. He looked around and saw that things weren't quite right in Washington. So he stood up and decided that he was going to do his part to put our government back on the side of the people, and it took guts and a lot of hard work, but with grassroots support."[13]

Much cynicism drove Palin's address. When running for vice president in the year prior to the rise of the Tea Party, Palin publicly ridiculed community organizers by contrasting her mayoral background with President Obama's past activism in Chicago: "I guess a small-town mayor is sort of like a 'community organizer,' except that you have actual responsibilities."[14] Just two short years later, Palin framed herself as a prominent national figure in the Tea Party. The blatant contradiction between Palin's 2008 and 2010 rhetoric suggests that she views the Tea Party as instrumental, a medium through which to gain national office.

A similar contradiction was seen in the actions and rhetoric of Freedom Works founder Dick Armey. Armey perverts the notion of a social movement by simultaneously framing the Tea Party as independent of partisan politics on the one hand, and reliant upon partisan victories for its identity on the other. Armey dedicated his political career to the strengthening of the Republican Party, and this goal is still at the forefront of his agenda. While depicting the Tea Party as independent of partisan forces, Armey also concedes that the purpose of Freedom Works–Tea Party activism is returning Republicans to control of Congress. Armey states that "this is a leaderless movement. That is its strength. If one person tries to get in front, they will be run over. . . . I believe this movement is by far stronger being an independent force pulling both parties to our values."[15] In this statement, Armey is careful to frame the Tea Party as a force promoting conservative rather than Republican values. Yet in other statements, Armey openly admits that directing Tea Party energy at forging an independent path from Republicans is counterproductive. He claimed that "starting a third party is exhausting to both energy and treasure" and admitted that his ultimate expectations for the Tea Party was that it would aid Republicans in picking up votes in states like Ohio, Pennsylvania, Florida, Arkansas, and Colorado during the 2010 midterms, and possibly gaining majority control of the House and Senate.[16] Tea Partiers across the country feel similarly, with a majority feeling that there is not "a lot" of difference between the Tea Party and the Republican Party.[17]

Elitist manipulation of Tea Party supporters is not always driven by ambitions for higher office. Other major figures simply appear to be ignorant of what makes up a real social movement and are largely unconcerned with the Republican Party's elitist manipulation of Tea Partiers. For example, Illinois Republican Institute spokesperson and Tea Party promoter John O'Hara is the author of one of the most prominent national books on the so-called movement, *A New American Tea Party*, yet his book has little to say about what makes up a social movement.[18] O'Hara allots more than 230 pages to describing the ideology behind the Tea Party and why its politics are preferable to those of the Democratic Party, yet the promise of the work to describe the "counterrevolution against bailouts, handouts, reckless spending, and more taxes" is unfulfilled; the book contains few details on specifically how this "movement" arose in the United States. The details are not provided because they do not exist. Revealingly, as the most prominent spokesperson for the Tea Party, O'Hara does not even reference any aspects of social or political organizing until the brief final chapter, "Rules for Counterradicals." In that chapter, O'Hara does not chronicle the details of the rise of the Tea Party; rather, he makes vague references to the importance of online networking in encouraging rally turnouts. Social networking does not constitute evidence of a social movement, although one would be unaware of this after reading O'Hara's book. O'Hara states that "action cannot stop at rallies. . . . Rallies are not ends in themselves, but means of asserting voice with a specific purpose: publicity, solidarity, and pressure in the name of tangible results."[19] The political activities that O'Hara endorses include calling political officials, writing letters to an editor, voting, joining a grassroots organization, and contributing to local organizations. The final two recommendations constitute central elements of a social movement, yet they represent just a few sentences in a 259-page book that is almost completely devoid of any substantive discussion of *how* the Tea Party has been able to organize, and why anyone should accept the claim that it is a social movement.[20]

ELITISM AND THE CULT OF SECRECY

Secrecy is another integral part of local top-down organizing on the part of Tea Party elites. Secrecy hinders the emergence of a bottom-up movement. Information on Tea Party "activist training" in the city of Chicago—

specifically on where training was taking place and at what time—was not made publicly available prior to sessions. Individuals were forced to RSVP if they wished to attend. This approach provided group organizers with maximum power to control turnout size, but also likely depressed turnout by adding bureaucratic hurdles to potential participants. Similarly, an organizer for the Palatine meetings refused to share information online about future campaigns, citing the ever-present "danger" of "infiltrators" intent on taking the "movement" down from the inside. This claim was particularly ironic, considering that one local organizer openly admitted to "infiltrating" Obama organizing meetings in 2008 to learn how to canvass for Tea Party causes, and admitted that he saw nothing immoral about this.

Perhaps the most extreme example of elite manipulation of rank-and-file Tea Partiers was seen in the activities of self-proclaimed Illinois Tea Partiers running for seats in the House of Representatives. Illinois electoral candidates such as Adam Kinzinger, Joe Walsh, Randy Hultgren, Joe Pollack, and Bill Brady readily and publicly adopted the rhetoric of the Tea Party and were widely referred to as "Tea Partiers" in national reporting, and as part of the "grassroots" rebellion against the Washington establishment. Such reporting was, however, deeply flawed in that these candidates had little interest in attending local Tea Party planning meetings. We never encountered a single one of them in a monthly planning meeting in any of the cities we observed in the spring, summer, and fall of 2010. These candidates were more than willing to speak regularly at local rallies and events due to their public relations value (and the limited commitment involved), but they were unwilling to get involved in any of the arduous groundwork required of any social movement. These officials were invoking the Tea Party brand without contributing to its mobilization. The lesson drawn from their actions serves as a warning for those claiming associations between Tea Party electoral victories and the rise of the Tea Party as a "movement."

The deceptive, authoritarian approach to activism was not restricted to meetings, but applied to "Town Hall" venues as well. The Tea Party's Schaumburg Town Hall, which was devoted to the discussion of healthcare reform, was tightly controlled so that the event served as a public relations initiative for Republican Joe Walsh, rather than as a forum for questions and discussion. Numerous presenters spent nearly the entire two-hour event exploring the esoteric details of the healthcare bill, while refusing to allow questions or discussion until the last fifteen minutes.

Well over half of the Q&A time at the end of the event was taken up by presenters' long-winded answers, leaving five to ten minutes in a two-hour forum for public dialogue. This outcome was all the more problematic for a public forum in what the moderator (Joe Walsh) promised was "simply a means of getting information to the public" and allowing them to ask questions about healthcare reform.

Tea Party organizers' secrecy also extended to active manipulation of audiences. The Schaumburg Town Hall presenters, which included a number of doctors and an insurance agent, claimed an expert knowledge of the Democratic healthcare bill in their presentations. Their credentials were supposedly self-evident, considering that their fields were directly relevant to the proposed legislation and fell within the larger realm of private healthcare. The presenters, however, dominated the event by exploring extremely detailed clauses of the healthcare bill that were difficult to follow for a lay audience. We had spent much of the fall of 2009 and spring of 2010 actively writing about healthcare reform in progressive media throughout the United States, and the details of reform explored by these presenters were actively misinformed.[21] The presenters focused on arcane passages of the bill, rather than talking more generally on its basic components. Audience confusion during the presentation also arose because the presenters made unwarranted claims that the expansion of Medicaid and the expansion of private health insurance and care under Obama's reforms constituted a "socialist" threat. This conclusion was rejected in national business reporting, which framed the reforms as "boons" for the private healthcare industry.[22]

Attendees at the Schaumburg healthcare rally were expected to accept warnings about impending "socialized" medicine on faith, even though none of the clauses discussed in the presentation were remotely related to creating a government healthcare plan to replace private care. One speaker warned about nonexistent "death panels" and about "stealth rationing," while refusing to discuss the rationing that already exists under private health insurance plans. As "evidence" of the dangers of Obama's "socialized medicine," one Tea Party presenter publicized statements from Centers for Medicare and Medicaid Services head Donald Berwick (appointed by Obama), who in the past expressed support for the United Kingdom's healthcare system. This strategy represented blatant Tea Party fear mongering, as the Medicare and Medicaid programs are *already* socialized and single-payer based, yet overwhelmingly popular among the general public. The "revelation" that the top administrator for an already socialized program believes in healthcare as a common good should have surprised no one. The manipulation of the audience was not restricted merely to conspiratorial warnings about "government takeovers" of healthcare. Our later discussion with another Tea Party organizer revealed that the "experts" who presented at the Schaumburg Town Hall had not even finished reading the healthcare legislation prior to lecturing the public about its "dire" and "socialist" content. Such admissions were not openly made at the time of the presentation.

The "Email Blast" Strategy: Compensating for Tea Party Apathy

Until this point, an important question has remained unresolved. If Tea Partiers were failing to organize across a wide variety of cities, and the cities they did establish a presence in were poorly coordinated, then how did the group's leaders manage to attract even the modest turnouts seen in April 2010 rallies? The answer to this question becomes clearer after engagement with the few local chapters that were organized. The approach adopted by Tea Party organizers was as follows: send out "email blasts" gathered from those who had visited local Tea Party websites hoping to attract a large turnout at rallies; and invite high-profile Republican candidates for the same reason. As a strategy, so-called Tea Party candidates' co-optation of the Tea Party brand at speaking rallies was very successful.

The two-pronged approach provided organizers with the most bang for their buck: organizers were not bogged down with time-consuming in-person meetings, and this gave the impression to the general public of a mass uprising among Tea Partiers who turn out for their photo ops. The email PR blast approach was discussed openly at a Palatine chapter meeting we attended. The main organizer—who announced he was stepping down from leading the chapter—explained that he no longer had time for monthly meetings because online networking was far more successful. He boasted that the Palatine website received 2,500 hits a month (compared to the 20 to 25 who attended meetings), and he personally sent out 81,000 emails per month attempting to galvanize support for attending local rallies. This approach had succeeded in *"generating a lot of noise"*—his words—by encouraging attendance at demonstrations and in garnering media attention, although the rallies were not followed up by mass participation in planning meetings. Increasing local participation in meetings, however, was not the goal. As the organizer admitted: "I didn't think I could just blast an email and people would come [to rallies] but they did." With his initial assumption proven wrong, the organizer now spoke of his goal of encouraging "more than a thousand" supporters to come to a local July 3 rally, which he speculated would be successful if he was able to secure prominent Republican speakers. The organizer explained that he spent much of his time "on candidates," encouraging public support and coordinating public rallies to bring further public attention to these figures.

The largest weakness local Tea Party organizers suffered from was their unwarranted expectation that a movement could emerge with little or no sustained face-to-face action. The goal was simply to "generate a lot of noise," rather than to build a sustainable grassroots movement that would become a coherent national federation. The PR-based approach succeeded in drawing public attention to the Tea Party and creating the mistaken impression that it was a social movement, but it also obscured the lack of broad-based participation in the group.

Simply sending out emails and attending the occasional rally was seen as sufficient in influencing the political system. Furthermore, many Tea Party leaders we observed indicated a genuine dislike for collectively based activism. They did not feel they should be expected to organize outside of a few large PR-style events, which were intended to create a heavily mediated public impression of a grassroots uprising and encourage greater turnout in the 2010 midterms. This approach has been very effective in garnering sympathetic media attention and in influencing public opinion, and less effective in mobilizing masses of people in a sustainable way.

As those who have engaged in grassroots activism understand, coordinating and sustaining local meetings is difficult and time-consuming, and the results are unpredictable. Local Tea Party organizers appeared to understand this reality on at least some level, which is likely why they chose the alternate route of coordinating online "email blasts" for PR-based events. This alternative approach is symbolic of the Randian, neoliberal approach to political activism. It assumes that "movements" can be transformed into "private expressions" and coordinated via personal email correspondence that encourages simply showing up once or twice a year at major rallies. This type of movement, however, dismisses the notion of *sustained, collective* responsibility and action. This much is clear in the issues on which local coordinators were campaigning. The major issue (as reflected in its name, **T**axed **E**nough **A**lready), is *individual* taxation of Tea Partiers. Another prime issue is healthcare reform, in which Tea Party supporters assume that the poor should be individually responsible for healthcare. The group opposes attempts by the federal government to expand Medicaid, as was done through the 2010 Democratic healthcare reform bill.

At the local level, issues discussed at Tea Party rallies were overwhelmingly personal in nature. To the extent that they promoted any activism, local organizers were preoccupied with mini-campaigns such as encouraging Tea Partiers to post "Don't tread on me" flags on their lawns on the Fourth of July, individually calling their school districts and complaining about "school indoctrination," opposing a local bond issue that would have increased income taxes, and finally, relying on private Republican voter rolls to canvass neighborhoods to attract conservatives to the polls. Resistance on the part of meeting attendees to even these limited personal political actions further demonstrates the neoliberal nature of the "movement."

TEA PARTY RALLIES
AND REPUBLICAN ELECTIONEERING

In their study of social movements, Frances Fox Piven and Richard Cloward conclude that major changes to the status quo are won primarily through grassroots disruption and mass defiance, rather than through formal organization building.[23] This finding is problematic for those who see the Tea Party as a movement, since it is lacking in grassroots institutions. The Tea Party relies primarily upon the Republican Party for its policy platform, and on elite local and national Republican activists and national right-wing media pundits to influence public opinion and electoral outcomes.

A close examination of the height of organizing in April 2010 reveals that rather than being concerned with mass defiance Tea Party chapters were dominated by partisan electioneering interests. The few local chapters in the Chicago area that were active in the run-up to the April 15, 2010, tax day rally listed few ways to become involved besides attending occasional local rallies. The major suggestions from the Palatine website included signing online petitions, attending the April 15 rally, and attending local Sarah Palin and Michele Bachmann visits. Few of the local websites that claimed to be politically active throughout the metropolitan area (prior to April 15) provided information for regular local chapter meetings taking place before or after the tax day demonstrations. The suburb of Palatine was one of the few that listed information for meetings for the eight million people living in Chicago suburbs, which were to be centrally located at the Hyatt Chicago Place in the suburb of Schaumburg. In other words, in the month run-up to the April 15 rally, the allegedly decentralized Tea Party had virtually no base of regular participants and relied on a highly centralized meeting system, with only one meeting per month in just a few of the hundreds of municipal jurisdictions in the Chicago metropolitan area. These findings should strike those who have any experience in local movement activism as suspicious. The vast majority of the antiwar and environmental groups with which we have been involved over the last decade met regularly (often once per week, although certainly not less than once every month) and were the products of community organizing. By "community organizing," we mean that one did not have to travel outside of the town to get to the meetings, as was the case with the Tea Party. When those associated with the leftist groups with which we were involved attended national or regional protests, they did so as participants of their local communities.[24] These movements were not reliant on national pundits, officials, and other elite-oriented actors to sustain their agendas, as is the case with the Tea Party.

THE APRIL 15 CHICAGO RALLY:
A MOVEMENT IN NAME ONLY

An examination of the most prominent of the Chicago area's April 15 protests reveals important details about what passes for grassroots participation. The Tea Party of Chicago spearheaded the largest metropolitan April 15 protest, yet its website listed just three events in the run-up to April 15: an April 13 sign-making session (in which less than a half-dozen people attended), the city protest in Daley Plaza on tax day, and a local speaking event for Michele Bachmann in Oakbrook—one of the smallest and wealthiest of Chicago's suburbs—at Ditka's Restaurant. The Ditka event was elitist in light of its location, its sponsorship by the Republican Party, and its $75 entrance fee, in addition to a $15 door charge.

Attending the April 15 Chicago protest in Daley Plaza left the critical observer with a strong impression that the Tea Party is not a movement. Those who attended a D.C.-based antiwar protest from 2002 through 2007 would have immediately seen a plethora of local groups congregated in the capital, with heavy tabling and leafleting and pamphleteering. If one attended the Chicago Tea Party protest, the contrast was immediately evident: no tabling, no leafleting. After attending the Chicago demonstration, we were able to gather no more than a single leaflet, and saw no more than a single group that was tabling, and that group was doing nothing more than selling Tea Party T-shirts.

Locally based affinity groups make up a major part of social movements, especially those relying on direct action and civil disobedience. These groups are tightly knit, representing community interests, and express their own unique political views and expressions. As Jeffrey Juris writes in *Networking Futures*, affinity groups were instrumental in the direct action across the globe that disrupted and shut down numerous protests against neoliberal capitalist institutions such as the International Monetary Fund, World Bank, and World Trade Organization.[25] We were engaged with affinity groups in our own observation of, and participation in, anti-corporate globalization protests in Washington during the 2000s. Their role in promoting grassroots civil disobedience was nowhere to be seen in the Chicago area Tea Party "organizing" we observed in the spring, summer, and fall of 2010.

In discussing the 1999 anti-WTO protests in Seattle, Juris explains that activist preparation among affinity groups and other activist networks "involved more than seven hundred organizations in daily forums, teach-ins, and demonstrations. The overall mobilization was organized by a broad coalition of direct-action groups, environmental NGOs, and labor unions."[26] Similar educational action and preparation was not evident in any of the rallies or meetings we observed throughout the Chicago area in 2010. These events demonstrated no evidence of efforts from grassroots educational groups, affinity groups, or direct action networks. Rather, rallies were seen by Tea Partiers primarily as means of providing a megaphone for Republican candidates running for Congress. In short, the contrast between bottom-up social networking and activism on the left and top-down partisan electioneering and PR on the right could not have been starker. Tea Party supporters were unwilling to participate in grassroots organizing, let alone engage in direct confrontation, civil disobedience, or nonviolent direct action.

A closer look at the speaking list for the city of Chicago's April 15 rally cemented the Tea Party's status as a covert Republican operation. Candidates running for Congress represented five of the fifteen speakers, none of whom were Independents, and all of whom were Republican. The speakers were careful *never* to reference these candidates as running for the Republican Party. Speakers consistently made the point that this "movement" had nothing to do with partisan politics, and that it was genuinely grassroots. Speakers complained that some saw the Tea Party as a front for corporations and Republicans, while the crowd booed away such assumptions as little more than a simple-minded conspiracy theory. For those concerned with the Republican origins of the Tea Party, however, the signs were clear. The themes from the speakers consistently echoed those of the Republican Party and business interests, celebrating free markets and complaining about the inherent corruption of "big government." While John Tillman of the right-wing Illinois Policy Institute went as far as to promise a "revolution," he fell back on oft-repeated Republican rhetoric demonizing congressional Democrats and Obama "socialism," and celebrating the need for affluent taxpayers to keep more of their own money. By the end of the march, the message—delivered implicitly and explicitly—was this: one need *not* engage in regular activism in the future, but simply vote in the fall midterms for the Republican candidates who attended the rally. A group fronting for Republican interests could not have offered a more consistent message.

Far from representing the poor and downtrodden of the inner city and suburbs, the Chicago rally was awash in a sea of plaid and flannel shirts and black and tan khakis. Seldom have so many white, over forty, balding men been seen in one location, save perhaps a Republican convention. This revelation is instructive when assessing who this "movement" represents. The white, male, affluence trend was apparent at all Tea Party meetings we attended. The vast majority of participants were older than forty or even fifty. Most all were white, even in suburbs where nearly half of the population or at least a very large minority are black or Hispanic. White privilege was also a main staple of the September 9–12 Tea Party rally hosted in the Chicago suburb of Morton Grove. As with other meetings, the demographic was overwhelmingly one of well-dressed and relatively affluent whites.

The September 2010 9–12 rally was significant in that it was the bluntest indication of the fusion of Republican politics, Fox News punditry, and Tea Party activism. The 9–12 Project originated in a "movement" begun by former Fox television host Glenn Beck, and it seeks to organize the right around the values that allegedly brought Americans together after the 9/11 terrorist attacks. Aside from adopting the right-wing appeal of Fox News, the Morton Grove rally also served as a rallying point for Illinois Republicans, as four of the five speakers advertised were Republican electoral candidates, including gubernatorial candidate Bill Brady, and Republican congressional candidates Joe Walsh, Joel Pollak, and Cedra Crenshaw. Speakers who were not running as Republicans were just as likely to support the Republican Party. Steven Tucker, founder of the Truthaboutobamacare.com website, spoke at the rally—as well as at the Schaumburg "Town Hall" presentation discussed earlier—making demonization of the Democratic Party his primary goal, and refusing to level any criticisms against Republicans. The 2010 national 9–12 rally was orchestrated by Republican operatives organized by the Republican-driven, Dick Armey–founded Freedom Works and the Republican-allied Koch brother industrialists.[27]

The September 2010 Morton Grove 9–12 Rally recycled the same candidates who spoke during the Chicago 2010 April 15 rally, the only difference being the addition of even *higher*-profile status quo Republican gubernatorial candidate Bill Brady. Speakers at the rally spoke of no specific activist initiatives in which audience members could get involved outside of voting for Republican candidates. The only leafleting and pamphleteering that took place at the rally came from Republicans running for office. This further solidified the event as PR for *the very same* small group of Republicans who had announced their candidacies during the Chicago April 15 Tax Day rally. *All* attacks on the political system at the Morton Grove rally were directed specifically against Democrats; no attacks were leveled against Wall Street or Republicans in relation to the 2008 bailout, or in relation to any other potential criticisms of Republicans. This blatantly Republican approach displayed a certain logic and consistency, however, considering that this is precisely what one would expect from a rally promoting Republican candidacies

EYE ON THE PRIZE: PARTISAN ELECTIONEERING
AS THE TEA PARTY'S FOUNDATION

The Tea Party and Republican Party are inherently intertwined. Quinnipiac University polling reveals that three-fourths of Tea Partiers

were either Republican or leaned Republican as of 2010. Pew Research
Center and CNN polling data from 2010 also revealed that 82 percent of
those who strongly supported the Tea Party self-identified as either
Republican or Republican-leaning, while 87 percent of Tea Party activists
indicated that they prefer to vote for Republican candidates.[28] In short,
public claims from conservative and mainstream pundits that the Tea
Party is not fundamentally a Republican operation are unwarranted and
contradicted by the available evidence.[29]

Local evidence reinforces the Republican orientation of the Tea Party.
There was a consensus at the meeetings we attended that the chief goal of
organizers was to return Republicans to power in Congress. One Chicago
organizer reminded his audience of the partisan nature of their operation:
"November is *everything* [emphasis added]. Our efforts need to be
focused on a get-out-the-vote drive." These meetings took on a partisan
quality, as was the case in one instance in which the organizer spent nearly three hours reading a canned PowerPoint presentation that instructed
the activists who attended on how to canvass local communities with the
help of databases provided by the Republican Party. Tea Partiers were
instructed to promote Republican principles such as "limited government," "balanced budgets," the dangers of "reckless spending," and "constitutional principles," but never to concede in front of those they were
lobbying that the ultimate goal was to return Republicans to power.
Further instructions included a warning to activists: "Don't let them
[Chicago and suburban residents] know you're a Republican." This
approach was deemed vital, since Republicans were seen as being widely
delegitimized by the public. This approach was also visible at
Schaumburg and Palatine meetings in which presenters consistently vili-
fied Democrats and heatlh care reform proposals but never made a single
critical comment against Republicans.

The strategy for Republican victory in 2010 involved a plan to dis-
credit the Democrats, thereby enabling a Republican victory by default.
Tea Party organizers complained that in the 2008 election the traditionally Republican DuPage County (in the Chicago suburbs) went
Democratic. They promised, however, that with some hard work Tea
Partiers could "turn it back" to the Republicans. How this was to be
accomplished was through a highly centralized, top-down approach.
One Chicago organizer reminded his audience at a Tea Party "activist
training" session that canvassing operations were to proceed through the
use of "robo script" in which canvassers would read a pre-designated

script seeking to portray Tea Partiers as "moderates" who were concerned with the "bipartisan" problem of government unaccountability.
This bipartisan focus, however, was immediately contradicted by the
admission that speaking about issues traditionally owned by Republicans,
such as "balanced budgets," would prompt those whom Tea Partiers were
lobbying to vote for Republicans, without having to explicitly mention
that canvassers supported the Republican Party. As the organizer
explained: "Get them interested in the principles and they'll know who to
vote for." This statement spoke strongly to the effort to elect establishment-oriented Republicans in Illinois, considering that this organizer
openly admitted that he did not vote for the Tea Party candidate for the
Republican gubernatorial primary, but rather chose to support a more
"electable" Republican candidate. This organizer's private admission that
he did not consider the state's Tea Party–Republican gubernatorial candidate Adam Andrzejewski to be viable was never conceded during rallies, when this same organizer publicly lectured attendees that a stronger
voter turnout for Andrzejewski would have ensured his victory.

A thoroughly authoritarian notion promoted by Tea Party organizers
was that activists contacting prospective voters were *not* free during the
canvassing process to talk about issues they deemed important if those
issues were at odds with what organizers believed were acceptable
Republican talking points. Acceptable talking points included any arguments that focused on the country's economic troubles or blamed
Democrats for a worsening economy. One leader explained: "You may be
a big pro-life person, but you're not going to want to talk about that."
Intead, the focus needed to be on constitutional principles, limited government, free markets, and individual freedom. The warning was clear:
"Don't raise controversial issues." Among the specific policy issues arbi-
trarily deemed "uncontroversial" by organizers included Republican
attacks on Social Security for "going broke," support for another round of
tax cuts in a state that already resides in the bottom third of the country in
tax rates, and business-inspired attacks on "union thugs," "public sector
unions," and "government employees" who, nonunion Chicagoans were
reminded, "make more than you do." Attempts to predetermine what
issues were and were not acceptable were not new to Chicago Tea Party
organizers, as this approach was also promoted by Armey's Freedom
Works at the national level.[30]

The focus on "electable" Republicans throughout Chicago squares
with our analysis in chapter 1 demonstrating the many ways in which

Tea Party Caucus members and upstarts are representative of the political status quo in Washington. The concern with supporting establishment Republicans suggests that the Tea Party is not interested in fielding new candidates independent of bipartisan politics. That the vast majority of Republicans currently in office openly support corporate welfare in defiance of free markets was not a significant concern at meetings. One organizer in Palatine lectured the audience that Tea Partiers should never "go for the perfect" candidate, as personified in Tea Party candidates who claimed free market principles but had little to no corporate funding and institutional support from the Republican Party. Rather, Tea Partiers should "go for the win" by supporting "electable" status-quo oriented candidates. Such recommendations were not openly challenged by attendees.

Tea Party leaders admitted that the goal of their electoral efforts was not to enfranchise new voters who had been left behind by an unrepresentative political system. Empowering marginalized prospective voters was seen as an active *threat* to their efforts to return Republicans to office. Voter rolls for the city and suburbs provided by the Republican Party to the Chicago Tea Party allowed activists to distinguish between those who were relatively more inclined to vote Republican—those self-identifying as independent, moderate, or Republican-leaning—and those who were less likely to vote Republican, including Democrats and strong liberals. Activists were instructed to appeal to the swing groups, and were reminded that they were appealing not to the disadvantaged but to those of privilege. During the canvassing meeting we observed, one organizer spoke of the registration "problem" in Illinois and elsewhere, where Democrats were supposedly seeking to register the poor and those "on welfare" in greater numbers. These groups were understood as potentially dangerous, although they traditionally do not vote in great numbers, because they would lean Democratic if they did vote. Universal voter registration was deemed a major threat by Tea Party organizers at the canvassing meeting, but one that "we don't have to worry about just yet" in organizing for the 2010 midterms.

The near impossibility of organizing an effective Republican canvassing campaign in a city as staunchly Democratic as Chicago was the first sign that the city's Tea Party chapter was lacking in seriousness. Another sign was that the "activist training" for canvassing communities with millions of people included just one attendee (in the major meeting we observed) who actually hailed from within the city limits. Those familiar

with canvassing operations understand that they require massive numbers of volunteers to have any effect on getting out the vote within a city
with nearly three million people and a metropolitan area with more than
9.5 million people. As one Chicago Tea Party organizer admitted, "We're
not doing [communal] canvassing" because "we don't have the
resources." Rather, the goal among the small handful who turned out at
the meeting was to make use of the Republican "voter vault" program,
which includes names, addresses, and contact numbers of previous voters, and allows them to contact individuals who might lean toward voting
Republican via email or phone.

We are not suggesting that Tea Party activists are satisfied with the status quo of the Republican Party. Ideally, Tea Partiers would like to see the
dwindling number of moderate Republicans thrown out of the party, and
be replaced with far rightists who increasingly make up the vast majority
of the party's rank and file in Washington. At meetings in which "electable" candidates were supported by Tea Party leaders, participants conceded that, in an ideal world, even more conservative candidates would be
fielded and would win. It was common to hear attacks on "RINOs," or
Republicans in Name Only. Clearly, then, Tea Partiers wanted to see the
Republican Party move in an even more conservative direction than it
already has. What was most problematic about such statements, however,
is that the party is *already* dominated by far-right reactionaries. These
officials are strongly committed to dismantling the welfare state, ensuring
further deregulation, and working toward the emergence of a one-party,
Republican-led state. Republican Tea Partiers were blissfully ignorant of
the already-existing polarization of the Republican Party to the far right.
Their complaints about the allegedly moderate nature of their party are
representative of their ignorance of political reality in an era of extreme
partisan polarization.

CONFLATING ELECTIONEERING
WITH SOCIAL MOVEMENTS

It is true that, in other cities, far-right Tea Party candidates did replace
less reactionary candidates in a number of primary races. Candidates like
Rand Paul, Sharron Angle, and Christine O'Donnell, among others, are
clearly more conservative than more moderate Republicans, and one has
elite Tea Party activists to thank for the rise of this new generation of rad-

ical conservative Republicans. Willingness to campaign on behalf of Tea Party Republicans in a variety of congressional districts, however, is not the equivalent of movement organizing. Mass participation in canvassing and electioneering can potentially make up *one part* of a larger social movement, but such activities, in and of themselves, are not representative of a grassroots movement. Our review of national evidence suggests that the lack of participation observed in Chicago chapters is not an isolated pattern, but representative of a more general pattern throughout the country. Tea Party electoral victories appear to be unrelated to movement politics. Those Tea Party upstarts who won office were more reliant on extensive campaign contributions and regular campaign ads than they were on mass-based get-out-the-vote drives coordinated by (nonexistent) groundswells of Tea Party activists.

The lack of Tea Party participation at the rank-and-file level is compatible with a strong performance of many Tea Party candidates in primary elections, contrary to popular depictions. Midterm elections typically energize only a very small group of ideologically committed partisans. Primaries are defined through mass-mediated campaigns and fundraising for candidates that are dominated by big business. Strong voter turnouts in favor of Tea Party candidates in the 2010 midterms is not evidence of a groundswell of "movement" activism, since conservative and Republican-leaning independent voters are likely to turn out and vote even for radical Tea Party candidates when provided a choice between them and Democratic candidates. Furthermore, comparatively low voter turnouts in midterms make it easier for radical conservative candidates to win than is the case during presidential elections, which typically benefit from a larger, less homogenous voter pool.

REGIONAL DIFFERENCES AS SELECTIVE EMPOWERMENT?

Some will no doubt criticize our Chicago study as a single case, not necessarily representative of the country as a whole. This potential criticism neglects the fact that our case study merely serves as a supplement to the larger, extensive national survey, which demonstrates that Tea Party chapters across the country are few and far between and largely inactive as a grassroots phenomenon. It is true that there is geographical variation in the Tea Party across the country. However, none of the differentiation that

is empirically documented reinforces the claim that the group is a movement. We have already discussed the failure of local chapters to regularly
organize across 92 percent of the chapters claiming a turnout for the April
15, 2010, rally. Problems for locations that did actually witness organization are also evident on the institutional and participatory levels.

At the institutional and participatory levels, geographic differentiation is
revealing of the selective appeal of the Tea Party. Institutionally, the Tea
Party Caucus in the House of Representatives prior to the 2010 midterms
was concentrated within only a few areas of the country. Of the 52 members, most (36) hailed from the South (including the Southeast with 20 representatives and Southwest with 16 representatives). Far fewer Caucus
members resided in other regions, with just one Tea Partier in the
Northeast, six in the West, and nine in the Midwest. Similarly, Tea Party
activists are more likely to be concentrated in the South, and then in the
Midwest and West, while their presence in the Northeast is far weaker.[31]
None of these statistics suggest that the Tea Party, especially its congressional caucus, is far-reaching in terms of a mass presence outside of the South
and Midwest. Victories for Tea Party upstarts in the 2010 midterms were
similarly lopsided in their concentration, with nearly half concentrated in
the South, and just 3 percent and 8 percent of victories in the West and
Northeast, respectively, although representation did increase in the
Midwest, with 40 percent of victories coming from this region.

At the participatory level, national survey data suggest that Tea Party
organizing, while scattered and generally remaining at low levels, stood in
2010 at three people for every 10,000 throughout the country. Activism
that did occur is concentrated far more throughout the South and parts of
the West. Relatively affluent "boom town" areas that are higher income and
primarily white share the greatest concentration of the low levels of activism
that exist. The Tea Party presence is radically lower in central cities and
minority-heavy counties, which are characterized by higher levels of poverty and black and Hispanic segregation.[32] In short, Tea Party organizing is
geographically selective in addition to being concentrated in areas that are
more elitist and less attuned to the needs of minorities and the poor.

MAJOR LESSONS

This chapter and the last presented considerable evidence that the Tea
Party is not a social movement: it is manipulated by elite Republican and

business interests. The false impression of the Tea Party as a grassroots uprising is largely due to clever marketing of a small number of Republican officials, Tea Party activists, and media pundits. Tea Party events appear at first glance to be an outgrowth of a decentralized mass uprising, but a closer investigation finds that these rallies are public relations stunts, organized by Republican operatives and heavily attended as a result of superficial online social networking. In short, the Tea Party is more smoke and mirrors than a genuine populist revolt.

A recent study identifies the growing prominence of "creative participation" among political actors who lack the mass participation base needed for a social movement but wish to engage in the political process nonetheless.[32] One could certainly classify local and national Tea Party activists as creative participants, perhaps among the most creative in U.S. history, in the sense that their actions represent what appears to be the first time, perhaps in world history, that a centralized political party, aided by a small number of elite activists, artificially constructed a movement from the top down and convinced the public that it represents a genuine mass uprising.

The Tea Party and the Republican Party were fundamentally intertwined from the beginning of the group's rise to national fame. The Tea Party was always seen as an instrument for returning Republicans, albeit more conservative ones, to political power. We do not accuse local Tea Party activists of intentionally deceiving the American public about their participation in a mass "movement." This analysis is institutional rather than conspiratorial. Local activists have long insisted on the genuine nature of the Tea Party as a movement, not because they are set on deceiving the public, but because they are fundamentally ignorant as to what constitutes a social movement.

The neoliberal Randian ideology that drives modern-day Tea Partiers explicitly shuns the major components that are necessary for a bottom-up social movement. The American right's lack of familiarity with social movement politics has enabled Tea Party activists to falsely imagine their group as a sort of underdog, as a movement that is fighting from the outside against a corrupt political system. Nothing could be further from the truth, considering that from its inception the low levels of local Tea Party activism have been amplified by the mass media, corporate funding, and the Republican Party.

Individual Tea Party operatives may be naive as to what constitutes a social movement, but one should not conclude that Republican officials and national Tea Party elites who are active members of the Republican Party apparatus share that ignorance. The rise of the Tea Party represents a conscious effort on the part of Republican elites to *rebrand* the party just in time for the 2010 and 2012 elections. This portrayal is not conspiratorial. Republican officials probably have little interest in what makes a genuine social movement and likely spend little time contemplating the matter. Rather, they saw a growing general public anger with the political system, amplified in the right-wing media war on the Democratic Party, and decided to take advantage of it in their attempts to win office in 2010 and beyond. In their attempts to ensure Republican victories in Congress, conservative pundits, Republican activists, and Tea Party candidates exaggerated the generally low levels of local organizing and comparatively meager turnouts at local and national rallies, at least when compared to left-leaning protests over the last ten years. They had a strong political incentive to do so at a time when the public was already planning on punishing the Democrats for a stagnating economy and high levels of unemployment.

Republicans were disgraced in 2006 and 2008, when the public came together to end the party's majority status in Congress and to elect a Democrat to the White House. The Bush administration was intimately associated with the failed dergulatory politics that caused the economic crisis, and that link between Republican politics and economic decline remained in the public mind for years. To overcome this major hurdle, Republicans and Tea Partiers sought to repackage their party as the "party of the people," specifically through the rise of the Tea Party phenomenon. Republican officials and conservative activists understood that the public viewed their party with the same disdain it held for Democrats. The solution to this problem was the construction of a "fresh" new "movement" on the right—one that claimed to represent Middle America but was in fact deeply reactionary in its politics. Republican strategists are well aware that the public typically views social movements as an "outside" force in the political process, one that is fighting against government corruption and in favor of greater public accountability. The perceived power of social movements to shed light upon official wrongdoing was obviously seen as a valuable resource for ensuring the return of a disgraced party back to power.

The Tea Party represents the next chapter in the Republican Party's dwindling control over, and manipulation of, the populace. During this time of enduring economic crisis and stagnation, the Republican Party is only able to retain its hold on government through rebranding itself as an "outsider" force in politics, which relies on unfounded fear-mongering over Democratic "tyranny" and "socialism." The party's loss of power over the American people represents a potential milestone in American history, with the "crisis of confidence" in government now reaching epic proportions.

THREE

The Counter-Revolution *Will* Be Televised: The Tea Party as a Mediated Rebellion

Chomsky and Herman's propaganda model for the mass media predicts that reporting on domestic protest groups will idealize those that support dominant political and business interests. Social movements that fall outside of the bipartisan range of opinions are consistently ignored. A group like the Tea Party, which is strongly supportive of Republican and business interests, should receive extensive and sympathetic coverage. This prediction is strongly borne out through the analysis provided in this chapter, which finds that the Tea Party receives far higher levels of coverage than social movements on the left, and that coverage ranges from extremely to largely sympathetic, depending on the media outlets in question.

The Tea Party's popularity is a product of the amplification and publicity provided by the mass media. Previous academic studies sit well with the conclusion that the Tea Party "movement" is largely media constructed. Movements receive varied levels of attention from journalists based upon their embrace or rejection of the acceptable spectrum of opinion in Washington. Those that fall within this spectrum are celebrated, and those outside of it are ignored.

THE 2010 MIDTERMS

The 2010 midterm elections were widely heralded as evidence that Obama had reached too far to the left. One prominent example of this was CNN's Anderson Cooper, who reported that President Obama was "struggling [in the aftermath of the election] to answer the question: does he get it? Does he get what happened last night? Does he believe some of the policies he's pushed have been pushed back by the American people? . . . The question remains, are voters simply tired of what he's trying to sell them?"[1] The public, reporters consistently suggested, was coming together to punish Democrats for their miscalculation of the public mood and calling for further "moderation" in future public policymaking.[2] This narrative was problematic, however, in that it relied on public opinion polling that revealed a vague opposition to some Obama policies such as "the stimulus" and healthcare reform, though ignoring competing surveys showing that the public was actually supportive of the specific components of these Democratic policies.[3]

The problems with journalists' conventional wisdom were of little concern to Tea Partiers, who had succeeded in promoting their own conservative narrative in the run-up to, and aftermath of the 2010 midterms. As MSNBC's Chris Matthews tellingly reported, "The biggest story of the campaign was the rise of the Tea Party."[4] Reporting about the Tea Party was widespread in 2010, as Matthews's metaphor suggested. The bottom-up rebranding of the Republican Party as the party of the people (via the Tea Party) was commonly seen in news stories, editorials, op-eds, and letters to the editor in major newspapers and television outlets. A LexisNexis search reveals that in the two months prior to the November 2 elections and in the week following the elections (from September 1 through November 7, 2010), the Tea Party was described as at least one of the following—as in "revolt" or "rebellion" against the political establishment, as "insurgent" or representing an "insurgency" against Washington politics, as "grassroots," and as a "movement" in 135 pieces in the *New York Times* (60 a month), in 120 *Washington Post* articles (53 a month), in 127 MSNBC programs (56 a month), and 149 Fox News stories (62 a month). Another study of media coverage found that reporting on the Tea Party as outside of the "Republican establishment" and as a "social movement" was a regular occurrence in the run-up to and immediately following the midterms. Such references appeared in dozens of articles and stories in a variety of news outlets I examined for this book.[5]

A closer examination reveals that reporting regularly depicted the Tea Party as an "outside" political force. The *New York Times* reported following the midterms that the Tea Party was seeking to *"make the transition* from a protest movement to a power on Capitol Hill" at a time when it expressed "a wary relationship with Republican leaders in Congress" (emphasis added). Such conclusions were at odds with the fact that the majority of Tea Party officials *already* held office as part of the House Tea Party Caucus (52 Tea Partiers were already in the House Caucus, compared to more than three dozen Tea Partiers who were elected to the House in the midterm elections). Such reporting was also inaccurate considering the comfortable (if at times conflicted) relationship between the Tea Party and the Republican Party.[6] Other news outlets took the *New York Times*'s lead, as CBS estimated on election night that the Tea Party was "sending at least 36 members to the House," ignoring the members of the Tea Party Caucus who already held office and were reelected.[7] The estimates provided by the media, while underestimating the Tea Party presence in government, nonetheless served the mass media's dominant narrative of depicting the Tea Party as an "underdog" fighting the "establishment."

Reporters showed little interest in the already existing links between Tea Partiers and Republicans. The *Washington Post* reported prior to the elections that the two groups were in conflict: "Call it a civil war, an insurrection or merely an insurgency. By any measure, the establishment leadership of the Republican Party has lost control and is now being pulled along toward an unpredictable, uncertain future."[8] NBC reported that Republicans "are now entering unfamiliar territory with their new partners, Tea Party activists," while the *New York Times* blogged after the election that "The G.O.P. leadership is still going to be constrained (hopefully in positive, deficit-reducing ways, rather than negative, let's-shut-down-the-government ways) by the activists who helped put them in power, and there will probably be an even stronger crop of Tea Party insurgents running against incumbent Republicans in the 2012 Senate and House primaries."[9] In looking to the future, Fox News led the way in speculating about the Tea Party's future:

> Anything could happen from now until the presidential election in 2012, and it remains to be seen whether a movement that prides itself on being outside the establishment will front its own Tea Party presidential candidate, revolutionize the Republican Party or merely fade back into the

background. Leading Tea Partiers vowed to keep up the pressure on their favored new lawmakers to fight a Washington establishment they say is broken and doesn't work for the best interests of the American people.[10]

THE UNREPORTED RESISTANCE

Marginalization of progressive social movements comports well with what late historian Howard Zinn referred to as "the unreported resistance." This resistance is censored because of its willingness to challenge the foundations of the bipartisan, free market capitalist system and its refusal "to surrender the possibility of a more equal, more humane society."[11] The forgotten social movements of the past and present could be accurately labeled "unworthy protests," following the dichotomy drawn between Noam Chomsky and Edward Herman's "worthy" and "unworthy" victims of U.S. violence. In laying out their propaganda model, Chomsky and Herman were concerned with how victims of U.S. and allied violence are largely unreported in the mass media, whereas the victims of enemy state violence—real or imagined—receive extensive attention and the perpetrators of such acts are subject to endless moral outrage.[12]

THE RISE OF MEDIATED REALITY

The vast majority of Americans do not have direct experience with most issues they read about in the news. As a result, the ways in which their experiences are mediated are crucial in influencing which issues they deem to be important and how they think about them. The mass media help political and business officials in "setting the agenda" for which issues will be discussed and which will be ignored, and in the way issues are portrayed, or "framed."[13]

The megaphone held by media pundits and reporters is instrumental in directing both negative and positive attention to the Tea Party. Even media outlets that frame the Tea Party in negative terms confer legitimacy on the group due to their willingness to certify it as a legitimate mass uprising. Contrary to the "liberal media" argument, one sees substantial vocal support for the Tea Party in the press, particularly among conservative pundits in print, television, and right-wing radio. The mass media, even when offering significant criticisms of the Tea Party, have generally depicted the group in a favorable light by drawing regular and sympathetic attention to it.

CONSERVATIVE PUNDITRY LEADS THE WAY

Conservative pundits lead the way in fomenting the image of the Tea Party as a populist uprising. In a May 2010 op-ed titled "The Tea Party's Allegiance to No One," Kathleen Parker of the *Washington Post* suggests that the group is independent of partisan politics. Parker announced that the Tea Party brought "power-to-the people," and that "no one doubts the sincerity or power of the Tea Party anymore." As proof, she referenced the group's "Contract from America," a list of Tea Party principles and public policy demands, to which "any serious Republican must subscribe, nay, sign in blood."[14] Charles Krauthammer argued in the *Washington Post* that "liberals" in Congress and the media missed this uprising because they spent the Tea Party's first year "either ignoring or disdaining the clear early signs of resistance" in "town hall meetings of the summer [2009]. With characteristic condescension, they contemptuously dismissed the protests as the mere excrescences of a redneck, retrograde, probably racist rabble."[15] Some support also appeared on the op-ed page of the *New York Times*, where conservative David Brooks declared that the "antigovernment right" was being "mobilized," representing "a characteristically raw but authentically American revolt led by members of the yeoman enterprising class."[16]

Conservative print media were strongly favorable toward the Tea Party, framing it as qualitatively different from other groups designated as on the fringe. In the *Wall Street Journal*, Peggy Noonan distinguished between the Tea Party—seen as a "populist" group that shares "antipathy" for "the increasing size, role, and demands of government"—and conspiratorial rightist groups like the John Birch Society, known for its "radical and ill thought through" politics.[17] The editors of the *New York Post* distinguished between extremists like Timothy McVeigh and the Tea Party, the latter having "injured nothing—save the sensibilities of those who would see America entombed in government debt."[18] The editors for the *Washington Times* warned of a suspected "plot" on the part of some progressive "saboteurs" to "crash" Tea Party protests in April 2010, such methods being "part of the typical liberal playbook to silence opposition to the left-wing agenda." "Liberals," the editors warned, were committed to a radical agenda "to ostracize skeptical thought and intimidate those brave enough to stand against the bureaucratic juggernaut."[19]

The strongest support for the Tea Party is found in right-wing radio and television. Fox News invites numerous Tea Party organizers on its programs to promote future rallies and events. Fox also regularly interviews Tea Party protesters on various public policy issues, and Fox News commentators and contributors are listed as "Tea Party Sponsors" on TaxDayTeaParty.com.[20] Fox News is the most followed of the cable news mediums, and right-wing pundits are the preeminent ideological force in American political radio.[21] Furthermore, conservative media pundits (alongside Republican officials) are increasingly successful in dominating "objective" reporting, as seen in "agenda setting" papers such as the *New York Times*, *Washington Post*, and others.

Rush Limbaugh celebrates the Tea Party as being composed of "genuine, peace loving, middle-American citizens of this country . . . who simply are trying to save what's left of their civilization."[22] Limbaugh's commentary extends to melodrama that promises Western civilization's doom, as he declared that the Tea Party is "the first time" that "everyday citizens" have "risen up since the Civil War."[23] In light of the numerous popular and usually progressive uprisings that have occurred in the United States, this is factually absurd. However, Limbaugh's comment is revealing, in that it demonstrates who the right does and does not consider legitimate "everyday citizens."

Sean Hannity is one of the most vigorous promoters of the Tea Party. He frames the group as "principle-focused, not party-focused," and his guests promise that this "authentic social movement" is dedicated to "empowering people." Hannity has interviewed congressional Tea Partiers such as Michele Bachmann, who argued that the Tea Party "is the movement that is bringing back the values, the principles, the core commonsense values that the Republican Party needs to stand on." Hannity dedicates multiple programs to exonerating Tea Partiers from any charges of racial bigotry, which have threatened to paint the "movement" as extreme and out of touch with modern-day America.[24] According to a LexisNexis search, Hannity dedicated the most programs out of any Fox host to discussing the "Tea Party movement"—38 programs, or nearly ten per month—in the four months running up to and following the April 15, 2010, national Tax Day protests.

Glenn Beck and Bill O'Reilly maintained a strong cross-promotional relationship, as O'Reilly's program followed Beck's in the Fox News lineup prior to the cancellation of Beck's program. O'Reilly and Beck consistently support the Tea Party in their programs. O'Reilly, while framing the Tea Party as composed of a very small number of "loons," explains that he "has always admired Americans who get involved in trying to improve their country. And that is what most Tea Party people do. They're regular folks who are fed up" with government spending and escalating debt. The Tea Party, O'Reilly reminds viewers, is instrumental in "getting under the skin of the liberal establishment" that supports a short-term increase in debt in the name of promoting economic recovery.[25]

Beck vigorously supports the Tea Party, probably more so than any other pundit on the right. He promotes Tea Party rallies in his programs and receives generous support from Tea Party members, among whom nearly 60 percent retain a positive view of Beck.[26] Beck erroneously concludes that the Tea Party is not only supported by Middle America, but is, in terms of its ideology, an integral part of mainstream America itself. In one program, he maintained that "the Tea Party movement *is* the majority of Americans. Whether you stand with the Tea Party movement or not, the idea of government 'get out of my way' is quintessential America."[27] A LexisNexis search finds that Beck leads the way in mentioning the Tea Party in his programs. During the four months in the run-up to and following the April 15, 2010, national Tax Day protests, Beck ran nearly fifty stories covering the Tea Party—an average of twelve per month, or more than one every three days.

It is not surprising that Fox News and right-wing radio are leading promoters of the Tea Party. Conservative claims that "the media" are uniformly "liberally biased" against the Tea Party are unfounded in the context of the above findings and when considering sympathetic coverage in non-conservative media. By early to mid-2010, the Tea Party was the subject of dozens of stories per month in the mass media.[28] As Figure 3.1 suggests, reporters at "objective" papers such as the *New York Times* and *Washington Post* increased their coverage—that is, any story, letter, op-ed, or editorial including the words "Tea Party"—to more than ten and twenty stories respectively in April 2009 in reaction to that month's national Tax Day protests.

Coverage at MSNBC reached nearly 30 programs a month, and Fox News directed twice as much attention to the Tea Party, with more than 70 programs that month—or two and a half per day. Coverage fell in May, June, and July 2009 after the Tax Day rally, but it began to increase dramatically by the fall of 2009 with the "Town Hall" Tea Party protests across

FIGURE 3.1: The Tea Party in National Media: (2/2009–10/2010)

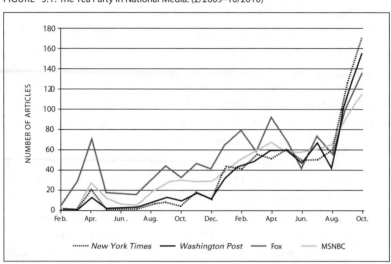

Source: LexisNexis

the nation. Coverage reached a new high by April 2010, during the second Tea Party Tax Day rally. Attention eventually declined following the April 2010 tax rally, remaining at relatively high levels in the summer of 2010, and escalating to an all-time high in all media outlets in the run-up to the midterms that fall. By October 2010, the media outlets examined here were running between four to six stories referencing the Tea Party every day, hardly evidence of the marginalization claimed by conservatives.

Center-right pundits and pollsters such as Scott Rasmussen and Douglas Schoen complain that the mass media are liberally biased against the Tea Party. They argue in their book on the Tea Party, *Mad as Hell*:

> Questions were immediately raised by members of both the political and media establishment about the extent to which the Tea Parties could truly be considered a grassroots uprising.... From the beginning, critics questioned the extent to which the Tea Parties truly represented grievances shared by a majority of the American public, writing them off as an "Astroturf" movement organized by Republican politicians and right-wing media.[29]

Rasmussen and Schoen's analysis is entirely anecdotal, failing to provide any empirical evidence. A close analysis of media reporting finds the exact opposite trend of that seen in Rasmussen and Schoen's claims.

TABLE 3.1: Framing the Tea Party: Social Movement vs. Astroturf
(July 2009–June 2010)

News Outlet	Total Stories on Tea Party as a "Movement"	Total Stories on Tea Party as "Astroturf"	Ave. Stories Per Month on Tea Party as a "Movement"	Ave. Stories Per Month on Tea Party as "Astroturf"
Washington Post	220	3	18	.25
New York Times	190	1	16	.1
Fox	461	43	38	3.6
CNN	595	15	50	1.25
MSNBC	315	22	26	1.8
NBC	72	0	6	0
ABC	63	3	5	.25
CBS	45	0	4	0

Source: LexisNexis

Mass media outlets frame the Tea Party very positively across the board. Seventy-five percent of Fox News programs following the April 2009 tax day rallies and prior to the April 2010 rallies (from February 2009 to April 2010) referred to the Tea Party as a "movement," as compared to 64 percent of *Washington Post* stories, 57 percent of *New York Times* stories, and 55 percent of MSNBC stories. Even the most "liberal" outlets such as the *New York Times* and MSNBC framed the Tea Party as a movement in the majority of their stories.[30] Stories were radically more likely to portray the Tea Party as a "movement," as opposed to "Astroturf." A review of Tea Party coverage for the year of July 2009 through July 2010, summarized in Table 3.1, finds that, across American television and newspaper outlets, the Tea Party was far more likely to be framed as a mass movement.

Closer analysis of reporting on the Tea Party demonstrates that they adopt a sympathetic line toward the group, similar to, but less blatant than that seen in right-wing media. The *Wall Street Journal* reports that the Tea Party is independent from the Republican establishment: it is "aggressively non-partisan" and "demand[s] ideological purity" from the Republican Party. The paper reports that Republicans are experiencing "a classic dilemma faced by parties in the minority—tension between those who want a return to the party's ideological roots and those who want candidates most likely to win in their districts."[31]

Agenda-setting newspapers follow Fox's example on the Tea Party. In January 2010, the *New York Times* framed the Tea Party's upcoming national convention as a "coming together" of the Tea Party's "diffuse," "grassroots groups" that express fierce "antigovernment sentiments." The paper drew critical attention to the controversies surrounding the Tea Party's February 2010 Nashville convention, due to alleged profiteering (from figures such as Sarah Palin, who charged $100,000 to speak) and a $549 attendance fee for Tea Party members to attend. Despite the controversies and the unflattering coverage, the *New York Times* depicted the Tea Party as decentralized, contentious, and diverse, while conflicts at "the convention reflected some of the factitiousness of the Tea Party movement."[32] Similarly, the *Washington Post* reported at the time that the Tea Party was "decentralized," its convention representing a convergence of a "fractious," "sprawling movement, made up of hundreds of disparate 'tea party organizations.'" This "grassroots movement exploded across the nation last year in revolt against President Obama's economic policies and healthcare agenda and reached a critical milestone as hundreds of conservative activists converged here for the start of the inaugural National Tea Party convention."[33]

National magazines took a virtually identical position to the agenda-setting papers. Even when they focused on negative aspects of the Tea Party, reporting characterized the group as authentically populist. In a story titled "How the Tea Party Could Help All of Us," *Newsweek* explained that "the Tea Party folks are mad, and their fury is often expressed in irrational and ugly ways." Nonetheless, "the goal of the [2009] Tea Party convention was, at least in part, the recovery of the spirit of the American Founding."[34] *Time* magazine described the Tea Party as outside of electoral politics: it "is not a political party . . . and maybe never will be. Rejecting the idea—widely held by Democrats— that a government of brainy people can solve thorny problems through complex legislation, the Tea Party finds its strongest spirit among conservative Republicans."[35] *U.S. News and World Report* framed media attention to the Tea Party as "minuscule. . . . Big media, especially TV networks, seem to be going out of their way to diss the conservative-leaning Tea Party movement as they work overtime to cheer on the Obama administration."[36]

U.S. News and World Report's claims about the marginalization of the Tea Party could only be made by ignoring empirical mountains of contrary evidence. The major flaw of *U.S. News and World Report*'s argument is that it uncritically cites a study by the conservative Media Research Center (MRC), which alleged that broadcast news outlets "ignore[d]" the Tea Party. This study, however, refused to wait until the April 15, 2010, rallies were over to analyze the intensity of media reporting.[37] Had the MRC bothered to analyze coverage *following* the rallies, it would have seen that the Tea Party received massive attention. The Tea Party received front-and-center attention in April, as the results of a CBS-*New York Times* poll covering the group's members were featured at the beginning of the *CBS Evening News* on April 14, and the national Tax Day rallies were featured at the start of *ABC World News* and *NBC Nightly News* programs on April 15.[38] In total, the Tea Party was referenced in 54 different news programs on the three networks during the month of April 2010, compared to 39 stories devoted to "antiwar protests" at the same networks during the month of February 2003 in the month before the invasion of Iraq. The disparity in coverage of these competing social protests amounts to 28 percent less coverage for the anti-Iraq protests. In short, television journalists devoted prominent attention to the Tea Party protests in the day prior to and the day of the April protests. Conservatives would be hard-pressed to ask for much more in terms of prominence of coverage.

The Tea Party receives sympathetic coverage in comparison to social movements on the left that drew tens to hundreds of thousands of participants *without* the help of corporate funding and Republican Party officials at the national, state, and local levels. The data in Table 3.2 provide a brief summary of various protests (four leftist and one on the right) that could be characterized as part of social movements in terms of their size, participation, and sustained action over a number of years.[39] Compared to the Tea Party, the four leftist movements received dramatically less coverage, despite the fact that many existed for far longer or were characterized by at least equal or far larger turnouts.[40]

My analysis is reinforced by another study done by FAIR (Fairness and Accuracy in Reporting), which found the marginalization of leftist social gatherings during the media's preoccupation with the Tea Party. Julie Hollar found that a fall 2009 march on Washington, with tens of thousands of gay, lesbian, bisexual, and transgender activists, received significantly less coverage than the Tea Party marches in April 2010. Similarly, the February

TABLE 3.2: Mass Media Framing of Social Movements (Number of
           Articles Referring to Each Protest as a Part of a Movement)

News Outlet	NY Times	Wash. Post	Fox	MSNBC	Total	Tea Party-to-Protest Ratio	Estimated Turnout
Seattle 1999 WTO Protest	0	0	0	0	0	106:0	50,000
Global 2003 Iraq Protests	15	11	8	14	48	2.2:1	6–10 mil.
Cancun 2003 WTO Protest	0	0	0	0	0	106:0	10,000
Washington 2004 Women's Rights March	2	4	0	0	6	17.7:1	500,000–1 million
National Tea Party Marches 2010	17	22	38	29	106	1:1	100,000–200,000

Source: LexisNexis

2010 Nashville Tea Party Convention received far more attention than the U.S. Social Forum, a convention of leftist and socialist activists, which drew 15,000 to 20,000 attendees, compared to just 600 at the Tea Party convention. But the Forum received just 1.5 percent of the coverage of the Tea Party convention in a sample of ten national news outlets.[41]

Reporters also masked the Tea Party's failures when they ignored its deterioration and decline in the fall of 2010. The collapse of the Tea Party's LibertyXPO convention in Washington in the fall of 2010, for example, was ignored in national reporting. A LexisNexis search finds that neither the *New York Times* nor the *Washington Post* ran a single story on the meeting's collapse in September 2010, while directing strong attention to the earlier, though comparatively lightly attended Nashville conference in February of 2010.[42] The collapsed October 2010 Tea Party convention in Las Vegas was almost completely ignored at a time when reporters preferred the narrative of an ascendant and insurgent Tea Party. The failed convention was covered in just one story in the *New York Times* and one story in the *Washington Post* in the last two weeks of September.[43]

These comparisons demonstrate a strong uniformity across elite print outlets and partisan cable news outlets in their prioritization of the Tea Party over leftist social movements and gatherings. The lesson is clear: a top-down phenomenon like the Tea Party, whose messages are promoted by the Republican Party, is deemed from two to more than one hundred times more worthy of being seen as a social movement than social movements on the left. This pattern is the result of the utility of the Tea Party's message to those who hold political power in Washington and on Wall Street.

MEDIA COVERAGE OF THE TEA PARTY
FOLLOWING THE APRIL 2010 PROTESTS

Attention to the Tea Party increased to even higher levels in the second half of 2010. After the April Tax Day rallies, reporting on the Tea Party shifted to a focus on the 2010 midterm elections, as self-proclaimed Tea Party candidates garnered extensive media attention. In a high-profile example, national media covered the question of whether the Tea Party was gaining steam as related to the primary successes of Rand Paul, Sharron Angle, Nikki Haley, Christine O'Donnell, and Ken Buck.

Although Haley received an endorsement from Sarah Palin, the *Washington Post* reported that "Republican operatives in South Carolina said Haley's surge" resulted from "her conservative-reformer message and support from 'Tea Party' groups."[44] The Associated Press reported that "Tea Party activists flexed their muscle in South Carolina, pushing Haley ahead of three rivals in the Republican gubernatorial primary."[45] A LexisNexis database search found references to "Nikki Haley" in dozens of stories during the first two weeks of June 2010, during the run-up to the South Carolina primary election. Coverage of Christine O'Donnell was substantial, with the *New York Times* mentioning her in 35 pieces and the *Washington Post* including her in 32 pieces in the first three weeks of September alone after O'Donnell won the Delaware Republican primary in mid-September. O'Donnell was seen as a "dissident," who "upset" candidates within the Republican Party, and as an exotic outsider who dabbled in witchcraft in her younger years.[46]

A number of news reports and pundits conceded that the Tea Party was a movement, but pondered whether it had begun to decline. The *New York Times* reported in late September 2010 on a Tea Party "plagued by infighting among groups, with sponsors and speakers [of the February national convention] dropping out right up until its opening hours," and with many Tea Party organizations having "slid in their participations and

donations across the country."[47] United Press International reported that
there were "few Tea Party victories in [the] primaries."[48] Liberal commentator David Corn of *The Nation* argued that the Tea Party may be
"losing its strength" and "is not as popular as it once was."[49] Corn wrote
in the company of other liberal pundits that this "movement" was in
decline. He cited a June 2010 *Washington Post*/ABC poll, which found
that 50 percent of respondents had an "unfavorable impression" of the
Tea Party, "an increase from 39 percent in March . . . this makes sense. At
first, the TP movement could be seen as a patriotic uprising with a time-
tested and honorable moniker . . . but in recent weeks, the—shall we say—
excesses of the Tea Party have been on display." Corn was referring to
Tea Party senatorial candidate Rand Paul's comments that private businesses should be allowed to ignore the Civil Rights Act. Also controversial at the time was Republican Senate candidate and Tea Partier Sharron
Angle (running in Nevada), who indicated support for eliminating the
EPA, Department of Education, and Department of Energy, and called for
the privatization of Social Security.[50]

THE RAND PAUL PHENOMENON

Rand Paul's candidacy gained prominence following his victory in the
2010 Republican primary. Commentators such as Rachel Maddow of
MSNBC and Joan Walsh of Salon.com skewered Paul because of his support for rolling back the government's protection of basic civil rights for
minorities.[51] These liberal pundits attacked Paul following his statement
that private businesses should have been exempted from the 1964 Civil
Rights Act's prohibition on racial discrimination and his dismissal of
debates about historical segregation because they are "obscure." Paul flirt-
ed with claims that private businesses should enjoy the "right" under the
First Amendment to discriminate based upon the color of a person's skin.[52]

Despite Paul's comments, he enjoyed success in the Kentucky
Republican primary. Media outlets across the country ignored his incendiary race statements through the election, only discussing them after he
won the primary. Paul's stance on civil rights was a matter of public record
when Louisville's *Courier-Journal* ran an April 25, 2010, editorial rejecting his candidacy. The paper deplored Paul for his "repulsive" and
"unacceptable view of civil rights," and his saying that though "the federal government can enforce integration of government jobs and facilities,

private businesspeople should be able to decide whether they want to serve black people, or gays, or any other minority group."[53] While a LexisNexis search shows that Rand Paul was mentioned in 66 national newspaper articles from April 25 to May 19, not one paper mentioned his position on the Civil Rights Act.

When Paul's opposition to public civil rights protections was re-exposed in NPR and MSNBC interviews (on May 19 and May 20, respectively), right-wing media outlets defended Paul. On *Fox News Sunday*, Sarah Palin attacked Rachel Maddow as "prejudiced" for her discussion of Paul's take on the Civil Rights Act.[54] In the *Wall Street Journal*, James Taranto lauded Paul's candidacy for doing "more good than harm" despite his making "a rookie mistake" by "answering the way he did" regarding the Civil Rights Act.[55] Neoconservative columnist William Kristol claimed on *Fox News All Stars* that Paul was a supporter of civil rights and reflected on his persona as an outside-the-Beltway figure who is refreshing in a town like Washington: "There is something attractive about him. I mean, he's plainspoken and seems like an honest, good-natured guy."[56] Fox News contributor John Stossel echoed Paul's position: "I'm in total agreement with Rand Paul . . . because private business-es ought to get to discriminate. And I won't ever go to a place that's racist and I will tell everybody else not to and I'll speak against them. But it should be their right to be racist."[57]

AGAINST THE REPUBLICAN "ESTABLISHMENT"

Reporting on the "outsider" status of the Tea Party was pronounced in the months following the April 15 Tax Day rallies. Table 3.3 presents evidence that, in the three months prior to the midterms, reporting on the Tea Party as a "movement" was widespread, with references to the group existing outside the "Republican establishment" appearing in dozens of news stories every month across the outlets in question. In short, the conservative claim that the Tea Party is regularly dismissed by journalists as an Astroturf affair is without merit.

Attention to the Tea Party was not always flattering. Nonetheless, the group did receive regular attention from journalists—far more than can be said for social movements on the left, which are routinely ignored in the media. News coverage from print and television outlets was, on the whole, very positive for a group that is lacking in basic participatory empower-

TABLE 3.3: The Mediated Tea Party: A Social "Movement"
Against the Republican Establishment"
News Coverage, August 1 to November 4, 2010

Media Outlet	No. of Stories on Tea Party as a "Movement"	Average Stories per Month/Day	No. of Stories on Tea Party vs. "Republican Establishment"	Average Stories per Month/Day
New York Times	135	45/1.5	98	33/1.1
Washington Post	136	45/1.5	159	53/1.8
MSNBC	137	46/1.5	88	29/1
Fox News	167	56/1.9	90	30/1

Source: LexisNexis

ment. Furthermore, the negative coverage of the Tea Party that did occasionally appear was more beneficial to the "movement" than little to no coverage. As the often repeated dictum goes: "Bad press is better than no press at all." This claim is not completely accurate, however, when applied to the Tea Party. The group received flattering coverage in American radio and cable news, and generous coverage from journalists.

THE TEA PARTY
IN THE LIBERAL CORPORATE MEDIA

Tea Party and conservative complaints about the "liberal" media appear most relevant when applied to narrow segments of the press, including the editorial pages of the *New York Times* and television outlets such as MSNBC, which specializes in narrowcasting to a small, liberal audience. At the *New York Times*, commentary was almost uniformly critical of the Tea Party. Tea Partiers were labeled "scaremongers" and "lowlifes" by Maureen Dowd and Bob Herbert, and Frank Rich focused on Tea Party "extremist elements and their enablers," such as Fox News's Glenn Beck.[58] The Tea Party was lambasted by Herbert as a "diversion from the suffering of those who are unemployed, such as those living in poverty in inner cities.... We need to pay less attention to the Tea Party yahoos and more attention to the very real suffering of individuals and families trapped in an employment crisis that is unprecedented in the post-Depression era."[59]

The editors at the *New York Times* never directly focused their attention on the Tea Party during the April 15, 2010, rallies.[60] Negative comments directed toward the group did emerge, however, when the editorial page covered tangential issues. In one editorial, the paper attacked Republican Senate candidate and Tea Partier Sharron Angle for her "alarming rhetoric" regarding "'Second Amendment remedies' and other teases about armed revolution. Her statements . . . when she was winning national attention dishing right-wing polemics—were some of the most offensive and inciteful to be heard in this year's welter of extremist alarums."[61] In an editorial titled "Limits of Libertarianism," the paper scorned Rand Paul for "denigrating several of the signal achievements of modern American society, including the Civil Rights Act of 1964 and the Fair Housing Act." Paul "helped to illuminate the limits and hazards of antigovernment sentiment . . . his views and those of other Tea Party candidates are unintentional reminders of the importance of enlightened government."[62]

Even when attacking the Tea Party, *New York Times* liberal columnists and editors concluded that it represented an independent and nonpartisan movement. Commentary was most intense surrounding the April 2010 Tax Day rallies. Paul Krugman envisioned the Tea Party as "anti-government," and Charles Blow framed it as "a Frankenstein movement—an odd collection of factions, loosely stitched together, where the head, to the extent that it exists, fails to control the body."[63] Rich saw the Tea Party as "exploited . . . by the Republican Party," and that "Tea Partiers hate the GOP establishment and its Wall Street allies, starting with the Bushies who created TARP, almost as much as they do Obama and his Wall Street pals."[64] Other columnists also repeated the myths that the Tea Party is nonpartisan and independent of government. Thomas Friedman depicted the group as full of political outsiders, as "a lot of angry people who want to get the government out of their lives and cut both taxes and the deficit."[65]

The editors of the *New York Times* worried prior to the 2010 midterm elections that it *could* get co-opted into the Republican sphere. They asked "how far" Republicans "will go in sidling up to the Tea Party and its more extremist protesters."[66] Charles Blow offered a similar interpretation, claiming that the Tea Party "may have some legitimate concerns (taxation, the role of government, etc.)," although "the anemic Republican establishment, covetous of the Tea Party's passion, is moving to absorb it, not admonish it. Instead of jettisoning the radical language, rabid bigotry, and rising violence, the Republicans justify it."[67] Supporters of this view are guilty of wishful thinking and self-delusion in light of revelations that the Tea Party is a direct manifestation of right-wing elements of the Republican Party.

The *Washington Post* mirrored the *New York Times* both in terms of its criticisms of the Tea Party and in its assumptions that the group is a social movement. The paper's editors decried the "growing strength of the [Republican] Party's Tea Party wing" as "making cooperation [across party lines] even more difficult."[68] The paper's main qualm with the Tea Party was its lack of "moderation." *Washington Post* editors focused specifically on the Tea Party's "purist" orientation, which appears "unsettling" in that it draws upon the inspiration of reactionary pundits like Glenn Beck, "the first true demagogue of the information age."[69]

In early 2010, *Washington Post* op-ed writers were adopting the same approach as seen in the *New York Times*. E. J. Dionne stressed the Tea Party's "grassroots rage," its "principled anti-government radicalism," and its "populism," reminding readers that "establishment Republicans are destined to disappoint them."[70] Eugene Robinson deemed "the movement's" rhetoric as "vitriolic" and "anti-government"—its approach "calibrated not to inform but to incite."[71] Finally, Colbert King emphasized the Tea Party's "outsized fear of a tyrannical federal government."[72]

During the same period, liberal television columnists at MSNBC followed the same standard set by pundits writing for major national papers. The outlet was strongly critical of the Tea Party's politics, while avoiding suggestions that it is not a movement. Rachel Maddow criticized the "conspiracy theories" prevalent among the Tea Party, which frame healthcare reform as socialist.[73] Ed Schultz targeted "Town Hall wackos" specifically for their attempts to associate healthcare reform with Nazism. Schultz's approach was decidedly partisan, as he vocalized his backing of Democratic political figures such as Representative Barney Frank, who responded critically during the fall 2009 Town Hall meetings to Tea Party "nut jobs" who sought to associate healthcare reform with Nazism.[74]

Despite the above criticisms, MSNBC's entire primetime lineup tended to see the Tea Party as a social movement. A search of the LexisNexis newspaper database finds that, between July 2009 and April 2010, nearly 130 separate programs referred to the "Tea Party movement." In contrast, editorializing that referred to the Tea Party as "Astroturf" appeared within this same period in just 16 news programs, and half of those were the work of just one commentator—Keith Olbermann. Olbermann was fond of characterizing the Town Hall protests of 2009 as artificial in terms of being directed by Republican interest groups and corporate interests, although his discussion of the Tea Party as an artificial movement scarcely extended into the 2010 period, when the group benefited from the greatest national media coverage. [75] Just one Olbermann program claimed the group was "Astroturf" from January through April 2010.

THE TEA PARTY
IN THE PROGRESSIVE-LEFT PRESS

Progressive (non-corporate) media I examined include publications such as *The Nation*, *The Progressive*, *In These Times*, *CounterPunch*, *Z Magazine*, *Monthly Review*, and the websites Alternet, Common Dreams, Daily Kos, and Huffington Post (formerly non-corporately owned), and range from liberal to radical in their politics. Though these media express dissident views found outside the bipartisan spectrum of opinions, their coverage of the Tea Party, with some exceptions, echoed that of the liberal corporate media. These outlets pursued one of two tracks in covering the Tea Party: they either sought to ridicule the Tea Party as harmful to the American political process or attempted to "find common ground" with the group in an attempt to build an alternative politics that challenged the bipartisan status quo. Most of these news outlets assumed that the Tea Party was a legitimate social movement working against the political-economic system.

Many in the progressive-left media sought around the time of the 2010 Tax Day rallies to work with the Tea Party. Katrina Vanden Heuvel, editor of *The Nation* magazine, wished to "have a sane conversation" with Tea Partiers "about taxes, the proper role of government and how to rebuild our economy." She promoted efforts to "constructively engage" the group—to "redirect the shared grievances of progressives and the more sensible Tea Partiers into a productive politics" to "build a broad-based coalition for economic change."[76] This approach was reiterated at Huffington Post, where Medea Benjamin sought "to begin a dialogue" with Tea Partiers in order to convince them to oppose escalating debt from increasing military budgets.[77]

Others at *The Nation* like Chuck Collins maintained that "like all social movements, the Tea Party wave is not monolithic"; many in this "movement" can "find common ground" with the progressive left.[78] John

Nichols hoped the Tea Party "stays true to a set core of principles that are rooted in distrust not just of big government but of big banks and big business." Nichols defended the Tea Party as a "genuine" movement, and "on the general principle that any honest dissent is healthy." Nichols repeated the myths found in corporate media, as he worried that the "movement" was becoming subject to "manipulation" by Washington-based political figures: "Old school Republican insiders are trying to hijack the rebel spirit of the movement and use its energy to advance their own electoral agendas."[79]

Much the same pattern was found among more radical writers in other progressive media. Alexander Cockburn, editor of *CounterPunch* magazine, lauded the Tea Party "mutiny," since the group represents "a boisterous populist faction, nominally within the Republican coalition but viscerally opposed to its establishment leaders."[80] David Rovics argued in *CounterPunch* that the motives of the Tea Party are legitimate: "These people who are often working two shit jobs to make ends meet whereas a generation ago one would have done just fine. They very legitimately feel disenfranchised. These are people with legitimate complaints, and dismissing them as racists or whatever other label people on the left want to put on them is simplistic."[81] Noam Chomsky argued that "these [Tea Partiers] are the people who ought to be organized by the left. . . . One thing to be done is don't ridicule these people, join them, and talk about their real grievances and give them a sensible answer, like, 'Take over your factories.'" As discussed in other academic analysis of the Tea Party, Chomsky's final comment about "taking over factories," although motivated by his commitment to socialist politics, does not comport well with the ideology of Tea Party activists, who are deeply suspicious of collectivism and unions, abhor socialism, and who support fiscal discipline for the "undeserving poor," all in line with "free market" rhetoric. Chomsky's insight regarding public outrage over the economic crisis and national wage stagnation (which spans a number of decades), however, remains relevant for the *broader public*, many of whom are supportive of a Tea Party that advocates free market policies that are harming Americans.[82]

Many editorials in progressive outlets were uncompromising in their condemnations of the Tea Party. In *The Nation* Leslie Savan took issue with the group's "know-nothing policies," and Glenn Ford of Black Agenda Report lambasted "any group whose unifying characteristic is daily engorgement on Rush Limbaugh and Glenn Beck" as "by definition, racist."[83] Ron Jacobs depicted the Tea Party in *CounterPunch* as "an angry group of people whose understanding of the political system in the capitalist U.S. fails to see the fundamental fact of that system: the government works for the corporations." Jacobs warned readers about "certain elements" of the group that "do share some racial and nativist prejudices with various Neo-Nazi and other fascist movements."[84]

More often than not, however, progressive media transmitted the conventional falsehood that the Tea Party is a mass uprising. A classic example was an article in Alternet, in which Adele Stan lectured readers about numerous "myths that help us avoid reality about the new right-wing politics." Among these "myths" Stan included claims that the Tea Party "is largely a creation of the media, which devotes too much coverage to the Tea Party's small constituency of malcontents ... [that it] is not an authentic grassroots movement; it's the creation of astroturf groups . . . [and as a result, it is difficult for the Tea Party to] win general elections."[85] These claims are representative of those seen in other left media. A review of more than 41 stories on the Tea Party appearing in leftist media in early to mid-2010—found in Daily Kos, *In These Times*, Huffington Post, *Progressive*, Common Dreams, *Z Magazine*, *CounterPunch*, Truthdig, *The Nation*, Truthout, and *Monthly Review*— concludes that 32 of the stories, or 78 percent, characterize the Tea Party as either "populist" in orientation or as a "movement." Writers for outlets such as *Truthdig*, *Monthly Review*, and *Z Magazine* did challenge the "movement" narrative, but these stories were a distinct minority when taking into account all stories examined.[86]

In this chapter I presented evidence that the Tea Party benefits from a number of favorable developments in the mass media, including: 1) massive, sustained attention; 2) strongly supportive coverage among right-wing pundits, reporters, and even many progressive-leftists) and 3) concessions among even the group's opponents that it is a bona fide social movement, working against the status quo. Perhaps most problematic in this analysis is not the finding that the media is uncritically disseminating falsehoods regarding the Tea Party, but rather finding so many prominent pundits on the left unable to recognize the Tea Party's elitist, top-down organization structure. That a majority of those writing in the media cannot distinguish between real and artificial movements is troubling for those calling for a renewed grassroots movement politics in order to pursue progressive change. Such ignorance will need to be addressed before any future progressive movement emerges.

FOUR

Mediated Populism:
The Tea Party Captivates Public Opinion

A propaganda model for public opinion should be able to account for the roles of material affluence and neoliberal ideas in influencing the public's policy attitudes. This model was described in detail in the Introduction of this book, and it is tested in relation to the mass media and the Tea Party in this chapter. An in-depth investigation into the sources of support for the Tea Party "revolution" in 2009 and 2010 demonstrates the tremendous powers of privilege and propaganda in establishing an emergent conservative national mood, and in stoking public opposition to liberal-left reforms in the area of healthcare. In the battle by business elites against such reforms, the mass media restrict the ideas to which the public is exposed and prevent Americans from considering progressive initiatives.

Prior to Barack Obama taking office, opinion pollsters reported that the public appeared to be near a tipping point in its opinions about government authority. Andrew Kohut of the Pew Research Center reported that the public was "pretty much evenly divided" about the proper size of government, as nearly equal numbers argued for "smaller" and "bigger" government. Just over a year later, Pew found that 50 percent of those surveyed "wanted a smaller government," compared to 39 percent who wanted "a bigger one."[1] The growth in popular opposition to government during this time was admittedly vague, considering that surveys of public opinion on specific programs show radically different opinions compared to surveys about the legitimacy of "government" more generally. In terms of overall public distrust of government, however, a significant shift appeared to be taking place.

The rise in a general conservative mood throughout the United States in 2009 and 2010 was closely associated with the resurgence of Republican officials in the 2010 midterm elections and the growing prominence of the Tea Party. The rise of the Tea Party was to a large extent aided by public anger over the economy and inadequate government response in terms of easing public suffering. At a time when the public was looking for someone to blame for the economic crisis, Tea Partiers were utilizing the mass media to blame "the government," as controlled by a Democratic president and majority in Congress. One of the strongest forces driving public support for the Tea Party was the media, which were primarily responsible for manufacturing a public rebellion against Democrats and liberal healthcare reforms.

THE TEA PARTY'S RISING STAR: MANUFACTURING A PUBLIC REVOLT

The American public became more supportive of the Tea Party and its messages in late 2009 and 2010. During this period, a number of justifications for supporting a "grassroots" Tea Party "revolution" were elucidated by Republican leaders and Tea Party activists, echoed in the mass media, and finally trickled down to an increasingly receptive public. The Tea Party was able to stoke public anger about the supposed dangers of "unprecedented," "runaway" Democratic spending, and the alleged threat of Democratic healthcare reform to the private sector. The failure (or unwillingness) of the Democratic Party to pursue a unified alternative vision for progressive healthcare reform and failure to ensure a strong economic recovery greatly contributed to the popularity of the Tea Party.

Democrats were conflicted between competing healthcare proposals; some, such as state insurance exchanges, were supported by conservative "Blue Dog" Democrats, while others such as the public option (or even universal healthcare) were preferred by more progressive members of Congress. As Democratic support for the public option eroded in mid- to late 2009, the media agenda predictably shifted to favoring conservative and reactionary voices of the right. This process helped to secure a victory for anti–healthcare reformers. Universal healthcare and the public option were eliminated from consideration in favor of corporate-friendly and market-based reforms. The Democrats' commitment to stimulus spending was also weak, at least compared to the greater stimulus spending supported by prominent liberals.[2] The relatively small size of the stimulus helped ensure weak economic growth, further exacerbating public anxiety at a time when unemployment hovered around 10 percent, housing foreclosures climbed to record levels, and the number of homes that were "underwater" remained at nearly one-quarter of all homes in the country.[3]

By early 2010, the Tea Party was making major inroads into Middle America. What had originally been a movement that appealed to more materially privileged demographics was speaking now to larger audiences, with the help of the media megaphone and local and national Republican operatives. By April, a *New York Times*–CBS poll found that 18 percent of adults—approximately 45 million people—shared some level of sympathy for the Tea Party.[4] Survey data from the Program for International Policy Attitudes suggested that half of Americans shared the perception that the Tea Party "was active in their community."[5] Although this perception is clearly contradicted by my and other observational studies, such misperceptions are not surprising considering the massive media attention to local Tax Day rallies throughout the country that took place in April 2010.[6] Journalistic portrayal of the Tea Party as the "common man's" rebellion likely helped encourage the public to overestimate the Tea Party's prominence.

The findings of the *New York Times* and CBS regarding the expanding appeal of the Tea Party were reinforced by polling that found that a sizable minority of Americans shared favorable views of the group. Polls from CNN, ABC, the *Washington Post*, and Quinnipiac found that between 32 and 41 percent of Americans shared "favorable" views of the Tea Party between January and April of 2010. *USA Today* and Gallup found that 31 percent considered themselves supporters by June, and a Pew Research Center poll in May found that 25 percent "somewhat or strongly agree[d]" with the group. NBC and the *Wall Street Journal* reported that 41 percent shared a "very" or "somewhat positive" view of the Tea Party phenomenon.[7] By the 2010 midterm elections, CNN polling found that 38 percent of Americans retained a "favorable" view of the Tea Party.[8]

The media's legitimization of the Tea Party was followed by the public's acceptance of the group as composed of "average" Middle Americans.

Fox News polling from February 2010 found that 51 percent of Americans thought the Tea Party was a "serious group," as compared to just 20 percent who designated it as on the "fringe."[9] The "serious group" characterization, although accepted by 69 percent of Republicans and 52 percent of Independents, was also embraced by 34 percent of Democrats. When forced to choose between the Obama administration and the Tea Party in a 2010 Rasmussen poll, 48 percent of voters said that "the average Tea Party member is closer to their views," while 44 percent said the same about Obama. Rasmussen polling found that 47 percent said they "felt closer to the views of Tea Party members than to Congress."[10] Rasmussen reported that 52 percent of voters believed that the "average member of the Tea Party movement has a better understanding of the issues facing America today than the average member of Congress."[11]

Public opinion has long been "socially constructed" through the polling process, in order to comport with surveyers' and political and business elites' preexisting political ideologies.[12] The way questions are worded inevitably influences how individuals respond to the questions at hand. Survey questions are usually constructed in such a way that they avoid probing the public about political opinions that reside outside of those expressed by political and economic elites. In the Rasmussen polls, questions were worded so as to restrict response choices to those existing within the bipartisan spectrum of opinion. Republican-advocated Tea Party themes were placed on one side of questions regarding who Americans sympathize with more, and Democrats were placed on the other side. Left unmentioned in such questions were progressive voices to the left of the increasingly center-right and corporatist Democratic Party, such as those advocating a public option or universal healthcare.

Rasmussen polls' wording for the Tea Party questions favored the group, at least when compared to more balanced questions from other polling groups. Unlike Rasmussen, competing polls asked whether or not individuals "supported" the Tea Party or whether or not they had a "favorable" view of it. Rasmussen questions exaggerate public support for the Tea Party due to their preferred approach of pitting the Tea Party against officialdom at a time when distrust of Washington was at record highs. Rasmussen could just as easily have worded its questions to ask the public what it thought about the Tea Party as a freestanding entity, without reference to officials, but this would have reduced support for the group.[13] Biased question wording is due to the conservative orientation of the Rasmussen organization, which regularly finds that the public is more conservative than other scholarly experts working in the area of public opinion.[14] The founder of Rasmussen is well known for framing the public as "libertarian" in its alleged opposition to government from above and its supposedly favorable view "self-government." In Scott Rasmussen's *In Search of Self Governance*, he argues that "the gap between Americans who want to govern themselves and politicians who want to rule over them may be as·big today as the gap between the colonies of England during the 18th century. . . . If we have to rely on politicians to fix [social] problems, the outlook for the nation would be bleak indeed. Fortunately, in America, the politicians aren't nearly as important as they think they are."[15] Furthermore, Rasmussen is a regular contributor to the right-wing Fox News network, which suggests he retains a vested interest in overestimating the public's conservatism.

Rasmussen's biased survey wording stands in contrast to more professional polling done by the nonpartisan Pew Research Center, which provided respondents with the choice of supporting the Tea Party, Republican Party, Democratic Party, Green Party, Libertarian Party, or some "other group."[16] When questioning of the Tea Party was worded in this way, support for the group fell to just 14 percent in the spring of 2010, rather than the nearly 50 percent found by Rasmussen.

While support in Rasmussen polls exaggerates Tea Party support, this does not mean that the group was unpopular among a significant minority of Americans. Six different polling questions asked over a number of months by various organizations in early 2010 (Pew, CBS–*New York Times*, *USA Today*–Gallup, CNN–ORC, AP–GFK, and ABC–*Washington Post*, and Fox News) finds that, depending on question wording, support ranged from one-fifth to more than one-third of Americans, and that support was growing. In all seven polls the same wording was repeated for each individual question across a number of months, allowing for generalization about the growing prominence of the Tea Party. Reviewing these polls, we can see that the Tea Party gained support among the public in *all* the questions in which the group was surveyed during the first six months of 2010. The average increase in support across all the polling questions was five percentage points from January through November of 2010. Such small growth over such a relatively short period is the norm in studies of public opinion, which has typically shown either remarkable stability or incremental change.[17] Figure 4.1 reproduces findings from the Pew Research Center, which tracked growing support for the Tea Party from March 2010 through the midterm elections.[18]

FIGURE 4.1: Changing Perceptions of the Tea Party, 2010

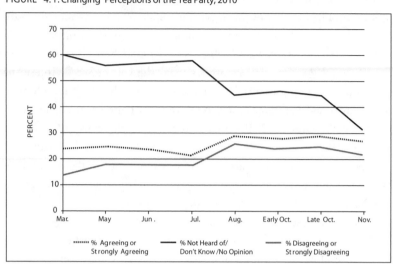

Source: Pew Research Center

Of course, opposition to the Tea Party also increased during this peri-od at a similarly proportional rate. Additionally, the percentage of those with no opinion of the "movement" or who had "not heard of it" declined dramatically, as undecideds balkanized into supporters and opponents. Importantly, support for the Tea Party was growing during this period, however, and support still surpassed opposition. Figure 4.1 indicates that 27 percent of Americans agreed with the group as of November 2010, compared to 22 percent of Americans who expressed disagreement.

Support for the Tea Party extends beyond general approval, with pub-lic agreement also seen in polling exploring the group's relationship with government. A review of the two most authoritative policy-related polls of the Tea Party and the public, conducted by the *New York Times*, CBS, and the Pew Research Center, demonstrates this point. In the *New York Times*–CBS poll from April 2010, an overlap was found between opin-ions of Tea Party supporters and the public at large on 20 of 30, or two-thirds, of all questions related to public policy, support for political lead-ers, and opinions of political institutions.[19] Similar results were apparent in the April 2010 Pew Research Center poll, with an overlap between Tea Party opinions and those of the general public on 72 percent of all policy, public official, and government institution-related questions.[20] An "over-lap" in opinion was defined as any time in which either a majority or plu-rality of respondents from both groups (the public and Tea Party supporters) provided the same answer to a polling question. Polling questions addressed a variety of topics, including opposition to government as "wasteful and inefficient," as "too big and powerful," as going "too far regulating business," as having "a negative effect on the country today," and opposition to attempts to expand the "size of government."

Overlapping opposition to government was also found in negative approval ratings of Congress, and against Obama's attempts to "expand the role of government too much" and his "handling" of healthcare reform, the budget deficit, and the economy. Overlap in policy positions covered issues such as skepticism of the effects of the Democrats' 2009 stimulus, opposition to illegal immigration, support for limiting legal immigration, and positions on abortion and gun control.

WHAT IS BEHIND THE LARGER APPEAL
OF THE TEA PARTY?

Much of the overlap in public and Tea Party opinion is related to questions that are general to the extreme, covering philosophical issues such as distrust of government and concerns over government intrusion into individuals' lives. It is on this level that the Tea Party is effective, as much of the public sees it as opposed to government corruption and the lack of official representation of the American people. It seems fitting that the "movement" would speak to the public on this generic level considering that most Americans reportedly did not know much about the Tea Party in early to mid-2010.[21] About half of Americans expressed no opinion of the Tea Party in April 2010, and the most common responses from those who did express reasons why the public supports the Tea Party cited a general "concern about the economy" and a "distrust of government overall."[22] The Pew Research Center's 2010 report, titled "Distrust, Discontent, Anger and Partisan Rancor," includes a subsection documenting the rise of support for the Tea Party. As the report found, "By almost every conceivable measure Americans are less positive and more critical of government these days." This position is congruent with the rhetoric of Tea Partiers, among whom three-fourths claim "it is a major problem that the government interferes too much in people's lives."[23]

Andrew Kohut of the Pew Research Center highlights the timely emergence of the Tea Party in a period when other economic instability is contributing to growing public anxiety. Kohut identifies a "perfect storm of conditions" contributing to public anger, including "a bad economy, backlash against Washington partisanship," and "epic discontent" with officialdom.[24] Kohut's claims must be understood in light of near all-time highs in public distrust of government. As of April 2010, 80 percent of the public distrusted, and 75 percent were either "angry" or "frustrated," with the federal government.[25] Feelings that the government is "pretty much run by a few big interests looking out for themselves" reached as high as 60 percent of the public in the post-2000 period, while favorability scores for the Republican and Democratic parties reached as low as 36 percent and 43 percent respectively by 2010.[26] In short, the Tea Party's message of government distrust was ideally positioned to capitalize on the public's antipathy toward Washington.

The Tea Party enjoys a rising prominence at a time of economic instability. The out-of-power party regularly gains seats in midterm elections during times of economic hardship.[27] As the economy falters, as GDP and personal income decline, and as unemployment grows, Americans blame the president's party when voting, since he is the most prominent and visible national political figure. In the 2008 presidential election, for example, Barack Obama surged in the polls in the wake of the economic crash. Obama's electoral advantage increased by more than seven percentage points in the polls from September to October 2008, precisely at the time when the economic conditions were rapidly deteriorating.[28] At a time when President Bush was in the White House, Americans blamed Republicans for the state of the economy. So it was to be expected that the Republican Party would gain a significant number of seats at the expense of the Democrats in 2010. A stagnating economy and high unemployment favored the Tea Party's message as the American public was growing disenchanted with the president.[29] When the smoke cleared, Republicans, as expected, had gained a massive number of seats in Congress.

A close examination of the 2010 midterms demonstrates the importance of the poor economy in explaining Democratic losses. The economy was the foremost issue of concern for voters. Exit polling found that the issue remained the primary focus for 62 percent of voters, with approximately 90 percent describing the economy as "bad" and expressing "worry over the coming year." Four in ten explained that their personal finances had worsened in the year prior to the midterms, with the vast majority leaning toward the Republican Party. At the level of electoral outcomes, one can see evidence of voting that was "retrospectively" driven by punishing the party in power.[30] For example, states that saw the strongest declines and the weakest growth in personal income from 2008 to 2010 were consistently more likely to go to Republican candidates.[31]

Democratic losses in the midterms were not only the result of a weak economy, they were also the product of lower voter turnout among the less privileged and liberal-leaning groups and higher turnouts among the relatively affluent and conservatives. Exit polling from the Pew Research Center found that voters were statistically more likely to be "conservative, white, and angry," more likely to earn more than the national median income, and more likely to be Republican.[32] Those most pleased with the electoral outcomes were relatively affluent or conservative—disproportionately Republican, white, and earning more than \$75,000 a year.[33] In short, the 2010 midterms were a major victory for conservatives, and a significant sign of disengagement by liberal and underprivileged demographic groups.

THE PUBLIC-TEA PARTY DISCONNECT: DISAGREEMENT AT THE POLICY LEVEL

The Tea Party's message grew in prominence in 2009 and 2010. This did not mean, however, that it was embraced across-the-board. A majority of Americans did *not* support the Tea Party when asked in public opinion polls. By early 2010, the so-called movement had failed to make an impression—positive or negative—on 40 percent of Americans.[34] Support for the group was confined to a significant minority for nearly all survey questions, as reflected in Figure 4.1. Many rejected the Tea Party as too far out of line with their political and social beliefs and leaning too far to the right. A review of the CBS–*New York Times* and Pew polls from April 2010 suggests that the majority of Americans disagreed with the group when it comes to policy-*specific* questions. The polls found that most Americans rejected the Tea Party's notion that it is not the federal government's responsibility to create jobs during recession. The public also had a less charitable view of the Republican Party than self-designated Tea Partiers. Whereas only 38 percent of the general public retained a favorable opinion of the Republican Party, that number stood at 54 percent for Tea Partiers.[35] Polling from 2010 found that Tea Party supporters were more likely than the general public to be Republican and conservative and less likely to blame former president George Bush and Wall Street for the nation's economic problems.[36]

On the level of specific policies, Americans reject the preferences of Tea Partiers. As shown in CBS–*New York Times* and Pew polls, the public was far more likely to support government requirements that all Americans have health insurance, to approve of raising taxes on those earning more than $250,000 a year, to support the legal protection of gay marriage, and to favor increasing government spending to create jobs. The public is also more likely to disagree that welfare for the poor is enabling more poverty, more likely to oppose efforts to cut back [government] programs to reduce [government] power, to disagree that the government should cut the budget deficit instead of creating more jobs, and to disagree with claims that Obama 'favors the poor' and that he has 'increased taxes for most Americans.'[37] These are not small quibbles with Tea Partiers; they represent a fundamental disagreement with the group's members. Opinions of the Tea Party and the public do converge in opposition to Democratic healthcare reform, but this overlap is superficial. It is more the result of a manipulation of the public by Tea Partiers, the Republican Party, and the mass media rather than a legitimate point of consensus. When asked about healthcare reform in general, most Americans indicate opposition. When asked about the specific provisions of centrist-Democratic and other progressive reforms, however, the public tends to be strongly supportive.[38]

Another point of rejection between the public and the Tea Party relates to impressions of Democratic Party "socialism." Tea Party organizers routinely referred to President Obama as a socialist at meetings, events, and rallies I attended in the Chicago and Madison metropolitan areas. One head organizer of a Chicago Tea Party chapter even pointed to polling, in which 52 percent of Americans and 92 percent of Tea Party supporters suggested most Americans thought Obama was moving the country toward socialism. These results were taken by Tea Party members as validating the Tea Party's anti–healthcare reform message.[39] Though these individuals were correct that polls associate the Democratic Party with socialism, Tea Partiers missed the larger finding that much of the public still supported the party and the president along "socialist" lines. A substantial minority of Americans—36 percent—admit to viewing socialism "positively." This percent increased among Democrats and Democratic-leaners to a sizable 53 percent.[40] When asked to define what socialism meant to them, the most common responses among those polled was "government ownership or control" of major social and economic institutions.[41] A closer look at such institutions, however, finds that 50 percent of Americans think that the Social Security program is "definitely" or "sort of" like socialism, compared to 40 percent who think it is "not socialism." Similarly, expansion of Medicare, Medicaid, and Social Security is seen as "definitely" or "sort of like socialism" by 58 percent of Americans.[42]

National social welfare programs certainly are "socialized" in the sense that they are nonprofit, run by the government, and paid for through collective taxation and redistribution from rich to poor through a progressive federal income tax. However, these programs are overwhelmingly popular among the American public. Conservative attempts to privatize Social Security are opposed by a majority of the American public.[43] Public support for socialized government welfare programs is obscured in Tea Party rhetoric that attacks the Obama administration for its allegedly "socialistic" encroachment upon private property.

THE SIGNIFICANCE OF THE TEA PARTY

Tea Partiers consistently indicated in the events and meetings I observed throughout 2010 that their number–one priority was returning Republicans to majority control of Congress. To succeed in this objective, they did not need to convince liberals or progressives, or even the majority of Americans, of the legitimacy of their cause. National polling data demonstrated that Democrats in the general public, in addition to self-designated liberals, held unfavorable views of the Tea Party.[44] They were unlikely to vote for Republican candidates claiming the Tea Party mantle in the 2010 midterms.

Most Americans did *not* accept the messages of the Tea Party in 2010. Elections, however, are never decided by a majority of Americans. All that the Tea Party needed to do to ensure a Democratic loss in seats in the midterms was to mobilize Independents and centrist- to conservative-leaning moderates, in addition to self-designated Republicans and conservatives. These are the groups from which Republicans had lost electoral support in the last ten years, and they were the most likely sources of future support for the party. To influence the midterms, the Tea Party needed to galvanize opposition to the Democrats while retaining a fairly positive public image. This condition was satisfied by late 2009, as a *Wall Street Journal*–NBC poll found that the Tea Party was seen "very" or "somewhat favorably" by 41 percent of Americans, compared to the

Republican Party, in which just 28 percent expressed "very" or "somewhat favorable" views.[45]

Tea Party organizers understood that appealing to the Republican Party's moderate and conservative supporters was a key strategy for success. This much was clear in my attendance of the group's meetings, in which the heads of local chapters admitted that the Tea Party's primary goal was to see Republicans regain office and to appear in the public eye as if they were an independent, nonpartisan group. This goal was accomplished by focusing on specific issues, such as the "unconstitutionality" of healthcare reform, the importance of "small government," and the "unsustainability" of growing debt, rather than by explicitly supporting Republican candidates for office.

Organizers for the Chicago Tea Party chapter provided the most sophisticated plan for how to win Republican votes in the midterms. Working with Republican Party–supplied databases providing partisan and ideological information about local voters, the Chicago Tea Party announced a plan to target likely voters who identified themselves in previous elections as: moderates who leaned liberal, independent moderates, moderates who leaned conservative, and weak conservatives. Organizers admitted that there was no need to appeal to liberals and strong liberals, since they were unlikely to vote Republican. Conservatives and strong conservatives would not be targeted, since they were already likely to vote Republican.

It was openly conceded at Tea Party meetings I attended that the Republican Party was deeply unpopular. Organizers thought the best strategy for asserting Republican control of Congress was a win-by-default approach, whereby Tea Party organizers would not openly campaign for Republicans but would instead actively turn voters against Democratic candidates by opposing their "socialist" agenda. The objective was for Tea Partiers to appear among the public and in media reports as "moderate," rather than conservative, to maximize the prospect of Republican victories by winning votes from the political "center." If Tea Partiers "won on the issues," voters would know which candidate to choose "without us telling them" who to vote for.

The Tea Party derives most of its support from Republican partisans. Tea Party supporters are more likely to prefer Republicans over Democrats by a 2.6-to-1 ratio.[46] More than 80 percent of Tea Party supporters are either Republicans or lean toward the Republican Party.[47] Reciprocally, Republicans are more likely than Democrats and Independents to harbor favorable images of the Tea Party, more likely to say the Tea Party better reflects their values, less likely to think Tea Partiers are "fringe" in their politics, and were more likely to vote in the 2010 midterms for Republicans and Tea Party Republicans.[48]

The Pew Research Center chronicles what were ultimately successful Tea Party efforts to organize Republican supporters to vote in the 2010 midterms. Pew reported in August 2010, in anticipation of the November elections, that self-described Republicans were "more engaged in the coming election and more inclined to say they are certain to vote than are Democrats." Whereas 56 percent of Republicans as of June 2010 were "enthusiastic about voting" in the fall, the number fell to 42 percent for Democrats and Independents. This was the largest gap between partisans seen in sixteen years. Additionally, 64 percent of Republicans were closely following campaign news, compared to 50 percent of Democrats. Seventy-seven percent of Republican voters were "absolutely certain to vote," as compared to 65 percent of Democratic voters.[49] Republican activists were more energized in the run-up to the 2010 midterms than were the Democratic rank and file. As the elections drew closer, similar trends were evident. By late September, 50 percent of "likely voters" planned on voting Republican, compared to 43 percent who planned to vote Democratic. Similarly, 49 percent of likely voters who were Independents planned to vote Republican, compared to 36 percent planning to vote Democratic.[50]

Although Tea Partiers mobilized their Republican base, they also appealed to sympathetic Independents. The Republican Party lost significant support among former members of the party, many of whom flocked to the political center in the post-2000 period. Gallup survey data find that the percentage of Americans designating themselves as Republican or as leaning Republican declined from 2001 to 2009 by 5 percent, while those claiming to be Democrats or leaning Democratic increased by 8 percent. At the same time, the number of self-designated Independents increased from 34 percent to 37 percent.[51] Crucially, Independents voted disproportionately for Barack Obama in 2008.[52]

The Tea Party had some success in the last few years attracting a significant segment of the public *back* to the Republican Party. Sympathetic media coverage, along with growing disillusionment with Democratic control of government and anger over a stagnating economy, allowed the Tea Party the room needed to cultivate public support among swing demographic groups. As *USA Today* reported in July 2010, the public "backlash" against the Democrats in the last few years "significantly increased the number of voters who call themselves conservative. Although 37 percent of Americans described themselves as conservatives in 2008, now 42 percent do."[53] Another survey found that those planning to vote Republican in congressional elections increased from 39 percent to 44 percent of all voters between September 2006 and August 2010. Among the groups that became more supportive of Republicans were more privileged and conservative demographics such as whites, men, those 65 and older, and white Catholics.[54]

Independents appeared to be heavily leaning toward voting Republican in 2010. Pew reports that those Independents who were "highly frustrated with government are highly committed to voting this year, and they favor the GOP candidates in their district by a margin of 66 percent to 13 percent."[55] Independents "plan[ning] to vote Republican" were more enthusiastic about voting compared to Independents who planned to vote Democratic. More specifically, 55 percent of Republican-leaning Independents were enthusiastic about voting, compared to just 36 percent of Democratic-leaning Independents. Anti-incumbent sentiment was high in the run-up to November and exacted a negative toll on the Democratic Party. While a majority of Americans say they approve of their individual member of Congress, this trend changed by mid-2010. At that point, less than half of Americans indicated that they wanted to see their member of Congress reelected.[56] This finding was a recipe for disaster for the party in power.

The Tea Party drew from a large pool of former Republican supporters when cultivating support for its preferred candidates in 2010. As Gallup reports, the Republican Party lost supporters in nearly every demographic area in the post-2000 period, although the largest losses came in the following groups: college graduates, those between 18 and 29 and 50 and 64 years of age, midwesterners and easterners, ideological moderates and liberals, occasional churchgoers, the unmarried, whites, those earning between $35,000 and $70,000 a year, and those earning over $70,000 a year.[57] Renewed support for Republicans materialized from those who were formerly aligned with the party. The Pew Research Center reported in early 2010:

> Looking at the public as a whole, nearly half say the federal government threatens their personal rights and freedoms. . . . The percentage saying the government is a major threat to their personal rights and freedoms is now higher than when the question was first asked in 1995 and through-

out the early 2000s. This shift has come almost entirely from Republicans and Independents who lean to the GOP.[58]

EXPLAINING THE 2010 MIDTERMS

Skeptics may rightly wonder: If the Tea Party "movement" is largely smoke and mirrors, with little grassroots activism to thank for its success, then why study it at all? The Tea Party remains relevant in American politics because, as a mediated phenomenon, it is succeeding in galvanizing Republicans, Independents, and swing-voter demographic groups to turn out in favor of the Republican Party. As a public relations phenomenon, the Tea Party is vital in the rebranding of the Republican Party as a "populist," force. An examination of midterm exit polls finds that voters regularly cited the Tea Party as playing a major inspirational role in inciting electoral turnout. Tea Party supporters were more likely to register to vote than non–Tea Partiers and were more enthusiastic about voting. Tea Party supporters accounted for approximately 40 percent of all voters. The Tea Party phenomenon has encouraged its supporters to vote for Republicans. Approximately 80 percent of Tea Party supporters indicated that they planned to vote Republican even if there was no Tea Party candidate running in their local races in the House and Senate.[59]

Liberals at times lambaste America's working class for being taken in by Republican rhetoric that runs contrary to the material interests of the working class and poor. Liberal journalist Thomas Frank criticizes the poor and middle class for voting on morality-based issues such as outlawing abortion, teaching creationism, and establishing prayer in schools. Republicans promise to deliver on these issues but never do, he argues, while the party enacts economic policies that are detrimental to the interests of Americans.[60] In other words, poor and working-class voters are guilty of false consciousness, in that they vote for Republican candidates who work against them, seeking, for example, to cut social welfare spending that benefits them the most. Frank's interpretation of American voting has been subject to much empirical challenge by political scientists such as Andrew Gelman and Larry Bartels, who demonstrate that the poor are actually more likely to vote Democratic in both rich and poor states and across geographic regions and more likely to support liberal policy proposals under the understanding that Democratic policies—at least *relative* to Republican ones—are more likely to raise their living standards.[61]

Available evidence does not suggest that Frank is completely wrong, as close to half of middle-income voters have historically voted Republican across poor, middle-income, and rich states.[62] As Bartels explains, however, "white voters in the bottom third of the income distribution have actually become more loyal in their support of Democratic presidential candidates [in recent years]. Republican electoral gains have come not among 'poorer folks' but among middle and upper-income voters."[63] In the case of the 2010 midterms, support for Republicans was more the result of the mobilization of conservative and relatively affluent groups and the demobilization and lack of participation of liberal and underprivileged groups. Furthermore, Bartels demonstrates that public opinion among the poorest Americans on economic issues has not grown more conservative in recent decades. He finds that low-income Americans are much less likely to prioritize "culture war" issues than are higher-income earners.[64]

I present evidence similar to Gelman and Bartels's findings that the less affluent are more likely to support liberal-centrist and Democratic policies. The findings, however, must be qualified. Less affluent Americans certainly were more likely to support progressive positions in July of 2009, when Tea Party attacks on healthcare were beginning to materialize. However, as the Tea Party- and Republican-sponsored themes became more prominent in late 2009 and in 2010, such messages became more popular among the poor and less privileged. In line with Frank's argument, I find that extended media campaigns on behalf of conservative positions can be effective in convincing poorer and working-class Americans to subscribe to positions that are contrary to their material interests.

The Tea Party's appeal was concentrated most heavily among those with higher incomes and those heavily exposed to intangible hegemonic forces, as shown in Table 4.1.[65] Wealthier demographic groups and those exposed to conservative-hegemonic messages were the most supportive of Tea Party themes in 2009. Included in the list of demographic groups below are those that tend to be higher and lower levels of personal income, and those that are either more or less susceptible to conservative-hegemonic ideas.

The variables in this study that are differentiated by income include the seven factors listed in the first part of Table 4.1. Those factors differentiated by varied exposure to hegemonic messages and ideas include the final three factors listed in the second half of the table. The relationships I doc-

---

TABLE 4.1: Material and Hegemonic Influences on Public Opinion

VARIABLES DIFFERENTIATED BY INCOME
Race; Education; Income; Sex; Income-Based Evangelicism;
Race-Based Evangelicism; Political Efficacy

Higher-Income Groups (more conservative in policy attitudes)	Includes: whites; the highly educated; middle- and upper-income earners; men; middle- and upper-income Evangelicals; white Evangelicals; registered voters.
Lower-Income Groups (more conservative in policy attitudes)	Includes: non-whites; the less educated; lower-income earners; women; lower-income Evangelicals; non-white Evangelicals; non-voters.

VARIABLES DIFFERENTIATED BY EXPOSURE TO HEGEMONIC MESSAGES
Party; Ideology; Political Attentiveness

Higher Exposure to Hegemonic Messages (more conservative in policy matters)	Includes: Republicans; conservatives; the politically attentive (high media consumers).
Lower Exposure to Hegemonic Messages (less conservative in policy attitudes)	Includes: Independents and Democrats; moderates and liberals; the politically inattentive (low media consumers).

Source: Pew Research Center, 2009

ument between all ten variables, as related to income, hegemonic messages, and conservatism, are straightforward. Simply explained, those individuals hailing from "higher income groups" and those with "higher exposure to hegemonic messages" are consistently more likely to take conservative positions on public policy issues. In contrast, those from "lower income groups" and those with "lower exposure to hegemonic messages" are more likely to reject conservative positions on public policy issues.

Survey data limitations prevent me from analyzing the roles of Fox News consumption and health insurance status in influencing views of the Tea Party in early 2010, since the questions of media consumption and insurance are infrequently asked in polls and were not surveyed at the time. These two missing variables are explored in detail in chapter 6, where I assess their effects on opinions of Obama and Democratic health-care reform.

Table 4.2, drawing upon Pew Research Center polling in early 2010, finds that the Tea Party enjoyed its highest levels of support among

TABLE 4.2: Support for the Tea Party among Various
            Demographic Groups
            February 2010

Demographic Group	Percent Support	Demographic Group	Percent Support
Whites	41%	High Income ($75K or more)	43%
Non-Whites	19%	Middle Income ($50–$75K)	36%
Conservatives	60%	Low Income (Under $50K)	32%
Moderates	24%	White Evangelicals	54%
Liberals	9%	Non-White Evangelicals	21%
Republicans	64%	High-Income Evangelicals ($75k or more)	63%
Independents	40%	Middle-Income Evangelicals ($50–$75k)	45%
Democrats	9%	Low-Income Evangelicals (Less than $50k)	39%
Highly Educated	51%	Registered Voters	39%
Less Educated	66%	Non-Voters	25%
Men	43%	Fox News–Non-Fox Viewership	N/A
Women	34%	Political Attentiveness	N/A

Source: Pew Research Center

whites, Republicans, men, middle-income earners, white Evangelicals, wealthier Evangelicals, Protestants, and registered voters.

In short, material affluence and intangible hegemonic forces played a significant role in influencing opinions of the Tea Party, with the group appealing strongly to those hailing from more financially privileged backgrounds and those systematically exposed to conservative propaganda. Out of all the groups examined, individuals hailing from higher-income demographic groups were more likely to support the Tea Party in *every* category, with the exception of the highly educated, who were less likely to lend their support when compared to the less educated. The strongest factors influencing support for the Tea Party, after conducting a statistical analysis controlling for all the variables above, include party, ideology, race, and Evangelicism.[66] By "controlling for," I am referring to the statistical procedure, referred to as "multivariate regression analysis," whereby I measure the relationship between individual variables on the one hand and opinions of the Tea Party on the other, while holding other variables constant. Through this process, one is able to isolate the individual effects of each variable when compared to the other variables in question. For example, the statistical analysis I undertake is able to measure the effect of race (being white or non-white) on opinions of the Tea Party, after statistically controlling (holding constant) other variables such as income, sex, partisanship, and other factors.

In line with the predictions of the propaganda model for public opinion, intangible hegemonic forces are the most powerful factors indoctrinating the public in support of the Tea Party. With regard to support for the Tea Party, the differences between Republicans and Democrats and between conservatives and liberals were the largest for any variables, as shown in Table 4.2. An examination of the raw data demonstrates that, in terms of gross differences, Republicans were a massive 55 percentage points more likely than Democrats to support the Tea Party (64 percent supportive versus 9 percent supportive, respectively). Similarly, conservatives were 51 percentage points more likely than liberals to support the Tea Party. Gross differences within other demographic groups never reached more than between 9 to 33 percentage points, compared to the more than 50-point differences seen within the partisanship and ideology variables. For example, whites were 22 percent more likely to support the Tea Party when compared to non-whites.

While material and intangible forces played a major role in cultivating support for the Tea Party among higher-income groups and groups with higher exposure to hegemonic messages, the Tea Party also began making inroads with lower-income groups and groups less exposed to hegemonic messages (see Table 4.1 for a list of these groups) by mid- to late 2010. Table 4.3 tracks the growing support for the Tea Party among various demographic groups from March through April of 2010, a period when Tea Party coverage had reached its highest point yet. Aside from material factors, Table 4.3 also includes the intangible variable of partisanship (some variables discussed earlier in this chapter, unfortunately, are not included due to the differences in data availability between the Quinnipiac and Pew surveys used). Survey data for Table 4.3 from Quinnipiac polling show that growth in support for the Tea Party (expressed in terms of gross differences between groups) was slightly

TABLE 4.3: Growing Support for the Tea Party among
Various Demographic Groups
March–April 2010

HIGHER-INCOME AND HEGEMONIC GROUPS		
Percent Support for Tea Party (March 2010)	Percent Support (April 2010)	Percentage Point Increase in Support
Republicans — 47%	57%	+10%
Middle and High Income ($50-$100k) — 31%	35%	+4%
Whites — 33%	38%	+5%
White Evangelicals — 37%	44%	+7%
Highly Educated — 31%	32%	+1%
Men — 31%	37%	+6%

LOWER-INCOME AND LESS HEGEMONIC GROUPS		
Percent Support for Tea Party (March 2010)	Percent Support (April 2010)	Percentage Point Increase in Support
Democrats — 5%	5%	+0%
Low Income (Less than $50k) — 23%	26%	+3%
Blacks — 4%	7%	+3%
Non-White Evangelicals — Not Avail.	N/A	N/A
Less Educated — 27%	33%	+6%
Women — 25%	28%	+3%

Source: Quinnipiac

stronger among higher-income groups and those exposed to hegemonic messages, which averaged 5.5 percentage points in growth across-the-board. Relationships were weaker, although still positive, for lower-income groups and groups less exposed to hegemonic messages. Increased support among these latter groups averaged three percentage points.[67] In analyzing the Quinnipiac surveys, I did not engage in statistical multivariate regression analysis, since the full data was not made publicly available. Instead, I simply analyzed the gross differences in terms of percent of support for and opposition to the Tea Party among various demographic groups.

The strongest growth in the Tea Party's appeal was seen among the less educated, Republicans, men, and white Evangelicals. Some might note that such changes are relatively small, representing just a few percentage points, but this point negates the long-established fact that public opinion (as measured in surveys) has always been extraordinarily stable, rarely fluctuating by more than a few percentage points, if at all, per month. Such changes are common even when the public is responding to changes in the information environment, as was the case with regard to growing support for the Tea Party in 2010.[68]

Public support continued to grow in late 2010. By November, support had increased to 65 percent among Republicans (an 18-point gain from March), 41 percent among men (a 10 percent gain), 28 percent among women (a 3 percent gain), 10 percent among blacks (a 6 percent gain), and 39 percent among whites (a 6 percent gain). Similarly, the public's reported self-identification with the Tea Party was also growing. Drawing on public opinion surveys from Quinnipiac, Table 4.4 finds that the percent of those considering themselves a "part of" the Tea Party grew between March and April 2010 largely among more privileged groups, when reporting of national protests was reaching new heights. This reported participation in the "movement," however, is most certainly exaggerated in light of this book's earlier findings. Tea Party protests *did* spike in April of 2010, although my analysis of local chapters across the country demonstrates that participation at that time remained at very low levels.

The meager public participation in the "movement" cannot explain why the Tea Party received saturation coverage in the first half of 2010. Nor can it explain the growth in popularity of the group in late 2010. Tea Party activism was deteriorating from admittedly small initial levels during the fall of 2010 and in the run-up to the midterms, as various national Tea Party "protests" saw poor attendance and as national conventions in Las Vegas and Washington collapsed. Participation, in short, appeared to be declining across-the-board.

Some greater national force, then, was at work in uniting Americans in support of the Tea Party brand. That greater force was the mass media.

TABLE 4.4: Self-Identification with the Tea Party among Various
Demographic Groups
March–April 2010

	HIGHER-INCOME AND HEGEMONIC GROUPS		
	% Who Are a "Part of" the Tea Party (March 2010)	"Part of" the Tea Party (April 2010)	Percentage Point Change in Participation
Republicans	21%	27%	+6%
Middle Income ($50-$100k)	12%	16%	+4%
Whites	21%	22%	+1%
White Evangelicals	21%	22%	+1%
Highly Educated	14%	17%	+3%
Men	13%	17%	+4%

	LOWER-INCOME AND LESS HEGEMONIC GROUPS		
	% Who Are a "Part of" the Tea Party (March 2010)	"Part of" the Tea Party (April 2010)	Percentage Point Change in Participation
Democrats	5%	3%	–2%
Low Income (Less than $50k)	14%	13%	–1%
Blacks	7%	6%	–1%
Non-White Evangelicals	Not Avail.	N/A	N/A
Less Educated	14%	17%	+3%
Women	14%	14%	0%

Source: Quinnipiac

A MEDIATED REBELLION

The mass media thoroughly regulates Americans' interface with the Tea
Party. The vast majority of Americans have few direct experiences with
political issues and events of the day. Over the last few years, the mass
media appear to have pulled the public to the right on two levels: in terms
of assessments of the Tea Party and in attitudes on healthcare reform.

Coverage of the Tea Party reached a new high by April 2010, and by that point a majority of Americans—68 percent—reported having heard or read about the group "a lot," compared to 42 percent who had heard only "a little."[69] Portrayals of the Tea Party were positive in terms of the explicit support it received in the conservative media and repetition of the theme that it was a social movement. In April 2009, when the Tea Party first emerged, more than half of Americans—52 percent—said they were following the group in the news either "very closely" or "fairly closely."[70] By April of 2010, 77 percent of Americans reported following news of the Tea Party either "a little" or "a lot"—up from 68 percent in March of the same year.[71] Among those who were Tea Party supporters, 47 percent indicated in 2010 that their information about the group was derived primarily from television. By contrast, only 4 percent said their information came mainly from emails from friends or local chapters; only 1 percent listed meetings as their primary information source; and just 1 percent cited phone calls from those who are well informed about or members of the Tea Party.[72] Friend and family sources of information, however, should not be divorced from media at a time when respondents admitted that "the news" was their primary source of information on the Tea Party. Although only a small segment of Americans were getting their information on the Tea Party from friends, family, and acquaintances, much of that dialogue was likely the product of interface with media.

These data tell us that media reporting was the most important source of public information on the Tea Party. Furthermore, the public seemed comfortable enough with journalists' attention to the group. A plurality of Americans—41 percent—believed as of mid-2010 that regular coverage of the "movement" was the "right amount," compared to 24 percent who said attention was "too much." Twenty-nine percent said that the media paid "too little" attention to the Tea Party. In total, then, 70 percent of Americans took positions sympathetic to the Tea Party; they were either happy with already massive Tea Party coverage or felt that it should have been even more generous. Similarly, a plurality of Americans—46 percent—agreed in April 2010 that the framing of the Tea Party had been "fair," with just 17 percent saying it was "too easy." Twenty-four percent said the media had been "too tough." Again, these numbers suggest that 70 percent of Americans took a supportive position by either concluding that the Tea Party was being treated fairly or by desiring *even more favorable* coverage for a group that had already received extensive attention and sympathy from journalists.[73]

FIGURE 4.2: Mediated Support for the Tea Party (March 2010)

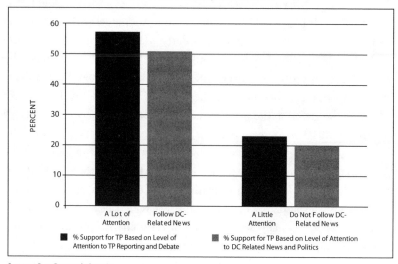

Source: Pew Research Center

In perhaps the most striking evidence of media influence, the Pew Research Center found that by mid-2010 support for the Tea Party was strongest among those who paid the most attention to the reporting on national politics and on the Tea Party. Among those following news related to Washington "very closely," 55 percent considered themselves supporters of the Tea Party, in contrast to the general public, of whom 33 percent supported the group.[74] Attention to the Tea Party was one of the leading issues covered in Washington-related news at the time. Increased consumption of Washington-related news was a statistically significant predictor of support for the Tea Party.[75] One might be tempted to say that this statistic proves little, since those who paid closest attention and who were the Tea Party's strongest supporters may also be more likely to be Republican or conservative. It could be the case, therefore, that conservatives and Republicans were *already* more likely to pay attention to Tea Party reporting and that media played a small role in influencing opinions, outside of providing information for supporters. The survey question does not ask about attention to the Tea Party; rather, it asks about attention to the news more generally, and conservatives and Republicans do not monopolize consumption of mass media, when compared to Democrats and Independents. Furthermore, my statistical analysis of public attention to the news (as shown in Figure 4.2) is able to control for individuals' political ideology and party (in addition

to a variety of other potentially confounding factors) yet still finds a statistically significant link between consumption of news related to
Washington and positive opinions of the Tea Party.[76] By statistical significance, I refer to an observed relationship between two variables that is
unlikely to be the result of chance variation within the larger population
of individuals who are surveyed.

Mediated support for the Tea Party manifested itself in other ways as
well. As seen in Figure 4.2, close attention to the national debate over and
reporting of the movement was also correlated with growing support.
The effects of attention to and consumption of news on the Tea Party is
not the result of other potentially confounding variables such as partisanship or ideology, either, since the relationship remains after controlling
these and many other variables.[77]

Such findings further drive home the point that the national debate
over the Tea Party, as reflected in the mass media, was heavily sympathetic to the group and its members. The results, then, are unlikely to be the
result of researcher bias, but reflect the pro–Tea Party biases in the press,
as measured through content analysis and through the effects of media
coverage, as seen in public opinion polls.

Mediated politics does not stop with the Tea Party phenomenon. The
power of media to manufacture dissent also covers healthcare reform.
Accompanying this debate is a consistent growth in public opposition,
corresponding closely with the rise of the Tea Party. At a time when the
healthcare industry was rebelling in order to obstruct progressive
reforms, journalists were more than happy to uncritically repeat Tea
Party–Republican propaganda.

FIVE

The Plot to Kill Grandma: The Tea Party, Mass Media, and Healthcare Reform

Reporters' thorough reliance on official sourcing is a fundamental component of American journalism. Corporate ownership and advertising also exert significant pressure on reporters to promote perspectives that are favorable to business interests.[1] It is not that reporters habitually feel they must ignore stories that are critical of business. Rather, the power of hegemony plays the dominant role in socializing journalists to refrain from seriously questioning corporate power. This does not mean that stories addressing corporate malfeasance and corruption will always be ignored. It simply means that there are a variety of institutional safety valves operating to ensure that challenges to business power do not become a staple of reporting. These forces are not conspiratorial, but institutional. In addition to corporate ownership and advertising, the editorial and peer pressures journalists face in the workplace are important. The indoctrinating powers at work in higher education play a role, as journalists learn about the importance of "objectively" fashioning stories that rely almost exclusively on the views of those within the bipartisan political-economic system.

All of the above factors are effective in pressuring reporters to view regular criticisms of business as akin to "rocking the boat." These pressures relate to the Tea Party and healthcare in that they reinforce a pro-corporate system that views attacks on private for-profit healthcare as an unacceptable threat to the established order. As a product of this system, the Tea Party itself played a vital role in suppressing progressive health-care proposals, screaming "socialism" and "tyranny" at even mildly liberal, pro-market reforms. These reforms were designed to *expand* the private market for healthcare services and increase the profitability of this sector, but they also exact minimal conditions on that system by prohibiting the exclusion of healthcare based on "preexisting conditions," modestly expanding Medicaid, requiring that for-profit health insurance interests provide coverage to all Americans, and by taxing the wealthy to pay for these initiatives. Even such limited reforms are seen as unacceptable by conservatives and business elites, because they potentially benefit the masses *as well as* the healthcare industry.

These attacks on liberal-centrist reforms serve another more important purpose. They effectively remove from consideration any government healthcare programs—such as a universal, Medicare-for-all plan or a public option. Ignoring progressive reforms (while lambasting liberal-centrist ones) serves as an ideological control, as exercised *against* the public. Tea Partiers' attacks have restricted the parameters of debate to a choice between mildly liberal pro-market reforms on the one hand and more extreme neoliberal reforms on the other, which grant maximum concessions to business and virtually nothing to the masses of Americans. By preventing consideration of progressive reforms, Tea Partiers are ensuring that for-profit systems with a financial interest in excluding the disadvantaged from healthcare will continue to operate into the indefinite future.

To this point, I have only documented the affection the Tea Party receives in various quarters of the national media and public. In chapter 3 I analyzed the favorable media treatment of the Tea Party as a populist uprising. Left unexamined are the ways in which journalists interact with Tea Party messages when it comes to the group's priority issue: national healthcare reform.

The Tea Party—Republican Overlap on Healthcare Reform

In 2009 and 2010, there was a nearly complete overlap between Tea Party and official Republican healthcare rhetoric. The convergence between anti-healthcare rhetoric was made possible by the standardization and uniformity of ideology on the American right, institutionalized as a result of the right's growing dominance of the mass media, and the rightward turn of the Republican Party.[2]

For decades scholarly studies charted the tendency of mass media to restrict permissible views to those expressed by the country's political elites. Journalists "index" the range of opinions expressed in reporting and editorializing against those declared by Democratic and Republican leaders.[3] As the American political system has moved further to the right, media coverage similarly shifts in a rightward direction.[4]

In the debate over healthcare, Democratic officials initially indicated rhetorical support for a public option that would provide government healthcare coverage to the uninsured. This plan was quickly abandoned in favor of an amalgamation of reforms characterized by the *New York Times* as "boons" for the private healthcare industry.[5] With the Democratic Party's pro-corporate shift, Republicans voiced positions even further to the right, warning of Democratic "socialism," "Marxism," "death panels," "rationing," and "big government takeovers" of one-sixth of the economy. In this environment and under the media "indexing" phenomenon, one would expect media reporting and commentary to be dominated at first by a mix of center-left Democratic policy proposals such as the public option and conservative counter-responses, and then quickly shift in a conservative direction following Democratic abandonment of the public option and the growth of the Republicans' visceral attacks against even piecemeal healthcare reforms.

A review of the arguments made by prominent Republican leaders demonstrates the overlap in Tea Party and Republican rhetoric.

"Unsustainable Debt"

Republican House minority leader John Boehner argued against Democratic healthcare reforms, maintaining that the government could not "spend money that we [the taxpayers and government] didn't have." Former Republican vice presidential candidate and Tea Partier Sarah Palin similarly warned against the "ever-expanding deficit," while remarking that "common sense tells us that the government's attempts to solve large problems more often create new ones."[6] Boehner's and Palin's claims were echoed at Tea Party rallies, which saw protests against "unsustainable debt" and "out of control" government spending that rightists claimed would cripple future generations. A common argument against healthcare reform that I heard at Tea Party events focused on the inability to "afford" healthcare reform.

The "Government Takeover"

Republican congressional officials such as Steve Buyer, John Fleming, and Jim DeMint erroneously warned that healthcare reform plans promoted by Democrats were the equivalent of "a government takeover of one-sixth of the economy." Along the same lines, Republican congresswoman and Tea Partier Michele Bachmann attacked the "government-run option" through the summer of 2010 onward.[7] These warnings became the rallying cry of Tea Partiers, even after Democrats abandoned the public option and decided to pursue corporate-friendly healthcare reform. Rhetoric at meetings and rallies I attended centered on warnings against "government healthcare" and "central planning," as allegedly personified by healthcare reform.

Obama, "Marxism," and the "Socialist" Takeover

Although they happened prior to the emergence of the Tea Party, former Republican presidential candidate John McCain's attacks on Obama for wanting to "spread the wealth" were representative of what was to come with Tea Partiers' conflation of tax cuts, "socialism," and "Marxism." McCain reacted critically to a comment made by Obama to "Joe the Plumber" in which Obama indicated support for tax cuts for most Americans. Obama explained that "when you spread the wealth around, it's good for everybody."[8] This comment was immediately misrepresented by McCain as evidence that Obama's redistributive policy sounded "a lot like socialism."[9] McCain framed the tax cuts, which were to be directed at most Americans, as a case of the unwarranted subsidizing of the undeserving poor. McCain argued, "Raising taxes on some in order to give checks to others is not a tax cut. It's just another government giveaway."[10] Republican National Committee chairman Michael Steele repeated similar warnings, declaring that Obama's healthcare plan represented "socialism." McCain's aversion to government subsidies directed at the poor and working class is repeated by Tea Partiers. Tea Partiers demonize Obama for being a "Marxist," although their conflating of socialism and Democratic policy proposals is a product of ignorance on the right.[11] Such ignorance was on display at *every* Tea Party event I attended.

The symbiotic relationship between the Tea Party and Republican Party complements the growing dominance of right-wing views in media. Whether one is talking about liberal sources such as MSNBC or the *New York Times*, or reactionary outlets like Fox News and the *Washington Post*, one sees striking similarities when examining coverage of healthcare reform.

"DEATH PANELS" AND THE PLOT TO KILL GRANDMA

Early coverage of healthcare was dominated by Republicans' conspiratorial rhetoric, which framed the Obama administration as out to deny life-saving medical treatment to the elderly and disabled. Nowhere was this development more evident than in journalists' response to Sarah Palin's coining of the term "death panels" to describe an end-of-life service provision in Democratic legislation. The controversy began after Palin posted the following message on Facebook:

> Who will suffer the most when they ration care? The sick, the elderly, and the disabled, of course. The America I know and love is not one in which my parents or my baby with Down Syndrome will have to stand in front of Obama's "death panel" so his bureaucrats can decide, based on a subjective judgment of their "level of productivity in society," whether they are worthy of healthcare. Such a system is downright evil. We must step up and engage in this most crucial debate. Nationalizing our health-care system is a point of no return for government interference in the lives of its citizens.[12]

Coverage of "death panels" became a mainstay of media coverage and consumed much of journalists' attention in 2009, as Figure 5.1 shows. Discussion of "death panels" appeared on MSNBC and Fox on average once per day in August and September 2009, while reporting at the *New York Times* and *Washington Post* reached similar levels.

The *New York Times* did correct distortions regarding "death panels," reporting in August:

FIGURE 5.2: Media Coverage of Town Hall Meetings and Healthcare (2009)

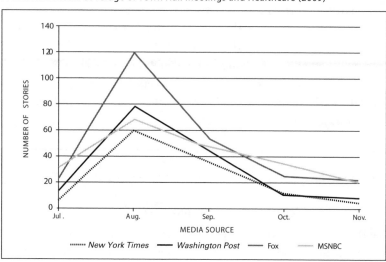

Source: LexisNexis

The stubborn yet false rumor that President Obama's healthcare proposals would create government-sponsored "death panels" to decide which
patients were worthy of living seemed to arise from nowhere in recent
weeks. . . . There is nothing in any of the legislative proposals that would
call for the creation of death panels or any other governmental body that
would cut off care for the critically ill as a cost-cutting measure. But over
the course of the past few months, early, stated fears . . . that Mr. Obama
would pursue a pro-abortion, pro-euthanasia agenda, combined with
twisted accounts of actual legislative proposals that would provide
financing for optional consultations with doctors about hospice care and
other "end of life" services, fed the rumor to the point where it overcame
the debate.[13]

A LexisNexis search finds that, within a week of Palin's Facebook
claim, other media followed the *New York Times*'s lead in correcting the
fallacious "death panels" claim. Other outlets correcting Palin included
the Associated Press, *St. Petersburg Times, Los Angeles Times,* and *USA
Today.* However, for every paper that refuted the claim, another paper
failed to report the correction. Among the papers failing to refute the
"death panels" claim in the week after Palin's comment were the
*Washington Post, Houston Chronicle, Pittsburgh Post-Gazette, Atlanta
Journal Constitution, Washington Times, San Francisco Chronicle,* and

Chicago Sun-Times. Furthermore, even the *New York Times*'s debunking of death panel propaganda was heavily mitigated by its continued obsession with the topic, as the paper published dozens of stories mentioning Palin's comment in the following months. This sustained attention granted Palin's formerly obscure claim a life of its own and played a large part in ensuring that the public option would not be seriously considered.

A slew of right-wing pundits embraced Palin's claims. Rush Limbaugh responded to criticisms of the death panels claim by arguing that Palin was "dead right on the issue": "The government's going to be in the position to decide who gets treatment and who doesn't" under a public option.[14] Fox News pundits Glenn Beck, Bill O'Reilly, Sean Hannity, and Laura Ingraham promptly and uncritically repeated Palin's warning within a week of the original claim.[15] Fox pundits reacted to reports that there were no death panels by revising the argument slightly to claim that government involvement in healthcare would cause care to be "rationed." Rationing, they argued, constituted "de facto death panels."[16]

MSNBC pundits Rachel Maddow, Ed Schultz, and Keith Olbermann challenged Palin's propaganda. However, by responding, they were allowing conservatives to dominate the national agenda.[17] Liberals' obsession with conservative propaganda translated into a tremendous amplification of these messages, far out of proportion to what was warranted in light of the lack of substance within these messages. Rather than spending time arguing for a universal Medicare-for-all program or a public option, liberals were left scrambling to correct conservative distortions in a national debate where many were convinced of the government's malicious intent. Following Palin's attack, the national discussion focused on the conservative question of whether or not Obama and the Democrats wanted to "Kill Grandma," rather than on the liberal perspective asking *how,* specifically, the national government could assist needy citizens.

ENTER THE "TOWN HALL" CRASHERS

Conservative narratives dominated coverage in August and September 2009, because of growing discussion of "death panels," and due to the rise in reporting of Tea Party "Town Hall" protests. Figure 5.2 demonstrates that media attention to the Town Hall protests spiked to more than 120 stories on Fox News for the month of August, and to between 60 and 80 stories in the *New York Times*, *Washington Post*, and MSNBC.

FIGURE 5.2: Media Coverage of Town Hall Meetings and Healthcare (2009)

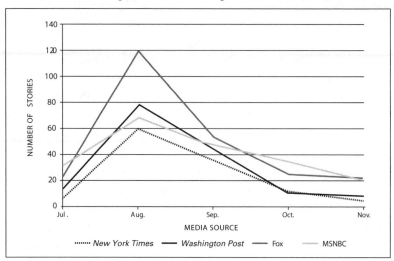

Source: LexisNexis

Attention to Town Hall demonstrators complemented reporters' fixation on "death panels," as Tea Partiers uncritically embraced conservative attacks on alleged government "rationing" of healthcare under a public option. Coverage of the Town Hall meetings eventually fell in September, although staying relatively high for that month. Attention to Town Halls and death panels dwarfed discussion of the public option in August.[18]

A LexisNexis search finds that, during August 2009, stories and programs on "death panels" and the "Town Hall" meetings combined appeared between 80 to 124 percent more often in the four outlets I examined than did stories on the public option. Clearly, conservative pundits were increasingly successful in dominating national debate.

Right-wing pundits presented the Town Halls as a rebellion of ordinary Americans against corrupt, backroom-dealing liberal elites. Fox News actively encouraged Tea Partiers to attend the meetings and disrupt them, as Chris Wallace, one of the network's leading journalists, worried about "a government takeover of healthcare" and lauded the "real public furor at these Town Hall meetings."[19] Sean Hannity celebrated the "healthcare uprising," in which the public came together to oppose "government run healthcare." He reminded his viewers that "this is your moment, your opportunity to stop this thing." Rush Limbaugh celebrated the protests as "real," "genuine voting American citizens" expressing public discontent with Obama. Hannity and Beck ran programs depicting the public, as allegedly demonstrated in opinion polling, as opposed to Democratic healthcare reform.[20]

The Republican Party's rhetoric regularly appeared in Fox's depictions of the Town Halls and the public option. Fox News host Greta Van Susteren interviewed Tea Party protesters attacking the Democrats for "forcing [healthcare] bills down our throats" and lamenting "being ramrodded" by liberal reformers, repeating the same language used by Republican leaders such as Sarah Palin, Michelle Bachmann, and John Cornyn.[21] On *The O'Reilly Factor*, Laura Ingraham derided Service Employee International Union "thugs" who allegedly "roughed up" Tea Partiers protesting healthcare reform.[22]

Reporting on the "Town Halls" suggested that the protests were manifestations of grassroots resistance. The *New York Times* reported "spontaneous opposition" to healthcare reform "that would only gain momentum as Americans learn more about the legislation."[23] The *Washington Post* reported on the "raucous town hall meetings," which were the product of an "anti-reform," "populist, anti-Washington *movement* . . . with few formal connections among the activist groups or with mainstream political organizations such as the Republican National Committee."[24]

LIBERAL MESSAGES (BRIEFLY) BREAK THROUGH

Conservative dominance of the media on healthcare was subsiding in September and October 2009. At this point, President Obama made "selling" Democratic reform a priority, realizing the dangers to his agenda as seen in conservative attacks on "Obamacare." Obama drew major national attention to Democratic reform proposals in a September 9 speech to Congress that received major attention in the media. He also tried to debunk right-wing propaganda that the government was planning on "killing Grandma."[25] This speech convinced many Americans of the need for action in terms of passing new healthcare legislation.

Presidents regularly attempt to influence public opinion by "going public" in their appeals and in directing positive attention to their proposals.[26] Obama made more than ten major speeches (more than one a week) during September and October 2009 related to issues of national healthcare.[27] His effort to "set the agenda" in the national press was successful, as discussion of the public option skyrocketed in media reporting. The number of news articles, editorials, op-eds, and letters mentioning the public option

FIGURE 5.3: Media Coverage of Center-Left & Conservative Healthcare Proposals, 2009–2010

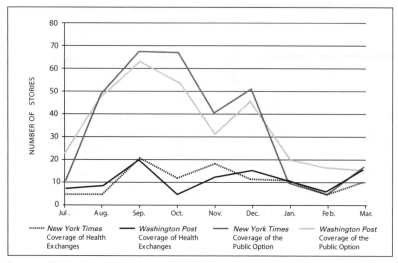

Source: LexisNexis

increased to between 60 to 70 a month between September and October 2009 in major newspapers (see Figure 5.3). Discussion of the public option dwarfed coverage of conservative Democratic proposals, such as set-ting up private, for-profit state insurance "exchanges" that would provide uninsured Americans with healthcare. Liberal elements within the mass media began to mobilize in favor of the public option. MSNBC's Ed Schultz vigorously promoted the public option, even after Obama indicat-ed that its inclusion was not vital for healthcare reform to pass.

Ex-MSNBC host Keith Olbermann publicly opposed Democratic healthcare reforms that did not contain a public option, and Rachel Maddow critically spotlighted Democratic Speaker of the House Nancy Pelosi for supporting the removal of the public option from a Senate healthcare bill.[28]

Editors of major national newspapers backed Obama on healthcare, regardless of whether Democratic proposals included a public option. The editors of the *New York Times* concluded that Obama "rightly called for sweeping healthcare reform" and claimed that "a new public plan option" would "compete with private insurance plans," "offer consumers greater choice," and "keep the private plans honest."[29] The editors at the *Washington Post* condemned refusals to exclude the public option from consideration as "crazy," but only because they assumed there was "no way to amass 60 votes with a public option in the [Senate] bill."[30]

FIGURE 5.4: Coverage of Progressive Healthcare Reform Proposals, 2009–2010

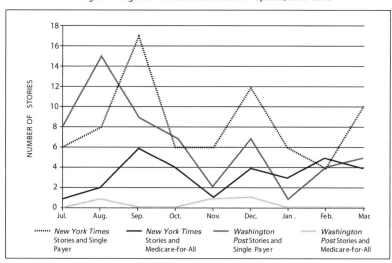

Source: LexisNexis

The window for discussion of progressive reform was closed once Democrats abandoned the public option. As Figure 5.3 demonstrates, discussion of the public option declined precipitously after October 2009 following declining political support. Other more progressive proposals never stood a chance without Democratic sponsorship. Figure 5.4 indicates that the "debate" over national healthcare reform in 2009 and 2010 was marked by an almost complete omission of a "single payer," "Medicare-for-all" system of universal healthcare. This option was invisible in the news. Universal healthcare, at the height of journalists' attention to it, received just 20 to 25 percent of the coverage received by the public option. Much of that coverage was not even from reporters. Of the 53 articles that ran in *the New York Times* discussing single payer care, 22 (or 42 percent) were letters to the editor from concerned readers who wanted to see the issue more seriously discussed.

With a lack of Democratic support for progressive reform, conservatives, representatives of the healthcare industry, and right-wing pundits opposed even limited reforms. Fox News led the way in condemning the corporate-friendly reforms passed in March 2010. The most salient theme in Fox coverage was the "cost" of the Democratic healthcare bill and the "debt" it would allegedly impose on current and future generations. Other prominent themes, although less salient, included warnings about healthcare reform as a "socialist," "rationing," "big government," "takeover" of healthcare, as seen in Figure 5.5.

FIGURE 5.5: Fox News and Anti-Healthcare Frames, 2009–2010

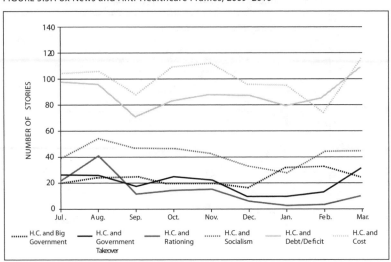

Source: LexisNexis

Newspapers and television outlets followed the Fox lead. Warnings about the "cost" of healthcare reform were a regular concern across many outlets (see Figure 5.6).

While Democratic leaders gained attention for presenting concrete healthcare reforms, Republicans played the role of obstructionists. There was no sustained media attention to concrete proposals from Republican officials when it came to promoting healthcare reform. Even conservative, market-based options like the state exchanges (where private health insurance would be sold by for-profit corporations) were shunned by the Republican Party. Democrats offered specific proposals for reform. Republicans, in contrast, offered specific objections that were designed not to pass constructive solutions to the national healthcare problem, but to derail Democratic proposals.

When Republicans offered proposals in the spring of 2010, they were non-starters for legislators seeking to expand healthcare coverage. These proposals would have increased the costs of care for the sick and provided no assurance that tens of millions of Americans who were uninsured would be guaranteed healthcare coverage.[31] Such "reforms" were designed to increase corporate profitability and reduce coverage for the indigent and poor.

FIGURE 5.6: Media on Healthcare Costs (2009–2010)

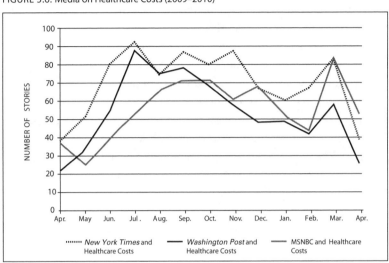

Source: LexisNexis

WHOSE VIEWS DOMINATED THE NEWS?

Conservative views tended to dominate reporting on healthcare reform. In assessing the arguments employed in the national healthcare debate, three liberal proposals were analyzed, alongside two conservative responses and one conservative proposal. Liberal-progressive proposals included any discussion of 1) Medicare-for-all, 2) single payer care, or 3) the public option. Conservative responses included a focus on 1) the cost of, and 2) the alleged debt/deficits resulting from reform, and 3) a conservative proposal for establishing for-profit state health insurance exchanges. Table 5.1 demonstrates that though all the conservative and liberal positions appeared in media discourse, conservative positions dominated across all the outlets I examined. The "costs" of, and "debt"/"deficits" allegedly resulting from reforms, appear as the first and second most salient themes in all the news outlets except MSNBC.[32] Even at MSNBC, two of the three most common frames are conservative. The public option is mentioned less than both "debt" and "cost" concerns in six of the seven outlets. Pointing out that MSNBC was *relatively* more balanced in its contemplation of competing conservative and liberal positions, however, must be carefully qualified, considering that the MSNBC audience is the smallest of all the outlets examined. The Fox News audience is three times larger than that of MSNBC, and the audiences of the

New York Times and *Washington Post* are approximately twice as large.[33] The three national networks individually boast between seven to 10.5 times more daily viewers than MSNBC.[34]

Progressive/ left reform in the form of a single payer, Medicare-for-all system is almost completely omitted from coverage. Single payer care was taken relatively more seriously on MSNBC, although only in that outlet. Furthermore, MSNBC's most prominent theme is a conservative one, focusing on the debt/deficit allegedly resulting from healthcare reform. When taking all these findings into account, it is clear that conservative perspectives enjoyed an advantage in national reporting on healthcare.

MEDIA PROPAGANDA, THE TEA PARTY, AND HEALTHCARE

Any discussion of healthcare reform should acknowledge the propaganda utilized by Republicans against liberal-centrist and progressive proposals. A single payer, Medicare-for-all program, in addition to the milder public option, was quickly dismissed from consideration, in large part due to Tea Party–Republican fear-mongering. Republican-business opposition to a government healthcare program was heavily propagandistic because it was promoted by those with no interest in increasing quality of care or health-care access for all. Conservative legislation, it should be remembered, pro-posed increasing cost of care and enriching corporate profits, while failing to guarantee coverage for all. Attacks on Democrats for establishing "death panels" were without merit. No such panels existed or would have been established through Democratic reforms. Such fear-mongering amount-ed to little more than vulgar propaganda.

Concerns over "rationing" under government healthcare were disin-genous. Conservatives and business lobbyists show no concern for the tens of thousands who die every year due to lack of access to healthcare in the U.S. private, for-profit system. Interest in the uninsured and poor has never been an integral part of their policy platforms.

Private healthcare apologists consistently ignore the inconvenient reality that the United States, as the only country with private healthcare in the first world, provides the worst quality of care for its citizens and at the greatest cost.[35] Universal healthcare systems, which provide health services as a public good rather than for private profit, provide better quality of care, as measured by numerous empirical indicators. The low

THE PLOT TO KILL GRANDMA

TABLE 5.1: Healthcare Perspectives and Proposals in Mass Media Coverage (2009–2010) (Average Number of Stories /Programs Per Month)

Paper/ Outlet	"Healthcare" and "Deficit" or "Debt" (July 2009– March 2010)	"Healthcare" and "Cost" (July 2009– March 2010)	"Healthcare" and "Public Option" (July 2009– March 2010)	"Healthcare" and "Exchanges" (July 2009– March 2010)	"Healthcare" and "Single Payer" (July 2009– March 2010)	"Medicare for All" (July 2009– March 2010)
NY Times	75	70	35	11	9	4
Wash. Post	64	54	35	11	6	.3
MSNBC	42	55	52	27	22	6
Fox	89	101	50	23	13	.8
ABC	20	33	15	6	1	.4
NBC	21	24	15	11	1	.3
CBS	24	31	16	7	2	.1

Source: LexisNexis

quality and high cost of U.S. care is no coincidence; it is the product of a system that places profit concerns over human need. Journalists' obsession with the "cost" of healthcare reform and the potential effects on "debt" and the "deficit" represent a propagandistic diversion from the real reasons corporate America and conservatives oppose reform. Such "concerns" over cost are not only propagandistic amid the already staggering (and still increasing) costs of private healthcare, which are consisntently ignored by conservatives. Cost concerns are also disingenuous in the wake of government's nonpartisan assessments that the Democratic healthcare reforms will *not* increase the deficit and would reduce even the national debt over a number of years.[36]

Universal healthcare, and even the public option, pose a threat to the private sector, as they would most certainly reduce costs, and improve quality of, and access to, healthcare. The potential loss of profits suffered by the healthcare industry represent the real reason for sustained journalistic, political, and business opposition to progressive reforms. Journalists' inability to acknowledge this basic fact ensures that an informed discussion of healthcare cannot take place within the confines of the corporate mass media. Journalists' intransigence in discussing the real reasons for opposition to healthcare are also contributing to public ignorance, as I document in the next chapter.

The dominance of Tea Party–Republican themes in the national discussion of healthcare raises serious questions about the state of media discourse and the rise of propaganda masquerading as "news." Pundits like Glenn Beck and Rush Limbaugh are demagogues, rather than newscasters or credible political analysts. The "big government" "takeover" of healthcare—framed as creeping "socialism"—is an important case in point. The public option, as it was originally proposed, represented a partial socialization of healthcare, not because the government would expropriate the assets of private health insurance companies but because it would provide insurance on a nonprofit basis and as a public service for those deemed uncoverable in the private market. This program would have made it more difficult for private providers, which would increasingly lose market share to the government program. It should be pointed out, additionally, that even the single payer, Medicare-for-all system represents only a partial socialization of healthcare. It would leave control of insurance in the hands of the government, while leaving private companies to profit from medical equipment, doctor-patient services, pharmaceuticals, and hospital care, among other areas of healthcare, as is the case today with Medicare.

Attacks by conservative pundits on Obama's "Marxism" are propagandistic.[37] Establishing a public option or Medicare-for-all system certainly is not socialist, as the term was envisioned by theorists on the left. Karl Marx advocated the nationalization and centralization of the means of production in the hands of the state. This process, under which *all* industries and private businesses would come under the control of the political system, would take place through a mass-based, bottom-up populist uprising and revolution, and an expropriation of private property.[38] The proposal to partially socialize *one part* of the healthcare system is far from Marxism. The public option merely sought to cover those left out of the private healthcare system, rather than to expropriate the property and assets of those invested in the private healthcare sector. Passing more progressive tax reforms, in which the rich pay a larger portion of their incomes in taxes for a public option, is also a far cry from Marxism.

The conflating of socialized welfare programs with revolutionary Marxism is characteristic of right-wing propaganda and ignorance. If anything, the public option was far closer to other already existing welfare programs such as Medicare and Social Security. A socialization of health insurance for the poor and uninsured represents a policy proposal similar to other socialized public programs, such as local libraries, police forces, firefighters, public roads, and a national military, with the major difference being that the beneficiaries are the poor, rather than the middle class. That conservative pundits framed the public option and other Democratic initiatives as far out of tilt with the norm of socialized public goods in the United States is a sign of how propagandistic the debate over national heatlh care has become.

None of the nuances above were conveyed in right-wing media propagandizing about nonexistent "death panels" or fictitious "government takeovers" of healthcare, or about mythical plans for a "socialist-Marxist" state. Nowhere was this manipulation more apparent than in the Fox News response to the Democrats' abandonment of the public option in favor of the corporate-sponsored healthcare bill that passed in March 2010. Democratic disowning of the public option was a sign that the party had given up on a government plan. This reality, however, was not accompanied by an acknowledgment from Fox News pundits that healthcare took a pro-market turn. Rather, the number of Fox News monthly programs discussing the "government takeover" of healthcare, warning of "big government" and "socialism," and discussing healthcare in relation to debt, the deficits, and cost, *increased* in early 2010 after the abandonment of the public option. Many of those paying close attention to Fox News would not be aware of the jettisoning of socialized care, of the market-based nature of Democrats' proposals, and of the Congressional Budget Office's conclusion that such reforms would *not* increase the budget deficit or debt—but would actually cut it by $28 billion.[39]

Political philosophers warn about the dangers of engaging in systematically distorted communication, in which the goals of discussion are instrumental, rather than intended to reach an understanding through the open and serious consideration of conflicting points of view.[40] An open approach was *not* the goal Fox pundits had in mind when they stoked public fear about death panels and government takeovers, and even in less blatant cases where they warned of escalating "costs" of reform and the increased "rationing" of care. These so-called discussions failed to even acknowledge the already-rampant rationing and rising costs of the for-profit system that left more than 50 million uninsured as of 2010, and under which approximately 20,000 to 40,000 people die every year because they lack health insurance.[41] By spotlighting the alleged costs that would accompany government reforms, the American right ignored the already occurring, massive increases in private healthcare costs and premiums that have been a reality for years.[42] By refusing to engage in an open discussion of the substantive points made by critics of private healthcare, rightist pundits limited the ability of the public to become informed regarding healthcare reform. By caustically demonizing and attacking those who disagreed with them, rightist pundits engaged in communication that was fundamentally uninterested in constructive engagement with opposing points of view. "Debates" over healthcare did not promote an open understanding and consideration of alternative points of view, but merely vindicated conservative pundits at the expense of other non-conservative positions.

The most extreme example of right-wing manipulation was seen in attempts to equate the Democrats with the Third Reich. Rush Limbaugh, for example, likened Obama's healthcare proposals to the fascism of Nazi Germany. Limbaugh compared the Obama administration's healthcare logo, which combined Obama's campaign logo with the ancient Greek symbol for medicine, to the swastika, wondering whether the logo constituted "a symbolic reference to Nazism." Limbaugh further celebrated a "Town Hall" protester's attempt to link Democratic healthcare reform with Nazism, declaring the attack to be "fabulous and fantastic and hilarious."[43] Glenn Beck created an analogy between Nazi Germany and Obama's America, under both of which "the state" would be allowed to make "life and death decisions" when providing healthcare. Beck referenced the fictional "death panels" as an example.[44] Beck also sought to associate leftist politics with extremism, conflating Nazism and Communism, and falsely arguing that both are the inevitable result of progressive politics.[45] A number of Tea Partiers adopted the Nazi analogy, comparing Obama to Hitler at Chicago metropolitan demonstrations I observed, and in national protests and Tea Party advertising.[46] These examples are not isolated incidents. A LexisNexis search from July 2009 through March 2010 finds that Nazism was discussed in programs covering healthcare reform on 51 separate occasions on Fox News.

Communication scholars Erin Steuter and Deborah Wills argue that "propaganda is not concerned with disseminating information but with rallying emotion." In *At War with Metaphor*, they maintain that "propaganda is the mechanism by which governments persuade the public of the evil of the enemy and the justness of its own cause." For propaganda to successfully appeal to audiences, it "must be pure, distilled, and unpolluted by contaminants such as complexity and subtlety." While Steuter and

Wills are discussing propaganda as it relates to political officials' manipulation and spin, the definition can be applied to the right-wing pundits described here.[47]

Right-wing propaganda is heavily cynical and postmodern in that it seeks to construct public opinion from the top down, with conservative political interests rather than empirical evidence determining the content of messages. Political communications scholar Geoffrey Baym approvingly points to comedian Stephen Colbert's criticism of the tendency of right-wing punditry to "privilege opinion over fact." These personalities provide, as Colbert argues, "the truth, unfiltered by rational argument." Baym analyzes the "right-wing political artistry that imagines problems and invents enemies to sell a predetermined, but often undisclosed political and economic agenda."[48] Baym's insights can be applied to the national debate over healthcare, in which Fox News and conservative radio pundits envisioned false threats of "death panels" and "government takeovers" while creating exotic connections between the Democratic Party and Nazism. These efforts, while clearly manifestations of right-wing paranoia and extremism, are promoted by individuals who present themselves as "objectively" informing their audiences about the "real world" of politics.[49]

MEDIA BIAS AND THE TEA PARTY

There is much disagreement about the nature of "mass media bias." Conservative media pundits, and a small number of media scholars argue that the media are consistently "liberal" in favoring labor, Democratic, and progressive interests.[50] Some on the left argue the opposite, that the media tend to lean in more conservative directions.[51] Other research fails to find a consistent liberal or conservative bias altogether.[52]

Though this study documents the conservative dominance of media coverage of healthcare by Republicans and the Tea Party, it does *not* demonstrate that the mass media are uniformly conservative across-the-board. Journalists tend to index, or tailor their reporting to the views expressed by political leaders. If there is an overarching bias that best describes media coverage of public policy, it is an *official source* bias. Under such a system, reporters are dependent upon the vigilance, or lack thereof, with which Democrats and Republicans express their ideological positions. When Democrats abandon progressive reforms such as the public option, one would expect to see reporting that briefly favors such views, then quickly pushes aside as political debate shifts to the right.

The media's bias in favor of official sources, in which journalists echo the increasingly conservative views of both parties, is not the entire story.[53] Pro-business biases also exist in reporting, with corporate ownership and advertising pressures playing a major role in suppressing views that challenge corporate power.[54] Under a hegemonic, propagandandistic media system, corporate ownership of the press plays a key role in ensuring that reporters dismiss healthcare reforms such as single payer care that challenge the foundation of private healthcare. Pro-business biases are built into reporting, in large part because the owners of corporate media are part of the same business elite that dominates the larger economic system.[55]

Analyses that discuss the pro-capitalist, structural biases of the mass media commonly fall under the hegemonic model of communication studies. Capitalist media are seen as commodities, aiding in the larger societal goal of selling consumerist values and promoting neoliberal ideas that seek to dismantle the social welfare state and impose a renewed privatization of public goods and services.[56] Corporate media regularly frame labor and American workers in a derogatory light, while depicting corporate business practices as responsible, productive, and virtuous.[57]

It is through hegemony that the pro-capitalist biases of political, economic, and media systems come together in the promotion of neoliberalism. Neoliberal capitalism, as defined by critical theorist Henry Giroux, embraces the notion that "the market should be the organizing principle for all political, social, and economic decisions. Neoliberalism wages an incessant attack on democracy, public goods, the welfare state, and noncommodified values," as they are considered threats to business power.[58] Giroux's warnings against neoliberalism are relevant to the restrictions placed on the media debate over healthcare. Conservative, market-based views are seen as the most desirable frames in reporting, whereas liberal proposals like the public option are downplayed, and progressive proposals like single payer, Medicare-for-all are not considered.

Progressive approaches to full or partial socialization of health insurance are strongly supported by the public, yet they receive meager attention in media. This marginalization is of major concern in a democracy. A majority of Americans revealed themselves as firmly supportive of the public option during the fall of 2009 and the spring of 2010.[59] Surveys questioning Americans about "universal healthcare" or "Medicare-for-all" find that majorities are supportive of this proposal.[60] That these approaches are not a part of the public debate suggests the tremendous success of American propaganda, and strongly validate the propagnda model.

MEDIA OBSESSION WITH THE TEA PARTY

As demonstrated in previous chapters, the available evidence as of late 2010 tells us that the Tea Party was not a social movement. One may wonder, then, why the mass media paid such incredible attention to its rebellion against the Democrats and healthcare reform, especially in light of the fact that journalists largely ignore progressive activists and their social movements.[61] While citizens' groups do receive regular coverage, progressive organizations usually find it difficult to break through to the mass public in terms of garnering sympathetic media coverage without official support.[62] When such movements are recognized by officials as having legitimate grievances, the mass media provide them with more sustained and sympathetic coverage.[63] The intimate connections between the Tea Party and Republican-business interests explain why the Tea Party has received dramatic and strongly sympathetic media attention. The Tea Party is not a social movement, yet its position within the bipartisan spectrum of "accepted" politics allows it to benefit from a low threshold set for what constitutes a social movement.

The term "movement" is thrown around loosely in media commentary. In the run-up to the 2010 midterms, the *New York Times* predicted "some kind of grassroots insurrection" in "every campaign" throughout the fall. These "insurrections" were to become increasingly common, the reporting went, due to the supposed fact that "it is exponentially easier now to assemble mini-movements and raise money online than it was in the pre-Obama days of 2006 when the political internet was in its infancy."[64] The *New York Times*'s lax standards for certifying a movement are based upon requirements as simple as raising significant amounts of money online and the identification of political campaigns that engage in populist rhetoric. Setting the bar so low for groups like the Tea Party virtually guarantees that they will be depicted as a social "movement." Conversely, no amount of mass organizing, protest, and insurrection on the part of legitimate social movements that are outside the bipartisan system is enough for these events to be regularly recognized in the news.

SIX

Manufacturing Dissent: Fostering Resistance to Healthcare Reform from the Top Down

A propaganda model for public opinion includes a number of material and intangible forces that are predicted to "filter" public opinion in favor of pro-business hegemonic views. In chapter 4 I documented the role of these filters in cultivating support for the Tea Party. In this chapter, I document the role of these filters in molding public opinion on the Tea Party's central issue of healthcare reform. Perhaps *the* most important filter of public attitudes on healthcare reform is the mass media. Although the Tea Party at first spoke primarily to a relatively narrow segment of American society, its Republican, pro-business appeal grew throughout late 2009 and early 2010. During this period, the Tea Party's anti-healthcare reform message increasingly took hold among the public. Fox News and other rightist media played a major role in fomenting public opposition to Democratic reform, although they were aided by so-called objective news outlets. American media, however, could not have pushed public opinion in such a critical direction if it were not for the unified efforts of the Republican Party and its junior partner, the Tea Party.

The 2010 election represented a classic manifestation of public ignorance, as encouraged by Republican–Tea Party propaganda. An in-depth survey by the Program on International Policy Attitudes (PIPA) found that the public was systematically misinformed on major policy-related issues.[1] Major points of public ignorance included:

- The erroneous belief, held by 68 percent of those surveyed, that the 2009 stimulus "only created or saved a few jobs," and another 20 percent thinking it "resulted in job losses." These findings translate into a staggering 88 percent of the public holding misinformed views on a stimulus that the Congressional Budget Office concludes created millions of jobs. The mantra that stimulus spending did nothing to help the economy is a long-standing theme of Tea Party-Republicans.

- The false impression that economists agree that healthcare reform will increase the deficit, a belief held by 53 percent of voters. This perception was belied by the Congressional Budget Office conclusion that healthcare reform would slightly *reduce* the deficit. Still, just 13 percent of voters thought healthcare reform would "not increase the deficit." Such views conform well to Tea Party–Republican claims that the United States "cannot afford" healthcare reform.

- An incorrect belief that the bank bailout was initiated by the Democrats. Forty percent of voters believed that the TARP bailout was initiated under Obama, rather than under former president George W. Bush. In reality, both Obama and Bush were supportive of the bailout, though legislation was spearheaded by Bush. The association of the bailout exclusively with Obama serves Republican–Tea Party propaganda, as it allowed Republicans to masquerade as the party of populism during the 2010 midterm elections.

- A fallacious perception that Barack Obama did not make tax cuts a central component of his policy platform. Fifty-four percent of voters wrongly assumed that there "were no tax cuts in the stimulus legislation" passed by Obama. Similarly, 86 percent of voters thought that "their taxes had gone up" (38 percent) or "stayed the same" (48 percent), and just 10 percent thought taxes had "gone down" since 2009. These perceptions were contradicted by the stimulus, the central component of which was tax cuts for the vast majority of Americans. The propaganda theme that Obama raised taxes for the masses is a central component of Tea Party–Republican rhetoric. Such rhetoric ignores the ways in which Obama emulated Republican policies by supporting tax cuts in his stimulus, and in the 2010 extension of tax cuts for the middle and working class, as well as business interests.

FIGURE 6.1: Political Misperceptions as a Function of Partisanship, 2010

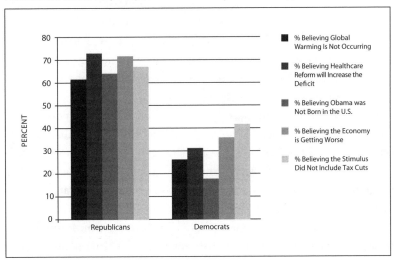

Source: Program on International Policy Attitudes

The PIPA survey provided some clues for uncovering the sources of this manipulation. The indoctrinating powers of partisanship are a source of ignorance, with those supporting the Republican Party being more likely to embrace misperceptions across a variety of issues, as reflected in Figure 6.1.

Much of the public thought that the election itself was a major source of manipulation, with political officials and their campaigns regularly disseminating propaganda. Other sources of perceived manipulation included the media, specifically Fox News and MSNBC, which were associated with a variety of misperceptions.[2] Additional factors are at work in confusing the public. The rise of conservative themes in the public mind throughout 2009 and 2010 arose significantly alongside the ascendancy of Tea Party propaganda in the media. This manipulation transcends individual organizations such as Fox and MSNBC to include media outlets across-the-board. Furthermore, other hegemonic and material forces also encouraged pro-business attitudes.

MEDIA EFFECTS ON OPINIONS
OF HEALTHCARE AND OBAMA

Growing opposition to healthcare reform is part of a larger schizophrenic pattern in public opinion, whereby Americans indicate their resistance to "big government," "welfare," and "healthcare reform" in general, but support specific social welfare programs such as Social Security, Medicare, Medicaid, the public option, and other cash subsidies to the poor.[3] This contradiction is the predictable result of a political system that foments public distrust in government and alienates most citizens from their own pro-welfare preferences. Americans still understand that social welfare programs benefit them, but they are increasingly subject to "anti-government" propaganda that creates a conservative national mood.

Polling from the Pew Research Center finds that most Americans remained uninfluenced by Tea Party endorsements of candidates running in the midterms. Tea Party critics may seize on Pew's findings that only 22 percent of Americans in the run-up to the 2010 elections indicated that a candidate being a Tea Party supporter made them "more likely to vote for" that candidate. What this criticism misses is that the Tea Party did not need to mobilize a majority of Americans to have a significant influence in the 2010 elections. Furthermore, 22 percent is a significant minority to be influenced by the Tea Party, as is the 44 percent of Republicans who indicated that a candidate's support for the Tea Party made them "more likely to vote for" that person.[4] In short, by narrowly appealing to relatively small demographic groups, the Tea Party succeeded in bringing in voters to the Republican Party. Attracting a determined minority made a tremendous difference in the 2010 elections, since midterms are traditionally dominated by small numbers of elite actors.

The Tea Party's significance cannot be restricted merely to its reputation. Even more important is the effect the party has on public opinion concerning policy issues. It is entirely possible that the Tea Party will be best remembered for its effects on *policy opinions*, in light of the group's success concerning healthcare reform.

The social factors influencing public opinion are potentially many. Some are material, such as the role income plays in molding political and economic beliefs. Others are based on more intangible forces. They are largely idea-driven, as seen in the power of political parties, ideology, political attentiveness, and media consumption. Many of the demographic groups I examined for this book are materially based, in that the people

within them are characterized by higher and lower levels of material affluence, as measured by personal income. Even those that are not differentiated by income are, at their foundation, driven by a materialist, neoliberal
ideology that establishes corporate profits and economic growth as the
ultimate goal of personal and public life.

As one might expect from this book's findings, material social forces
are instrumental in the proliferation of public opposition to healthcare
reform. Affluence, for one, plays a major role in the growing appeal of the
Tea Party and its messages. Perhaps the most important forces driving
sympathy for the Tea Party, however, are idea-driven. Support for the
group is driven most strongly not by personal income, the material affluence conferred through education, or by one's good fortune in benefitting
from health insurance. Rather, the most consistent forces driving support
include partisanship, ideology, media consumption, and political attentiveness (driven heavily by media consumption). These forces are strong
enough to convince even many of those with modest financial backgrounds to support a free market ideology that is overwhelmingly detrimental to their material interests.

In assessing Tea Party–Republican influence on the public, I analyzed
public opinion data from the Pew Research Center during the 2009 to
2010 healthcare debate.[5] I examined a number of variables delineated by
higher and lower levels of income, and by varied susceptibility to pro-
business, hegemonic ideas.[6] Included among the income-driven variables
are: race, sex, income, education, political efficacy (voters versus non-voters), class and race-based religious fundamentalism (higher- versus lower-
income "born again" Evangelicals, and white versus non-white
Evangelicals), and health insurance status (the insured versus uninsured).
Included among intangible variables are: Fox News viewership (Fox versus non-Fox viewers), ideology (conservatives versus moderates and liberals), partisanship (Republicans versus Democrats and Independents),
and political attentiveness (the attentive versus nonattentive). All of the
relationships discussed between these demographic variables and opinions on public policy are statistically significant.[7] In only one of the demographic variables—sex—does no relationship exist for any of the questions asked. For only one variable—education—is the relationship
between affluence and opinions of healthcare the opposite of what I
expected. With regard to education, those who benefit from higher levels
of education are actually *more likely* to support Obama and Democratic
healthcare proposals, with the less educated more likely to oppose both.

TABLE 6.1: The Tea Party, Obama, and Healthcare: List of Survey
Questions Used in Statistical Analysis

1.	Do you favor or oppose the health care proposals being discussed in Congress?
2.	Favor or oppose requiring all Americans have health insurance, with the government providing financial help for those who can't afford it?
3.	Favor or oppose a government health insurance plan to compete with private health insurance plans?
4.	Favor or oppose requiring insurance companies to sell health coverage to people, even if they have preexisting medical conditions?
5.	Favor or oppose requiring insurance companies to sell health coverage to people, even if they have preexisting medical conditions?
6.	Favor or oppose requiring employers to pay into a government health care fund if they do not provide health insurance to their employees?
7.	Favor or oppose raising taxes on families with incomes of more than $350,000 and individuals earning more than $280,000 (to pay for health care reform)?
8.	Favor or oppose taxing employees whose health insurance benefits are above a certain value?
9.	Approve or disapprove of the way Obama is handling his job as president?
10.	Approve or disapprove of Obama's handling of the economy, health care policy, the federal budget deficit, and tax policy?

Note: No. of significant variables included in this statistical analysis: party, ideology, income, education, voting status, race, health insurance status, Evangelicals by race, Evangelicals by income, and Fox News/non-Fox viewers (10); No. of times these variables can potentially predict policy attitudes: 130; No. of times these variables significantly predict policy attitudes: 64/130 question, or 49% of the time.

Source: Pew Research Center, July 2009 survey

The analysis herein suggests the profound importance of affluence (higher income) and exposure to hegemonic ideas in limiting openness to Democratic and liberal policy proposals. The demographic variables discussed (excluding sex due to its insignificance across-the-board) are statistically significant approximately one-half (49 percent) of the time in predicting whether respondents take more conservative or liberal positions on the 13 survey questions listed in Table 6.1. These 13 questions cover public opinion on President Obama, his job and public policy performance, and specific Democratic and liberal healthcare proposals. Sixty-four of the 130 demographic variables included within the statistical analyses of these 13 questions (10 independent variables multiplied by 13 policy questions equals 130 total variables) are significant in predicting opinions on Obama and healthcare. Of these 64 significant variables, 61 push in a more conservative direction, meaning that affluence is significantly associated with conservative attitudes. In other words, material and intangible hegemonic forces are associated with taking conservative opinions an overwhelming *95 percent of the time* for the significant variables examined. Only in the case of education are the more affluent (those with higher education) more likely to take liberal-leaning positions on Obama and healthcare. As we will see, this single exception is generally weak, however, and does not seriously contradict the predictions of my propaganda model.

It is important to examine whether demographic groups express a majority opinion (50+1 percent) either in favor of or opposed to Obama and healthcare reform. Tables 6.2 and 6.3 demonstrate that from July 2009 through March 2010 a majority of respondents in affluent (higher income) groups and in groups exposed to intangible hegemonic ideas were opposed to Democratic healthcare reform in *all* of the 27 questions surveyed during that time period. In contrast, a majority of respondents in less affluent (lower income) groups and in those groups less exposed to hegemonic ideas refused to oppose Democratic healthcare reform in 15 of 27 (or 56 percent of) questions surveyed. Such differences, especially among lower-income groups, suggest that the disadvantaged are quite capable of forming opinions in favor of their own material self-interest, at least in terms of supporting an expansion of healthcare coverage for uninsured Americans. Still, the finding that majorities in disadvantaged groups take conservative policy positions 43 percent of the time should not be ignored. This trend presents at least a partial confirmation of Thomas Frank's argument, originally discussed in chapter 4, that the less privileged are regularly manipulated into supporting policies that run directly counter to their material interests.

DETERMINANTS OF HEALTHCARE ATTITUDES

A closer look at individual groups provides greater detail on public opinion with regard to healthcare. This analysis further demonstrates the importance of affluence and intangible hegemonic forces as determinants of public attitudes.

1. Insured vs. the Uninsured

The uninsured were one group whose members clearly understood that Democratic-promoted healthcare reform would benefit them. As of July 2009, the uninsured were consistently less likely to oppose government healthcare proposals. In looking at gross differences, just 40 percent of the uninsured opposed the government on healthcare, compared to 57 percent of those with health insurance, a difference of 17 percentage points.[8] Significant gross differences between the insured and uninsured were seen in other areas as well. The uninsured were less likely to oppose a "public option," and less likely to distrust government in promoting healthcare reforms.[9] Clearly, the uninsured acknowledged that working-class and poor people were more likely to benefit under Democratic healthcare reform.

2. Higher- vs. Lower-Income Earners

Tea Party–Republicans were successful in appealing to higher income earners—but far less successful with those earning lower incomes. As of July 2009, higher-income respondents were more likely to oppose health-care reform than lower-income earners. Among those lower-income earners making under $50,000 a year, 50 percent opposed the government on healthcare, compared to higher-income earners making between $50,000 and $75,000, and more than $75,000, of whom 57 and 58 percent, respectively, opposed reform. Higher-income earners were also more likely to oppose taxing the wealthy to pay for healthcare and more likely to distrust the government on reform.[10] These findings could have been predicted after attending Tea Party meetings, as I regularly observed Tea Partiers at various events appealing to middle- and upper-income earners, warning against impending tax increases from the Obama administration. Tea Party speakers explicitly referenced higher-income earners as the ones that would be the hardest hit by Obama's alleged tax increases. Despite Tea Party and Republican success in appealing to those with higher incomes, they have been less successful in convincing those with lower incomes. It is this latter group that stood disproportionately to gain from supporting liberal healthcare proposals.

3. The Significance of Race

Race is another demographic in which the less affluent were more likely to reject Tea Party themes. In assessments of Democratic policies, non-whites were less likely to take conservative positions in July 2009. Among non-whites, 33 percent opposed the government on healthcare reform, compared to 59 percent of whites—a 26 percentage point difference. Non-whites were less likely to distrust the government on healthcare, less likely to disapprove of Obama's job performance, and his handling of the economy, healthcare, and the deficit.[11] Studies of race in the United States documented the gap between black and white wealth, and the dramatically different experiences of poor blacks when compared to more affluent whites.[12] Considering their diverging life experiences, it should be expected that both groups express significantly different positions on the expansion of the welfare state and on the performance of the United States's first African American president.

4. The Fox News Effect

Partisan news consumption is a classic intangible and hegemonic force that plays a central role in influencing public opinion. As a group, Fox News viewers are more likely (although not significantly so) to earn above the national $50,000 median income and are among the most strongly influenced by the Tea Party and Republican partisan messages. Like Fox News viewers, Rush Limbaugh listeners are not representative of the working class or poor, but closer to Middle America and the middle-upper class. The median Limbaugh listener is 53 years old; 93 percent are white; 34 percent make more than $100,000, at least half make $50,000 or more, and 40 percent make less than $50,000. Fifty-three percent attend church at least once a week; 78 percent are Republican; and 85 percent are conservative.[13]

Consumption of right-wing media is one of the most powerful explanations for the rise of the Tea Party. The Tea Party needs a megaphone to get its message across, and Fox News is happy to encourage anti-Democratic views by demonizing non-conservative perspectives. Limbaugh listeners are more likely to oppose Democratic officials and to support regressive taxation policies.[14] Fox viewers are far more likely to criticize Obama and Democratic policies. Fox viewership is associated with opposition to Obama and healthcare reform in every one of the 13 questions surveyed here.[15]

As of July 2009, 88 percent of Fox News viewers opposed the government on healthcare reform, compared to 47 percent of non-Fox viewers—a difference of 41 percentage points.[16] The effects of Fox News consumption on policy attitudes and opinions of officials are unique in relation to other television media. My review of more than five dozen polling questions asked by the Pew Research Center between 2004 and 2009 covering opinions of media, government, political officials, and public policy finds that Fox News viewership is a significant predictor of opinions in approximately two-thirds of questions asked. This finding stands in contrast to MSNBC viewership, which predicts that viewers will have liberal opinions in only 11 percent of questions, and CNN viewership, which predicts liberal opinions in only 13 percent of questions.[17]

NARROWCASTING REBELLION

Fox News casts a narrow net, appealing primarily to conservatives and Republicans. This audience became increasingly closed off from conflicting points of view over the last decade, due to the rightward shift of the Republican Party and its supporters' growing refusal to consider non-conservative political views. Kathleen Hall Jamieson and James Cappella speak of the media "echo chamber" through which conservatives develop their political attitudes.[18] This echo chamber consists of a tightly controlled message that emanates from business leaders and Republican officials, is transmitted through conservative punditry, and trickles down to sympathetic conservatives and the Republican rank and file.

Fox's messages are closely coordinated with political officials who disseminate key points in the Republican platform. Political scientists Jacob Hacker and Paul Pierson describe this process with regard to the Republican campaign to impeach former president Bill Clinton. Tom Delay, a former Republican congressman and architect of the Clinton impeachment, succeeded in

> stoking the outrage of an increasingly organized, coordinated and intense Republican base . . . Delay was using a network of conservative talk shows and party fund-raisers to generate pressure within the GOP. He would go on as many as ten radio talk shows a day, and his staff would blast fax talking points and tip sheets to perhaps two hundred such programs at a

time, revving up the conservative audiences that would then turn up the heat on their local congressmen.[19]

The Republican political establishment continues to organize a top-down rebellion against the Democrats, appealing to its base of supporters and providing ammunition for right-wing pundits. Conservative media watchdog groups highlight recent incidents in which the Republican Party quietly handed down talking points to Fox News employees. These points were then passed off as news stories to promote the Republican platform.[20] Right-wing pundits like Rush Limbaugh retain close personal ties to Republican elites. *U.S. News and World Report* concedes that "Limbaugh stays in private contact with key Republican operatives, and as a result, his on-air comments regularly promote party policy and strategy." The relationship is described by former Republican speaker of the House and Tea Party supporter Newt Gingrich as a "very loose alliance," although Gingrich also frames it as a "very close symbiotic relationship."[21] Of course, the uncritical dissemination of Tea Party–Republican talking points in the media is not accompanied by an admission that the pundits are serving as an unofficial propaganda arm for Republicans. This approach leaves Fox News viewers with the false impression that they are not being manipulated from above, but are forming opinions based on a reasonable assessment of "the facts."

Fox News viewers will react with derision to the negative characterization of them as closed off from competing viewpoints and as being manipulated from above. Such defenses are more fantasy than reality. Fox viewers represent a special group, as they are increasingly unwilling to consult *any* alternative media source that challenges their conservative views. Similarly, Limbaugh listeners are less likely to engage in liberal views.[22] Figure 6.2 demonstrates that a substantial minority of those who get their news primarily from Fox used to regularly engage in the views of competing television news outlets such as MSNBC, CNN, and other media. That changed following the 2008 election and in light of Obama's taking office, the rise of the national healthcare debate, and the ascendancy of the Tea Party. In 2004, nearly 30 percent of Fox News viewers also consulted other television media. By 2009, however, that number had declined to a minuscule two percent.[23] Such consumption patterns amount to a balkanization of conservative news audiences.[24] These individuals increasingly see "the media" as "liberally biased" and are turning away from considering alternative points of view in dramatic numbers.

FIGURE 6.2: Primary and Secondary News Consumption and Ideological Polarization

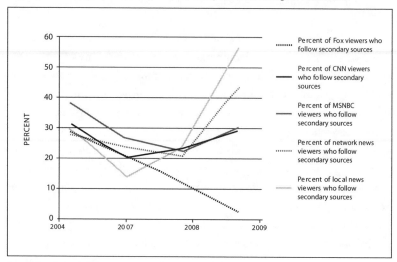

Source: Pew Research Center

5. The Power of Partisanship

Partisanship is one of the most powerful forces influencing public opinion. Individuals growing up in conservative households are socialized by
right-wing views that closely overlap with those of the Republican Party.
Since partisanship is often embedded in us from our early years, it is a
particularly influential factor in determining policy attitudes. Even more
powerful than Fox News consumption, partisanship is the most consistent predictor of opposition to Obama and the liberal political agenda. A
massive 87 percent of Republicans opposed government healthcare proposals, with just 22 percent of Democrats feeling the same—a 65 percentage point difference. Republicans are more likely to oppose Obama and
healthcare reform in *every* one of the thirteen questions in the July 2009
Pew survey.[25] In short, partisanship is one of the most important intangible forces that influence public opinion.

6. The Affluence Divide in Evangelical America

Journalist Chris Hedges documents in his book *American Fascists* the
strong support for conservatism among Evangelicals. Approximately half
of the 25 million Evangelicals in the United States can be classified as part

of the religious right.[26] At first glance, Evangelical, "born again" Christians express public policy opinions in line with Thomas Frank's false consciousness thesis. Evangelicals are less affluent than non-Evangelicals, yet slightly more likely to take anti-Obama positions in line with Tea Party rhetoric. Their support for Tea Party–Republican themes, however, is small compared to other demographic groups. Among Evangelicals as a whole, 66 percent opposed government healthcare reform proposals, compared to 55 percent of non-Evangelicals.

Frank's thesis as applied to Evangelicals is thrown into question upon closer inspection. Less affluent Evangelical groups are less likely to take conservative positions when asked about the *specifics* of healthcare reform. Non-white Evangelicals—making up one-quarter of the entire population, and representing a comparatively disadvantaged group in terms of income—are less likely to oppose Obama and healthcare reform.

The July 2009 Pew Research Center poll does find that lower-income Evangelicals (making under $50,000 a year) are more likely to oppose healthcare reform, and more likely to oppose Obama's handling of the deficit.[27] Fifty-eight percent of Evangelicals earning under $50,000 a year opposed government healthcare reform in July of 2009, and 78 percent and 73 percent of Evangelicals earning between $50,000 and $75,000 and more than $75,000 respectively felt the same—a difference of 20 and 15 percentage points. Similarly, 67 percent of Evangelicals earning under $50,000 a year opposed Obama's handling of the deficit, compared to 84 percent of Evangelicals earning between $50,000 and $75,000, and 83 percent of Evangelicals earning more than $75,000 a year. These numbers, however, are highly misleading. When asked if they support a government health insurance plan to compete with private health insurance, only 39 percent of lower-income Evangelicals are opposed. The dramatic discrepancy between opposition to government healthcare more generally, and support (among 61 percent of lower-income Evangelicals) for a government health insurance plan more specifically, is likely explained by the opaque nature of the healthcare reform debate. During this debate, it was unclear what reforms would be passed by Democrats due to the party's backpedaling on the public option and the conflicting healthcare bills floating through Congress.

When analyzing Evangelicals based on race, distinctions also emerge. Among white Evangelicals, 72 percent opposed healthcare reform, compared to just 36 percent of non-white Evangelicals—a difference of 36 percentage points. Opposition to a government health insurance plan stood at

57 percent among white Evangelicals, but at 28 percent of non-white Evangelicals—a difference of 29 percentage points.[28] Nonwhite Evangelicals were also less likely to oppose Obama's handling of the economy, his handling of healthcare, the deficit, and taxes, and less likely to distrust the government on healthcare reform.[29] In sum, Frank's warnings of false consciousness are of little utility when looking at Evangelical subgroups.

7. Ideology as a Political Guide

Along with other hegemonic forces, ideology is one of the most consistent determinants of political attitudes. Ideology is a strong predictor of policy attitudes with conservatism serving as a powerful force for promoting neoliberalism. Eighty-seven and 76 percent of those identifying as "very conservative" and "conservative," respectively, opposed government healthcare reform efforts as of July 2009. In contrast, just 47 percent of moderates and 24 and 23 percent of those claiming to be "very liberal" or "liberal" respectively indicated opposition. The difference across these groups, reaching as high as 54 percentage points, is among the largest for all the groups examined here. The growing differences between liberals and conservatives are documented by recent studies, which find that liberal-conservative polarization in the general public is at a historical high. The public is becoming better "sorted" ideologically, with Democrats holding more uniformly liberal attitudes and Republicans more conservative values.[30] Liberals and conservatives are well "sorted" ideologically on Obama and healthcare. Ideology is a statistically significant predictor of policy attitudes for *every* survey question examined here except one (concerning Obama's handling of taxes).[31]

8. Growing Conservatism among Voters

Little empirical evidence suggests that voters are disproportionately conservative from election to election.[32] Instead, the increasing partisanship among voters in 2009 and 2010 was the result of the mobilization of conservatives in the run-up to the 2010 midterms. Midterm elections are typically dominated by partisan elites. The galvanization of voters who oppose the president and the party in power is common during times of economic crisis and high unemployment. Such was the case in the 2010 midterms, when registered voters were more likely to oppose Obama and the Democrats. Opposition to healthcare reform in July 2009 was evident among 48 percent of non-voters, compared to 56 percent of voters—a difference of eight percentage points. Registered voters were more likely to oppose not only government healthcare reform but also disapprove of Obama's performance on healthcare, the deficit, the economy, and his overall job performance.[33]

9. Education as a Liberalizing Force

Education is the only variable in this analysis in which growing affluence is not associated with opposition to Obama. Previous academic studies found that those with higher levels of education are more indoctrinated in support of elite bipartisan politics.[34] In the case of assessments of Obama and healthcare, the highly educated are less likely to disapprove of Obama, in relation to his overall job performance and his handling of the economy, and less likely to oppose healthcare reform.[35] Such patterns, however, are rather weak, as opposition among the highly educated to Obama and healthcare reform still reaches a majority of Americans.

The highly educated, then, are only different from the less educated in that they are *slightly* less likely to disapprove of Obama when compared to the less educated. In July 2009, the highly educated were only one percentage point less likely both to disapprove of Obama's overall job performance and to disapprove of government healthcare reform proposals. This difference may be statistically significant, but it hardly appears relevant for all practical purposes. By March of 2010, highly educated Americans were only four percentage points less likely to oppose government healthcare when compared to the less educated, and both groups still expressed majority opposition. These differences are not all that relevant when compared to differences seen in other demographic groups.

Education is *not* a statistically significant predictor of attitudes on a government healthcare plan or a public option, as seen in the Pew Research Center's July and October 2009 polls. This finding is worthy of serious reflection, considering that proposals for a nonmarket-based government health insurance plan represent the strongest challenge to business power. On such questions, the highly educated are not significantly different from the less educated. In short, increased education is the only exception to a general rightward pull exacted by affluence, and it is not a very strong one at that. Minuscule to nonexistent differences based on education are nowhere near enough to overcome the powers of material and hegemonic forces.

TESTING THE PROPAGANDA MODEL
ACROSS POLICY ISSUES

A comprehensive review of Pew Research Center polling from 2004 through 2010 finds that the demographic variables analyzed are successful in predicting attitudes across a wide variety of policy issues over a number of years. As seen in Table 6.2, hegemonic variables such as ideology, partisanship, and media consumption are the most consistent predictors of attitudes on Obama and healthcare reform. These variables play a vital role with regard to a large number of policy issues, opinions of mass media, and approval of government and political officials.

As in the cases of the Tea Party and healthcare, more affluent (higher income) demographics are more likely to share conservative, pro-business views in nearly *every* question surveyed. These findings represent strong evidence of the powers of materialism and hegemonic forces in reinforcing establishment views. These policy issues include questions of foreign policy and war, social and moral issues, civil liberties, and government economic policy.

INCREASING APPEAL OF THE TEA PARTY

Tea Party–Republican ideology was less successful in reaching disadvantaged demographic groups in July 2009. The rise of the Tea Party as a media darling, however, took place from 2009–10. Any assessment of the group's appeal needs to examine evidence from this later period. Analyzing public opinion from 2009 through early 2010, I find, in congruence with Thomas Frank's thesis, growing support for Tea Party–Republican messages among the less affluent.

An effective way to measure whether messages are accepted by various demographic groups is to examine identically worded polling questions asked over a period of months or years. This approach diminishes measurement bias and helps ensure that researchers are not comparing apples and oranges by examining differently worded questions. I examined identical questions that were asked by the Pew Research Center in July and October of 2009 and March of 2010 covering public opinion on healthcare reform. Although I was only able to locate one question related to healthcare that was repeated throughout Pew polling, that question—covering whether the public supported Democratic healthcare pro-

TABLE 6.2: Forecasting Public Opinion: Affluence and Hegemony as
Predictors of Political Attitudes

Demographic Groups	% of time each variable predicts opinions of healthcare and Obama (13 questions)	% of time each predicts opinions of mass media (26 questions)	% of time each predicts public policy attitudes (131 questions)	% of time each predicts opinions of government officials (39 questions)	% of time each predicts opinions across all survey questions (209 questions)
Party	100%	58%	84%	95%	84%
Ideology	92%	46%	86%	85%	81%
Fox News Consumption	92%	62%	68%	62%	67%
Race	33%	15%	47%	80%	48%
Education	13%	46%	39%	26%	36%
Sex	0%	12%	41%	18%	30%
Income	20%	8%	24%	28%	23%
Evangelical	33%	19%	19%	31%	22%
Political Efficacy (Voting)	33%	8%	16%	13%	16%

Source: Pew Research Center Surveys, 2004–2010

posals—was *the* central issue being debated in relation to healthcare. As a general and vaguely worded question, it provides a useful test for measuring the public's "mood," and whether Americans were moving more to the left or right during the period in question.

Opinions of government healthcare reform became more critical across-the-board from mid-2009 through early 2010.[36] Tables 6.3 and 6.4 reveal two important patterns. First, as Table 6.3 demonstrates, more affluent groups and those with greater exposure to hegemonic forces were more likely to oppose Democratic healthcare reform. These groups expressed majority opposition to healthcare proposals. Eight of the groups characterized by greater material privilege or greater exposure to intangible hegemonic forces were more likely to embrace Tea Party–Republican messages on healthcare and Obama.

TABLE 6.3: Opposition to Healthcare Reform in Higher-Income and
Hegemonic Groups (July 2009–March 2010)

	Percent Opposed (July 2009)	Percent Opposed (Oct. 2009)	Percent Opposed (March 2010)	Percentage Point Change in Opposition
Republicans	87%	88%	90%	+3%
High Income ($75k or more)	59%	62%	60%	+1%
Middle Income ($50K–$75k)	57%	61%	60%	+3%
Insured	57%	60%	60%	+3%
Whites	59%	65%	65%	+6%
White Evangelicals	72%	81%	79%	+7%
High-Income Evangelicals (more than $75k)	73%	71%	75%	+2%
Middle-Income Evangelicals ($50–$75k)	78%	75%	68%	−10%
Highly Educated	55%	58%	57%	+2%
Registered Voters	56%	61%	60%	+4%
Men	58%	61%	60%	+2%

Note: The Fox News variable was not included in this examination because it was included
in the July Pew Research Center poll but not the October poll.

Source: Pew Research Center

On a second level, opposition to healthcare reform increased across
most groups characterized by material privilege and exposure to hegemonic messages. Opposition to Obama and healthcare reform increased
across 17 of the 20 categories examined in Tables 6.3 and 6.4.

These results are strong evidence of the propaganda powers of Tea
Party–Republican interests in convincing the masses to accept policies
that are detrimental to their well-being. The change in opposition only
averaged 2.2 percentage points across all the groups examined, although
such incremental changes, again, are the norm in public opinion. Such
aggregates, however, also neglect the drastically different sizes of the
demographic groups in question, making these estimates misleading in
that they *underestimate* growing opposition. When looking at the public

TABLE 6.4: Opposition to Healthcare Reform in Lower-Income and
Less Hegemonic Groups (July 2009–March 2010)

	Percent Opposed (July 2009)	Percent Opposed (Oct. 2009)	Percent Opposed (March 2010)	Percentage Point Change in Opposition
Democrats	22%	26%	25%	+3%
Low Income (Less than $50k)	50%	56%	56%	+6%
Uninsured	40%	53%	48%	+8%
Non-Whites	33%	37%	30%	–3%
Non-White Evangelicals	36%	34%	25%	–11%
Low-Income Evangelicals (Less than $50k)	58%	65%	64%	+6%
Less Educated	56%	62%	61%	+5%
Non-Voters	48%	46%	50%	+2%
Women	52%	58%	57%	+5%

Note: The Fox News variable was not included in this examination because it was included in the July Pew Research Center poll but not the October poll.

Source: Pew Research Center

as a whole, opposition to Democratic reforms proposed in Congress increased by eight percentage points in the eight months following the July 2009 Pew Research Center poll. The largest growth in the public's conservative "mood" was seen in growing opposition to Obama's "handling of healthcare reform," which grew by a remarkable 21 percentage points in less than a year, from June 2009 through March 2010.[37]

The evidence above suggests that, even within a number of months, support for the Tea Party backlash against healthcare reform grew significantly. A brief side point, however: Frank's harsh assessment of the poor and working classes may be too critical. The false consciousness thesis assumes that the poor and working classes, by opposing Democrats, are working against their own interests. It was *not* clear by late 2009 that the Democrats were pursuing healthcare legislation that would benefit the disadvantaged. Once the public option was abandoned by the party, there was little indication that any reforms were going to pass through Congress at all, let alone any that would benefit the poor and working class.

Considering the lack of transparency of congressional debate and the jet-tisoning of the public option, it may have been asking too much for the working class and poor to conclude that healthcare reform was going to benefit them. Factor in the scare tactics used in conservative media, and the vulnerable were even more likely to become skeptical of reform.

MEDIA EFFECTS AND HEALTHCARE REFORM

Growing opposition to healthcare reform and to the Democratic Party was driven by the mass media. In the rest of this chapter, I chart the pub-lic's growing opposition to healthcare reform as a function of their increased attentiveness to negative reporting on reform. Media outlets, both "objective" organizations and conservative media outlets alike, dis-seminated Tea Party–Republican messages amid the collapse of Democratic support for the public option, and in light of the uncertain prospects for a Democratic victory on healthcare.

Political scientists Jacob Hacker and Paul Pierson speak of the grow-ing power of the Republican Party to set the agenda for domestic policy. The ability "to dictate which proposals receive attention" is a "formida-ble political weapon" when combined with the power to block new poli-cies through institutional opposition and dominance of the media.[38] The Tea Party–Republican rebellion against healthcare is a clear example of both agenda-setting and political intransigence. Republicans successfully took universal healthcare and the public option off the agenda through their dominance of the mass media.

The mass media were the most important source of information on healthcare reform. National opinion surveying found that, as of late 2009, a plurality of Americans (41 percent) explained that what they see or read in the media is "important" in "forming opinions on healthcare reform." Media consumption ranked above "personal experiences" and "talking with friends and family," which 31 percent and 25 percent, respectively, listed as important.[39] Another survey found that 81 percent of the public turned to the news media "for details on" proposed healthcare legislation, compared to just 19 percent who did not rely on the media.[40] Reliance on mass media far outranked other sources; just 46 percent listed "family and friends" as a source of information, 7 percent listed their "employer," and 7 percent listed "church" or a "religious organization."[41] Furthermore, media certainly played an additional role in influencing dis-

FIGURE 6.3: The Agenda Setting Power of Media on Healthcare, 2009

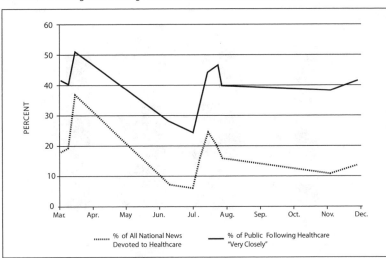

Source: Pew Research Center

cussions with friends, family, and others, considering that these individuals also relied heavily on the media for information.

The media power to "set the agenda" for which policy issues the public considers is documented in countless empirical studies.[42] Little
changed with regard to healthcare coverage. The media played the defining role in influencing what Americans saw and did not see regarding
healthcare reform. Surveys from 2009 and 2010 found a strong correlation between media attention to healthcare and public interest in the
issue.[43] The results of Figure 6.3, drawn from the Pew Research Center,
demonstrate the symbiotic connection between reporting of healthcare
and public attitudes, as the percentage of citizens who closely followed the
healthcare debate was closely dependent on fluctuations in coverage.[44]

Those who paid closest attention to the healthcare debate were deeply
influenced by reporting, not only in the intensity of their attention but in
their policy attitudes. Figure 6.4 highlights the intimate links between
public opinion and media coverage, revealing two important patterns.
First, those who paid the greatest attention to the national debate and
reporting on healthcare were more likely to oppose reform than those
who paid little to no attention. The relationship is at its starkest in July
and August 2009, and is statistically significant, after controlling for partisanship, ideology, and other variables.[45] Some critics will challenge

FIGURE 6.4: Mediated Opposition to Healthcare Reform (2009)

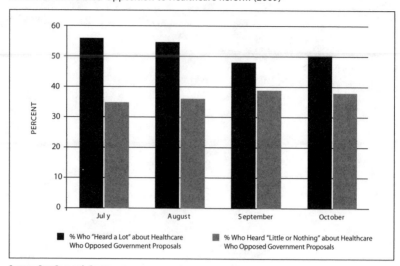

Source: Pew Research Center

these findings, suggesting that the national attention here is defined not by attention to media, but simply by whether individuals have "heard a lot," a "little" or "nothing" about healthcare.[46] This potential challenge is suspect against the fact that, as empirically demonstrated above, mass media remained by far the most important forum in which the public "heard a lot" about the details of healthcare reform. As already mentioned, more than 80 percent of those surveyed admitted that they were looking to media to form their opinions on healthcare. Furthermore, the national political debate over healthcare did *not* take place independently of coverage, considering the symbiotic relationship between media and the larger political system.

Monthly changes in public attitudes toward healthcare reform are very closely indexed to monthly fluctuations in positive and negative framing of healthcare as seen in media. Before exploring monthly trends in media coverage, one other point must be highlighted. Figure 6.4 suggests that the relationship between attention to the healthcare debate and opposition diminished significantly between July and October 2009. Those who paid close attention to the healthcare debate were still more likely to oppose government proposals by September and October, although there was a much smaller gap in opposition compared to earlier months. The weakened relationship raises an important question: What exactly was happening between July and October that diminished the power of conservative messages in the public mind?

Changes in public opinions of Democratic healthcare reform were closely linked to monthly fluctuations in media content. I provide evidence for this conclusion by examining national polling time series data from April 2009 through March 2010. This data, compiled from surveys undertaken by seven national news and polling organizations, demonstrates that the American public responded to the information provided by media, political officials, and Tea Party activists by increasing its opposition to reform.[47] Opposition grew at a time when conservative messages dominated media content. Thomas Frank argues that the public exudes a false consciousness, with working- and middle-class Americans irrationally opposing social welfare programs that benefit them directly. I argue, however, that this response was rational insofar as the public responded in exactly the way one would predict after being deprived of non-conservative points of view. In a political-media climate moving to the right, Americans were susceptible to alarmist rhetoric about "death panels," healthcare "rationing," and "big government" threats. Without the tools to resist, Americans responded predictably. Skepticism toward healthcare reform grew within the general public, although people remained sympathetic to specific reforms that would benefit them materially.

Public opinion was not static on healthcare. Figures 6.5 and 6.6 indicate that there were three periods of rapid change in public opinion from 2009 to 2010 regarding approval of Obama and healthcare reform. Rapid change is defined here as any increase in support or opposition of more than five percent over a single month. There are two spikes and one dip in opposition: the two spikes occur from July through August of 2009 and from January through February of 2010, and the dip occurs from September to October of 2009. Identifying the causes of these changes is not difficult.

As documented in Figures 5.1 and 5.2 from the previous chapter, the period from July to August of 2009—in which public opposition to Obama and healthcare reform spiked—represented the height of coverage

FIGURE 6.5: Growing Opposition to Healthcare Reform (2009–2010)

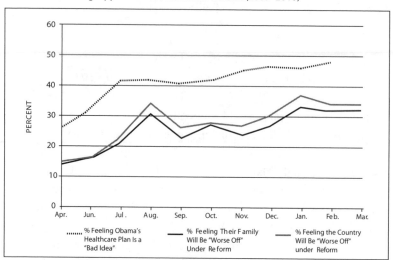

Source: Kaiser, NBC, and *Wall Street Journal* Surveys

of Tea Party Town Hall meetings and the peak in media attention to Sarah Palin's warnings about government "death panels,"

These warnings resonated with Americans, who were worried about the loss of health insurance and quality care in a time of economic crisis. This concern is rational for the working poor (and perhaps the middle class as well), considering national problems with growing job insecurity, and that health insurance is tied to employment for American workers. The high emotions running throughout the Town Hall meetings clearly struck a nerve with the public.

While a majority of Americans—53 percent—thought that the Town Hall activists were "rude and disrespectful," 61 percent found their protests "appropriate" in the context of their concerns over the costs of healthcare, a potential decline in quality of coverage and care, and anxiety over government "socialism."[48] The Tea Party was seen by a growing number of people as a boisterous but necessary group that was justifiably taking on a corrupt political establishment.

The August to September of 2009 period saw opposition to Obama and healthcare fall significantly, due in large part to Obama's highly reported speech to the nation and to Congress stressing the need for healthcare reform. This period saw the height of news coverage of the public option, document-ed in Figure 5.3 from the last chapter. The president's discussions of health-

FIGURE 6.6: Public Disapproval of Obama on Healthcare (2009–2010)

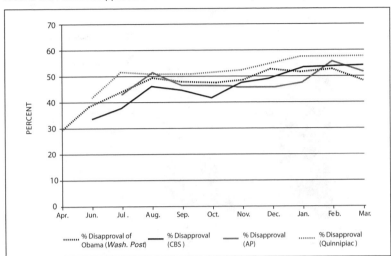

Source: *Washington Post*, CBS, AP, and Quinnipiac

care reform, along with growing media attention to reform, were successful in convincing many Americans of the need for reform. Growing approval was due in large part to the president's success in "going public," with his appeal for reform.[49] Fifty-six percent of Americans planned on watching the president's speech to Congress. Mass attention was associated with support for Obama, as approval for the president's handling of healthcare increased from 40 to 52 percent in the week following his address. Obama's 12 percent approval spike was most effective in galvanizing Democrats—among whom 85 percent supported his handling of healthcare. Obama also gained support among Independents and Republicans, although their support was less than that granted by Democrats. Most important, public support for the Democrats' most visible reform proposal—the public option—increased by 9 percent in the week following Obama's speech.[50]

Approval of Democratic reform was strong following Obama's appeal to the public. By early 2010, the public remained strongly supportive of liberal-centrist legislative provisions, as depicted in Figure 6.7.[51] Such support, however, was nullified by the fact that Americans were largely unaware of whether any of these proposals were included in Democratic reforms, and public uncertainty over whether any reforms would be passed at all. Conservative attacks on healthcare further incited public opposition to Democratic reform.

FIGURE 6.7: Public Attitudes on Healthcare Reform Provisions, 2010

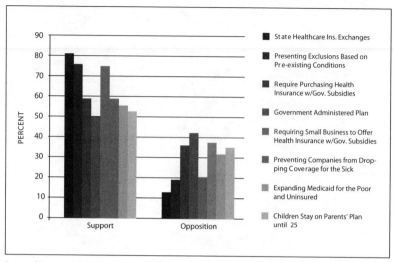

The above forces were starkest in their effects by early 2010. At this time, a majority of Americans indicated their opposition to Obama's handling of healthcare, and a plurality opposed Washington on healthcare reform, despite paradoxical majority support for the actual provisions undergirding Democratic reform.[52]

Early 2010 was a pivotal time for the healthcare debate. The final period of change in national opinion occurred during January and February 2010. Opposition to Obama and healthcare reform spiked, coinciding closely with the rise in reporting on the Tea Party, as seen in Figure 5.1 from the previous chapter. The Tea Party enjoyed its greatest coverage yet by January–February 2010, and its concerns appeared to resonate strongly with the public. The statistically significant relationship between attention to the Tea Party on one hand, and opposition to Obama and healthcare reform on the other, is seen in Figure 6.8.[53] This relationship remains, even after controlling for respondent ideology, party, and other factors. As Figure 6.8 demonstrates, those who paid the closest attention to reporting and debate on the Tea Party were more likely to oppose healthcare reform when compared to those who paid only a little attention or no attention.

The public grew increasingly opposed to healthcare reform for a variety of reasons. The strongest motivation evident in polling was fear over

FIGURE 6.8: The Tea Party Catalyst and Mediated Healthcare Rebellion, 2010

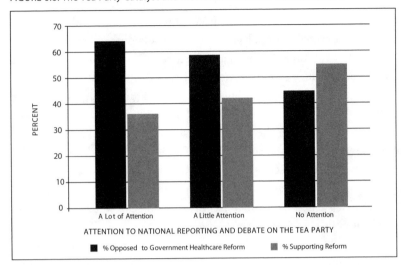

Source: Pew Research Center

the costs of reform. This strongly correlates with media coverage, in which "costs" were the most prominent oppositional theme. The prominence of cost concerns was seen most clearly in Gallup polling, which found in early 2010 that the three most important reasons for opposition to healthcare legislation were worries that "the federal budget deficit," "the overall costs of healthcare in the U.S.," and the costs respondents and their families pay for healthcare would all "get worse," if Democratic reforms passed.[54] Clearly, the cost and deficit justifications for obstructing healthcare reform struck a major chord with the public. These concerns would have been far weaker if it had not been for reporters consistently repeating Tea Party–Republican anti-reform themes.

This chapter documents the growing opposition to reform during July and August 2009, and increasing support in later months. These developments make more sense after reflecting upon the changes that occurred in media content. Coverage of death panels and Town Hall protests spiked from July to August, precisely at the time when the mass media were having their greatest effect in encouraging public opposition to healthcare reform. In contrast, the differences between those paying more and less attention to healthcare decreased significantly between September and October, when Obama began promoting reform, and when coverage of the public option was at its highest. Finally, opposition rose again when the Tea Party's coverage reached an all-time high in early 2010, when conservative media pundits were openly championing its cause, and when "objective" reporters and liberal-left pundits reported that the "movement" was a legitimate, grassroots phenomenon.

Communication scholars maintain that the media influences what issues people think about and how they think about them, but refuse to concede that the media also influence policy attitudes. This attempted distinction is artificial and unwarranted in the case of healthcare reform. Simply by dominating the agenda for issues talked about and how they were discussed, Republicans and Tea Partiers influenced policy preferences through the media. By transforming the healthcare debate into a discussion of "death panels," "rationing," government "socialism," and "cost," Tea Partiers and other Republican officials were able to direct public attention to the perceived drawbacks of reform. The terms of the discussion changed from focusing on what the government could do to help the uninsured, to whether or not the government would deprive Americans of lifesaving care. Republicans–Tea Party themes in the mass media were successful in promoting cynicism among an already distrusting public.[55] In this climate, Republicans, Tea Partiers, and conservative pundits increasingly warned Americans of the alleged dangers of reform.

Since the late 1960s, the American public developed a culture of distrust directed against Washington officials. These officials are seen as uninterested in representing the people. Public suspicion is well-founded. Political scientists Lawrence Jacobs and Robert Shapiro find that "politicians don't pander" in their communication efforts with the public. They lament the "lack of democratic responsiveness" in officials' efforts to manipulate, rather than pay heed to public opinion. Jacobs and Shapiro highlight the comments of former Democratic and Republican pollsters Frank Luntz and Dick Morris, who explain that political officials "don't use a poll to reshape a [government] program, but to reshape your argumentation for the program so that the public supports it." Jacobs and Shapiro undertake a case study of former president Bill Clinton's healthcare reform agenda in the 1990s, citing it as an example of officials seeking to mold public opinion around a preexisting policy. In that case, "Clinton rejected the Canadian single-payer system even though some polls indicated that it was supported by as much as two-thirds of Americans."[56] Further reflections from their study:

- "Administration officials found it inappropriate and 'wrong' to allow polling and public opinion to 'drive the process.' The president was elected, 'not to follow public opinion, necessarily, but to lead by making decisions about the best way to get an ultimate end point.' Clinton decided that the best strategy was to 'go out and sell a program to the public' and to 'lead public opinion,' rather than to follow it."[57]

- "White House officials persistently discounted existing public opinion when formulating health policy. The administration used information about public opinion to craft the presentation of Clinton's plan—a plan that had been formulated to reflect the president's philosophy, policy preferences, and political judgments," even though the plan was more in line with a market-based approach (rather than a single-payer approach), seeking to legislate mandatory employer healthcare for American workers.[58]

Subsequent examination of official representation largely reinforces Jacobs and Shapiro's findings, concluding that "presidents can usually disregard current opinion," as the commander-in-chief "will only want to pander to public opinion . . . if he expects to confront a very competitive electoral race in the near future." Presidents regularly "take unpopular positions," and they prefer not to openly advertise them for risk of public retribution.[59]

Jacobs and Shapiro's analysis stands the test of time when reflecting upon this book's findings. Officials in the Obama administration decided to push for market-based reforms by establishing for-profit state "exchanges" to sell health insurance to the uninsured over a public option or universal healthcare, despite polling that revealed majority support for these proposals. Since the public indicated support for *both* progressive proposals (such as the public option and Medicare-for-all) and liberal-centrist proposals (such as those shown in Figure 6.7), public opinion was clearly not the defining factor in influencing officials' choice of centrist over progressive reforms. The cost of official contempt for public opinion, however, is that the majority of Americans now widely distrust their leaders and the Washington establishment. Political scientist Marc Hetherington demonstrates in his study of public opinion that "declining political trust has played the cenral role in the demise of progressive public policy. . . . Decreasing trust in government over the last two generations has undermined public support for federal programs like welfare, food stamps, and foreign aid, not to mention the entire range of race-targeted programs designed to make equality between the races a reality. . . . Even initiatives like healthcare reform, which are less obviously redistributive and certainly not as racialized [as images of welfare], require trust in government to maintain support." As Hetherington empirically documents, the decline in the proportion of progressive-left laws passed from the mid-1960s through the post-2000 period is closely correlated with declining political trust in government. In other words, the prospects for passing liberal-left oriented laws is *greatest* during times when trust in government is highest, and lower whenever trust is declining.[60]

The demise of progressive healthcare reform, Hetherington argues, is not the result of some sort of "ideological right turn," an argument for which he finds little evidence.[61] Rather, the public was strongly supportive of government efforts to extend healthcare to the needy at the policy level, while remaining deeply distrustful of government in general. Many on the left may point out that *distrust* of government and officials should be seen as a vital component of a participatory democracy. This point is well taken, but it can also be seen as distinct from the broader question of whether the public can trust that the government is able to provide for the common good—as reflected in providing for social welfare programs.

MEDIA HEGEMONY
AND MANUFACTURED PUBLIC IGNORANCE

The decline in public trust in government is driven to a great extent by Republican–Tea Party efforts. This development is paradoxical, considering that Republican officials stake their careers on convincing the public to defer to the greater knowledge of conservative officialdom. The messages disseminated by Tea Party–Republicans reach the American public through sympathetic media. Republicans and business elites are the direct beneficiaries of "anti-government" propaganda, as they push forward with ever-expanding corporate welfare subsidies such as the bank and auto bailouts, and direct massive taxpayer dollars to foreign conflicts that are a boon for military industrial contractors. These subsidies demonstrate the contempt that business elites share for "free market" principles. Corporate welfare initiatives are rammed through Congress through the institutionalization of a political crisis culture. This culture is personified by officials who perpetually threaten the public with

Armageddon—as seen in warnings of complete economic destruction following the 2008 stock market collapse and in doomsday predictions
about mythical foreign "weapons of mass destruction"—in order to cultivate public deference for conservative pro-business policies.

Chomsky and Herman were primarily concerned in their study of the
mass media with how the government "manufactures consent" in the mass
media in line with policies that benefit political and business elites. Elites
also manufacture *dissent* to dissuade the public from supporting progressive policies. In this chapter I have been discussing the power of media to
manufacture public opposition to healthcare reform. The manufacture of
dissent is an apt description in light of the public's strong support for specific progressive and Democratic proposals, which coexisted alongside
growing opposition to healthcare reform. Public disapproval of Obama's
handling of healthcare grew steadily in 2009 and 2010, eventually reaching a majority of Americans. Approximately half felt the Democrats' healthcare reforms were "a bad idea" by early 2010, while the Americans who
opposed healthcare reform ranged between 55 and 57 percent within the
same time period.[62] Despite Americans' seeming opposition to reform,
public opinion was paradoxical. By November 2009, a majority of
Americans—61 percent—indicated that they supported the public option.
Democratic legislation passed in early 2010 served as a mass subsidy for
the private healthcare industry. These reforms, however, also provided
modest concessions to the needy, strengthening Medicaid for the poor,
curbing some of the worst excesses of the private healthcare system (specifically exclusions based on preexisting conditions), and strengthening that
system by requiring all Americans not eligible for Medicare or Medicaid to
buy health insurance in the private market.

Hegemonic forces work across many policy issues, and public confusion regarding social welfare is not unique to the healthcare debate. In
Why Americans Hate Welfare, Martin Gilens documents the public's
strong opposition to welfare, despite strong support for specific welfare
programs such as job training, Medicare, Medicaid, and Social Security.[63]
As Gilens concludes, "Contrary to popular belief, Americans are not
clamoring for cutbacks in government efforts to help the poor. Instead,
most Americans want government to spend more on these programs, and
most say they are willing to pay higher taxes in order to boost spending
for the needy."[64] These findings are confirmed in the analyses of other
public opinion scholars.[65] Such revelations may at first seem contradictory when compared to the data uncovered in this work, which demonstrate

that the public was increasingly opposed to expanding the social welfare state through healthcare reform. The answer to this seeming contradiction is alluded to in the title of Gilens's book, *Why Americans Hate Welfare*. The American right is effective in leading a media campaign to convince the public to oppose "welfare" as an ominous threat that allegedly retards the development of the disadvantaged. At the same time, this media campaign has not convinced Americans that their already existing support for specific social welfare programs, which benefit the masses by reducing poverty and ensuring comfortable livings for the middle class, are unworthy of support.[66]

In his classic novel *1984*, George Orwell described the process by which individuals simultaneously hold contradictory opinions as "doublethink."[67] Such confusion is promoted through the indoctrination of the masses, and through an extensive reliance on propaganda and manipulation. False consciousness lies at the foundation of any study of hegemony and manufactured dissent. A Tea Party–Republican inspired rebellion—when characterized by opposition to healthcare reform on the one hand and overwhelming support for the specific provisions of reform on the other—is a classic case of Orwellian doublethink.

False consciousness can only be established by thoroughly confusing the public. This condition was met in the case of the healthcare debate. The public demonstrated a strong interest in the issue, with 92 percent of Americans saying that it was "important," and 72 percent classifying the media's reporting on healthcare as "interesting."[68] Nearly half of Americans followed healthcare news "very closely" by late August to early September 2009. Public consumption was incredibly high when compared to public attention to other political issues.[69] While interest in healthcare was high, the public faulted the mass media for poor and confusing coverage. A majority of Americans see the mass media as generally unfair in their reporting of issues related to the poor.[70] Coverage of Democratic efforts to extend healthcare reform to the poor represents an example in which the media favored conservative positions against reforms that would benefit the disadvantaged.

Appraisals of healthcare media coverage were negative. From July of 2009 to March of 2010, only 21 percent felt news organizations did an excellent or good job explaining the "details of proposals"; 31 to 38 percent felt the same about the media's job in covering "the political debate"; and just 23 to 24 percent felt the media performed well in addressing the implications of reform "on people like yourself."[71] Strong majorities clas-

FIGURE 6.9: Increasing Confusion among Americans Following the National
Healthcare Debate "Very Closely," 2009

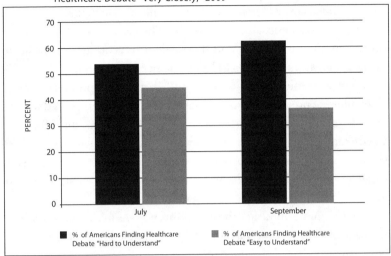

Source: Pew Research Center

sified the debate over healthcare reform as becoming "hard to understand" throughout the last half of 2009.[72] The problem of public confusion got worse over time. While the percentage of Americans following
healthcare coverage doubled from July to September 2009, the percentage of the public who found that the "issue remains hard to understand"
grew from 63 to 67 percent.[73] Figure 6.9 indicates that in July of 2009, a
majority of those following healthcare "very closely" said it was "hard to
understand," while an even larger majority of those who followed the
issue "less closely" felt the same.

By September 2009, the percentage of those following healthcare
"very closely" who said it was "hard to understand" grew *even larger*.[74]
In other words, those paying close attention to healthcare grew *more* confused throughout the fall of 2009. The increased confusion of the public
regarding healthcare will be disturbing to intellectuals committed to democratic government. My healthcare case study suggests that media coverage was detrimental to an informed understanding of the issue, as echoed
in the saying: "The more you watch, the less you know."[75] A majority of
those paying close attention to healthcare found the issue very difficult to
follow. To make matters worse, their difficulties increased dramatically
throughout 2009, as indicated by the surveys in Figure 6.9.

The media cannot solely be blamed for public ignorance on healthcare. Journalists were merely the passive transmitters of information from a congressional lawmaking process and a political system that are increasingly complex, esoteric, and inaccessible. The healthcare reform process was lacking in transparency, and this made it difficult for Americans to evaluate competing proposals. The opaqueness of reform was fostered by the lack of cohesion within the Democratic Party, which promoted a number of different proposals. Final legislation that Democrats passed was the product of reconciliation between competing bills in the House of Representatives and Senate, ensuring that the public would not know which version of healthcare reform would pass until the last possible moment. The final legislation was a complex, lengthy amalgamation of numerous reforms, making it difficult to understand.

The mystification of healthcare reform was useful for those inciting public fear over "death panels," "big government," "socialism" and "Marxism," and the "rationing" of care. Healthcare is naturally a very sensitive topic. It deals with life-and-death issues, and it could have been predicted (and in fact was predicted) that Republican–Tea Party scare tactics that warned of the end of healthcare as Americans know it would cause a public backlash.[76] Efforts to "expose" Obama's plot to "kill Grandma" resonated with a public that was fearful of losing healthcare coverage during a time of economic crisis, stagnant-to-falling income, and high unemployment. With little substance to draw on in the face of competing proposals for reform and the increasingly uncertain future of the public option, a divided Democratic Party was left in a vulnerable (largely self-inflicted) position in combating conservative disinformation.

RATIONAL OR IGNORANT PUBLIC? OR BOTH?

Many critics will point to the public's general opposition to healthcare reform and its support for specific provisions of healthcare passed by Democrats as evidence of public ignorance. A number of scholars in the area of public opinion subscribe to an "elite theory" of politics, which emphasizes the public's relatively low levels of knowledge on civic issues. Elite theorists claim that the public fails to form consistent policy preferences along liberal, conservative, or moderate lines, and those who do form coherent ideologies are largely reliant on the cues of political and business elites.[77] Other scholars challenge elite theories, framing the public as rational in its opinions. They find that Americans hold incredibly stable opinions, and that citizens formulate opinions that are quite insightful, based upon changes in available information and real-world events.[78] I find evidence of both elite and rational public theories at work. The public is both rational *and* ignorant in relation to healthcare reform. In line with elite theories, the public was confused about what the reforms entailed, and displayed ignorance concerning the specific proposals in question. Furthermore, most Americans opposed the Democrats and Obama on healthcare reform while strongly supporting the actual provisions proposed in bills in Democratic legislation. In line with the "rational public" argument, the public's job-approval rating of the president and opinions of the Democrats' handling of healthcare remained fairly stable across the months examined. When the public *did* change its attitudes, they were predictably in response to real-world fluctuations in media content. Public opinion became more supportive of healthcare reforms when Obama described the potential benefits of reforms, and grew more skeptical when faced with Republican–Tea Party propaganda.

Rational, mediated ignorance was the order of the day. In 2009 and 2010, the public was heavily propagandized amid fearmongering about Obama's efforts to "kill Grandma" and Tea Party warnings about government "tyranny." Under these circumstances, it is not surprising that Americans grew more hostile to Democratic proposals. At a time when public debate was biased against liberal and progressive healthcare reforms, conservatives manipulated public fears and turned the tide against encroachments on the private healthcare system. Democratic abandonment of progressive reforms in favor of complex and esoteric pro-market proposals helped ensure that public ignorance and resistance grew. The Tea Party played an instrumental role by inciting fear of a government already viewed suspiciously by most Americans.

CONCLUSION

The Post-Midterm Tea Party
and the Wisconsin Revolt

The tall tale of the Tea Party as a revolutionary "outside" force in American politics was pervasive in the post-midterm period in 2010. However, this description became even less tenable as Tea Party congressional leaders displayed their establishment-oriented positions, and as "mass" participation from group members reached new lows. This conclusion, written in August 2011, provides a brief glimpse of the Tea Party as it existed with Republican control of the House of Representatives. I reflect upon the top-down nature of the Tea Party by examining the elitism of the group's national leaders and its 2011 national conference, the conformist orientation of the Tea Party in Congress, and the anemic level of participation in the group in the era of the Wisconsin labor revolt.

THE POST-MIDTERM TEA PARTY "INSURGENCY"

Furthering its earlier narrative, mass media continued in the post-midterm period to frame the Tea Party as a revolutionary challenge to Washington. In one story on the February 2011 national Tea Party conference in Phoenix, the *New York Times* headline read "Tea Party Group Issues Warning to G.O.P." The story suggested, falsely, that the two were independent factions and that "Tea Party members who were here from across the country expressed deep displeasure with the nation's course, in particular the way Washington spends taxpayers' money."[1] The issue at hand was $61 billion in proposed spending cuts from Republicans in Congress, which Tea Party conference members considered "not severe enough." Similarly, the *Los Angeles Times* reported that "the conference did not provide a cozy environment for career politicians."[2] The *Los Angeles Times* repeated similar claims in its reporting of the 2011 Conservative Political Action Conference (CPAC), in which it referred to "the Tea Party's emergence as a new force inside the Republican Party."[3]

Media discussions of the Tea Party "rebellion" extended to policy debates and to the Madison, Wisconsin, protests. Concerning the congressional vote to reauthorize the PATRIOT Act, the *Washington Post* reported that "House Republicans suffered an embarrassing setback . . . when they fell seven votes short of extending" the bill—"a vote that served as the first small uprising of the party's Tea-Party bloc."[4] In political infighting over raising the federal debt limit, media commentary depicted a tension between the Tea Party and an allegedly moderate Republican Party. David Brooks of the *New York Times* remarked that "the Republican Party may no longer be a normal party. Over the past few years, it has been infected by a faction that is more a psychological protest than a practical, governing alternative."[5] Stephen Stromberg of the *Washington Post* remarked that "Tea Partiers will have reason for disappointment" in the context of his assumption that Republicans would not entertain a default on the government debt. Tea Party Republicans threatened to default on the debt if Democrats failed to abandon proposed tax increases, and if they refused to agree to significant cuts in Social Security, Medicare, and Medicaid.[6] These characterizations, however, were far from accurate descriptions of Tea Party-Republican politics. Brooks's rendition rested on his unawareness of the decades-long drift of the Republican Party to the far right—well before the emergence of the Tea Party phenomenon. Stromberg's comments reveal a profound ignorance of the reality of Republican politics. There remained little difference between Tea Party and non-Tea Party Republicans on the debt issue: both threatened to default on the national debt if their demands on taxes and senior welfare programs were not met.[7]

On the issue of the Wisconsin labor protests, the *New York Times* reported on an April 2011 Madison protest entailing attacks on Republican Governor Scott Walker. A limited number of Tea Party counter-protesters also appeared at the rally. Reporting on the event, the paper

declared "the passionate arguments went right on, each side claiming the
upper hand, the larger crowd, the right side of history." Such framing,
also repeated during an earlier February protest in Madison between
"dueling protests" of anti–Scott Walker demonstrators and Tea Partiers,
inaccurately depicted the situation in Wisconsin as split between equally
energized Tea Partiers and labor supporters.[8] Most noteworthy was one
New York Times reporter's comment that the protest in question "looked
like just another day in Madison" in light of the state's "polarized" political climate.[9] Such framing was highly distorted, suggesting that Tea
Partiers were keeping up with labor protesters in terms of their turnout
and public presence.

TEA PARTY ELITISM: NATIONAL LEADERSHIP

The "grassroots" Tea Party myth continued throughout 2011, although it
was directly belied by new evidence of elitism at the national leadership
level. One study from early 2011 documented the compensation of high-
level Tea Party representatives, finding that their incomes were at or very
near the top 1 percent of American income earners.[10] Sal Russo, the head
of the national Tea Party Express, reported an income of more than
$800,000 in 2010 for his Tea Party public relations and media-related
activities. Matt Kibbe, the president of FreedomWorks, earned more than
$300,000 in 2009 for his work with the group and its affiliates. Fellow
FreedomWorks representative Dick Armey earned $500,000 a year for
his Tea Party-affiliated activities. Finally, Tim Phillips, the president of
the Tea Party-affiliated Americans for Prosperity, reported an income of
more than $250,000 for 2009 for his Tea Party activities.[11] Such high
incomes reveal the tremendous elitism that defines the Tea Party at its
highest levels. Revenues raised from the Tea Party are serious indeed and
suggest that the group's leaders remain heavily establishment oriented,
despite their populist rhetoric.

THE PHOENIX CONFERENCE

The year 2010 saw the collapse of the Tea Party's planned October conference in Las Vegas. That collapse suggested that the Tea Party was not
the vigorous grassroots movement supporters described. At a time when

such a national conference was most needed to bring together Tea Partiers and aid them in coordinating their attempts to influence the midterms, the Tea Party's leaders were disorganized and unable even to muster support for a meeting of local chapters. The year 2011 saw a formal resurgence of the Tea Party, as they held their February convention in Phoenix, attracting approximately 2,000 attendees. Comparatively speaking, the turnout was far smaller than other national organizations that have received far less media attention. The progressive World Social Forum (WSF) regional meeting in Detroit in mid-2010 witnessed a turnout of approximately 18,000, and the main WSF meetings for 2011 drew 75,000.[12] The WSF meetings were nearly invisible in the mass media, whereas the Tea Party convention received prominent coverage.[13]

An examination of the Phoenix conference reinforces the Tea Party's elitist elements. The most prominent speakers included important Republican political officials and other longtime Republican operatives, hardly the kind of people who represent a dramatic break from the status quo. These figures included Republican congressmen Joe Barton, Rob Woodall, and John Shadegg, and Republican presidential candidate Tim Pawlenty, as well as longtime Republican-conservative groups such as the Media Research Center and the Heritage Foundation. Financial supporters for the Tea Party convention fit the archetype of the "Astroturf" classification that critics typically associate with the group. Elitist, corporate financing for the Tea Party conference should not be surprising considering the effort of the Tea Party Patriots (the group organizing the convention) to raise more than $800,000 in sponsorships for the event. As *Mother Jones* remarked, "The primary summit sponsorship comes with a price tag of $250,000—an amount they're not likely to squeeze out of a bunch of rural Tea Party activists." The price for renting booths reportedly ran as high as $4,000 each, with their availability advertised regularly on the radio programs of pundits such as Rush Limbaugh and Sean Hannity.[14]

My review of the more than fifty groups that rented booths at the convention reveals the strong ties between the Tea Party and business interests. Of all the groups, 41 percent were classified as for-profit, meaning that their primary goal was making money from the Tea Party conference. An additional 35 percent of the groups were either funded by elite business interests or affiliated with national business interests that play a major role in supporting the Tea Party. Such interests included corporations such as Philip Morris and Exxon Mobil, various advertiser and mutual funds interests, business-funded ideological groups such as the Competitive Enterprise Institute, Republican business organizations such as FreedomWorks and the Sam Adam's Alliance, and wealthy industrialists such as the now infamous Koch brothers. Business-funded and allied groups and for-profit groups, then, constituted 76 percent of all groups funding the convention exhibit hall. Just 11 percent of groups displayed no visible ties to wealthy business financiers or interests, and another 13 percent did not provide enough information to evaluate them either way. In sum, available evidence suggests that the 2011 Phoenix Tea Party conference was heavily elitist in its reliance on corporate-funded, business-allied interests. The percentages above suggest that the convention's Astroturf financial supporters outnumbered grassroots groups by a ratio of approximately 7.5 to 1.

The Congressional Tea Party: Mr. Conformity Goes to Washington

It was widely assumed in reporting that the Tea Party "challengers" who won office for the first time in the 2010 midterms represented an entirely different political breed in terms of their willingness to challenge the Washington establishment. As of this writing (August 2011), few major bills had been voted on in the 112th Congress.[15] The legislation that was put to a vote or was near a vote, however, was of major importance. By early July 2011 these included the Republican attempt to repeal Democratic healthcare reform, the reauthorization of the PATRIOT Act, and the planned vote on raising the federal government's debt ceiling. Tea Party voting (or planned voting) on these bills, however, was in no way significantly different than that of non-Tea Party Republicans. The *Washington Post* preferred to characterize the Tea Party vote as an example of a "first small uprising" against Washington elites. This claim was more the result of lazy reporting than an accurate description of reality. In the final House vote on PATRIOT Act reauthorization, a meager six Tea Partiers voted against the bill, compared to 54 Tea Partiers who supported it. Just 10 percent of Tea Partiers in the House opposed the PATRIOT Act, compared to 9 percent of non-Tea Party Republicans, and 11 percent of all Republicans.[16] Such opposition is far from significant when comparing Tea Partiers to other Republicans. Evidence is more split in the Senate, with two of the Tea Party Caucus members voting against the bill—Rand Paul and Mike Lee—and two voting in support, Jim DeMint and Jerry Moran.[17] The relatively small number of Senate Tea Partiers, however, prohibits much generalization about that vote.

Voting on the 2011 House bill to repeal "Obamacare" and the planned vote on the Federal debt ceiling also revealed no differences between Tea Party and non–Tea Party Republicans. Every Republican member of the House voted in favor of repeal, suggesting no difference between the two groups.[18] A vote never took place in the Senate, where support was too weak for passage. Nonetheless, all forty-seven Republican senators indicated their support for repealing "Obamacare," suggesting no distinction between Tea Partiers and non–Tea Party Republicans.[19] As for the Balanced Budget Amendment, findings were similar to the voting on Democratic healthcare. As of this writing, all forty-seven Republican senators announced their support for such an amendment.[20] In the House, 93 percent of Tea Party Republicans co-sponsored the amendment as of July 2011, compared to 94 percent of non–Tea Party Republicans. These differences are not significant.[21]

In the lone case of the August 2011 vote on raising the national debt ceiling, Tea Partiers did exhibit a different voting pattern than non–Tea Party Republicans. On that vote, 53 percent of Tea Party Republicans voted for the debt ceiling increase, accompanied by $2.4 trillion in social spending cuts, with 47 percent voting against. This stood in contrast to 94 percent of non–Tea Party Republicans voting in favor of the ceiling raise, and just 6 percent voting against. This single exception to a pattern of overwhelming similarity between Tea Party and non–Tea Party Republicans, however, must be carefully qualified. First, a majority of Tea Party "insurgents" still voted *in favor of* the debt ceiling increase, countering claims that they are in revolt against the Republican establishment. Second, the lack of significant difference between Tea Party and non–Tea Party Republicans on voting for the Balanced Budget Amendment, which would call for radically larger cuts than those passed as part of the debt ceiling, suggests that there is little substantive difference in the policy preferences of the two groups. Some sort of disagreement does exist among Tea Party and non–Tea Party Republicans, as the debt ceiling vote demonstrates. It is a stylistic difference, however, as Republicans fight over the best *means* of achieving radical reductions in social spending, not on whether such reductions are needed or legitimate.

Tea Party intransigence, as seen in the debt ceiling vote, may eventually manifest itself in sustained media condemnations of the Tea Party.

This could take place *if* the Democratic or Republican Party begins to regularly criticize the group. This appears to have already happened to a very limited degree. By early August, 2011, news outlets were reporting statements from Democrats such as political strategist David Axelrod, Vice President Joe Biden, and Senator John Kerry who attacked what they labeled the "Tea Party downgrade," after Standard and Poor's reduced the U.S. credit rating from AAA to AA+ status following the Republican-Democratic debt ceiling fiasco.[22] Far stronger and more sustained criticisms will need to be voiced, however, for serious attacks on the Tea Party to become a main staple of reporting.

Furthermore, even if criticisms of the Tea Party as obstructionist do become a regular staple of reporting, they will do little to challenge the false discussion of the Tea Party as an insurgent or radical force in comparison to alleged Republican centrists. The attacks on the Tea Party as of mid-2011 obfuscated the real power dynamics in Washington at the time. News outlets were reporting by August 2011 that Democratic vice president Joe Biden and Democratic Representative Mike Doyle referred to the Tea Party as "terrorists," in light of some of the group's members opposing compromise with Democratic budget cut demands and for refusing to vote for a debt ceiling increase.[23] Attacks on the fictitious deviation of Tea Party Republicans from the "mainstream" Republican Party, however, merely perpetuate the media myth of the Tea Party as a revolutionary, outsider force. References to the group as extremist or terrorist are untenable in light of its relatively weak representation in government, as Tea Partiers account for just 25 percent of all House Republicans and 14 percent of all House representatives, and just 9 percent of Senate Republicans and 4 percent of all senators. Such numbers prevent the congressional Tea Party caucuses from exercising the institutional power to block legislation (at least by themselves) from passing either chamber of Congress. Actual obstruction in the congressional record is even smaller, with Tea Partiers voting against the debt ceiling bill constituting a minuscule 12 percent of House Republicans and 6 percent of all House representatives, and just 9 percent of Senate Republicans and 4 percent of all senators.

The finding that there is little substantive difference between Tea Party and non–Tea Party Republicans does not fit the mythic narrative of a revolutionary Tea Party. Journalists are more interested in perpetuating this myth, however, as seen in reporting in mid 2011on the debt ceiling and balanced budget amendment. For example, a report in *The Hill*, a congressional news source, spoke of House Speaker John Boehner and Senate Republican Leader Mitch McConnell's "Tea Party problem," as both came under "Tea Party pressure" to tie the raising of the national debt ceiling to the passage of a balanced budget Constitutional amendment.[24] Such framing of Tea Party insurgency was even more blatant in a *Washington Post* profile of Republican senator Mike Lee. As a sponsor of the balanced budget amendment and cofounder of the Senate Tea Party, Lee was portrayed as a longtime "political insider" who "refashion[ed] himself as a Tea Party revolutionary." His threats "to filibuster attempts to raise the federal debt ceiling" supposedly cemented his status as a leading Tea Partier, pushing the Republican Party in a more reactionary direction.[25] Of course, Lee is substantively no different on the debt and balanced budget amendment than 94 percent of non–Tea Party Republicans, who also support the amendment. This finding, however, is beside the point. The Tea Party was never about transforming the Republican Party. At its foundation, the Tea Party is a public relations phenomenon. As the *Washington Post*'s profile of Lee demonstrates, the Tea Party represents a rebranding of the Republican Party as "born anew" under the façade of a "grassroots" conservative "revolution."

Critics might counter that Republican uniformity in favor of reactionary policies was a response to the power of the Tea Party in the wake of the 2010 midterms. There is little reason to take this claim seriously, since it is entirely lacking in empirical evidence. Statistical voting studies, discussed in chapter 1, demonstrate that the shift to the reactionary right in the Republican Party has been taking place for more than three decades, with polarization away from the political center at historic highs in the post-2000 period. As my review of ADA voting scores found, the recent shift of the Republican Party even further to the right predates the rise of regular reporting on the Tea Party by one to two years, as seen in Figure 7.1 below. Mass reporting on the Tea Party did not begin until late 2009, while Republican polarization was already apparent in 2008.

A close examination of Figure 7.1 indicates that the polarization of Republicans in the last few years is no more severe than that seen at other times in the last twenty years. The spike in Republican extremism from 2008 onward is comparable to spikes seen in the House and Senate during the mid-1990s (1995 specifically), and during the late Clinton and early Bush years (the late 1990s to early 2000s). The mid-1990s were indeed polarizing, with Republicans committed to shutting down the federal government following their failure to secure major budget cuts.

FIGURE 7.1: Conservative Polarization of the Republican Party in Congress, 1991–2010

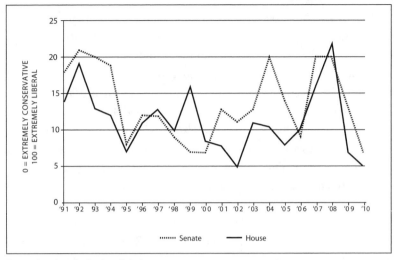

Source: Americans for Democratic Action

Similarly, the late 1990s and early 2000s saw a similar polarization with the emergence of an ardent Republican commitment to deregulation (of Wall Street particularly), followed by the rise of a strongly unilateral and militant Bush administration, which was viewed as one of the most polarizing presidencies in U.S. history. In short, polarization data suggest that the Tea Party "revolution" is not all that different from previous extremist periods in recent political history.

Contrary to the narrative depicting Republican polarization as a recent phenomenon, studies of congressional voting records suggest that the Republican shift was steady and nearly constant in the House of Representatives since the 1970s. The trend was similar in the Senate, with a mass rightward polarization from the 1970s through the early 1990s, followed by a leveling off of polarization in the mid-1990s, and by another significant polarization from the late-1990s through the present day.[26] Taking these findings into account, it is foolish to attribute so much power to the Tea Party as the primary cause of right-wing polarization. The ADA data I employ suggest that the Tea Party phenomenon *may* have had some effect in pushing the party to the right. However, the rightward shift documented in Figure 7.1, which was already taking place more than one year before the first days of the Tea Party, suggests that Obama's election itself and the rise of a Democratic

Congressional majority may have been a more important force in pushing Republicans to the right.

Congressional scholars see partisan division as a long-term rather than
short-term development. The most authoritative database that measures
polarization in Congress (as a function of voting) is DW Nominate, which
is coordinated by legislative scholars widely recognized as at the top of their
field. DW Nominate is regarded as a reliable measure of legislators' ideology, on a par with, and perhaps more authoritative than, the ADA voting
scores I employ in this book.[27] An analysis of Tea Party Caucus members'
voting records that makes use of the DW Nominate scores suggests that,
when it comes to political-economic issues, there are no significant differences between members of the caucus and non–Tea Party Republicans.

Statistical analyses of DW Nominate data suggest that there is no difference between Tea Party and non–Tea Party Republicans in terms of
their voting records. For example, in 2011 Republicans in Congress
began to pledge to vote for an increase in the national debt limit only if it
was accompanied by a "cut, cap, and balance pledge." That pledge
required supporters to vote for "substantial cuts in spending," "passage of
a Balanced Budget Amendment," and "enforceable spending caps." As a
hallmark of the Tea Party agenda, support for such an effort should have
sharply separated Tea Party and "moderate" Republicans. In reality, there
was no significant ideological difference between the two groups after
examining their previous voting records.[28] Furthermore, as legislative
scholars conclude, the average ideological scores of Tea Party
Republicans, as reflected in an analysis of all their past votes, are not substantively different from non–Tea Party Republicans.[29] In short, the idea
that there are competing moderate and Tea Party Republicans is a myth
perpetuated by the political-media system.

I argued that it is an exaggeration to claim that the Tea Party is a significant force in pulling the Republican Party to the right. My conclusion
may be *too generous* with regard to the power of the Tea Party, after reflecting upon legislative scholars' failure to find differences between Tea Party
and non–Tea Party Republicans. Such findings suggest that media coverage of an "insurgency" Tea Party is distorted, propagandistic, and far too
favorable to the group.

These findings should not be taken to suggest that the Tea Party phenomenon is unimportant. The Tea Party's main value is its power in
rebranding the Republican Party, rather than in changing the substance of
the party's ideology. The Tea Party provides cover for Republicans to

obscure their long-standing shift to the far right. "Moderate" Republicans can portray themselves as seeking to find a "middle ground" between their less extreme positions and the more extreme ones of Tea Party Republicans. This strategy allows the party's rank and file to mask just how extreme its politics have become in recent decades. The approach also allows the party to continue pulling the national political discourse to the right, as Democrats are pressured to grant even more concessions to an "outsider revolution" that is simply implementing the "will of the people." As a public relations gimmick, the Tea Party is effective in achieving these objectives.

THE TEA PARTY MEETS THE MADISON REVOLT

The 2011 Wisconsin labor protests represented a tumultuous time for American labor. Unions have been under sustained assault from government and business officials for decades, with Wisconsin's Governor Scott Walker's actions serving as the most recent example. In an effort to eliminate the state's public employee labor unions as a support base for the Democratic Party, Walker announced a "Budget Repair" bill that exacted savage cuts on labor in the name of avoiding a worsening economic crisis. His initiative demanded pension and healthcare concessions from state workers, while mandating a legal abolition of collective bargaining efforts above the consumer price index and prohibiting unions from collecting mandatory dues from members. Walker's initiatives were eventually passed in early March 2011 by a narrow 53–42 vote in the Wisconsin State Assembly and by 18–1 in the Senate. Although the reforms received majority support from government officials, they provoked a mass rebellion among the workers of the state, who were dedicated to derailing the reforms and, later, to removing Walker from office.

Walker's attacks on labor incited opposition from protesters who emphasized that the battle was one drawn by political choice, rather than economic necessity. Walker had deliberately exempted the police and firefighters' unions, which had granted him political support in his candidacy. This exemption prompted an outcry from other unions, which claimed that Walker's bill was, in reality, a war against the support base of his political enemies. Opponents of his bill also cited the governor's announcement of millions of dollars in business tax cuts (shortly prior to his assault on labor) as evidence that Walker had deliberately manufactured the budget deficit in order to provide cover for his longstanding war against Wisconsin labor. Other reasons for opposition included the argument that the short-term cuts demanded by Walker—in union pension and healthcare costs—could be realistically separated from long-term issues involving collective bargaining and union dues, which had no relationship to escalating state deficits.

Public opinion surveys found that resistance to Walker's anti-labor campaign was widespread across Wisconsin and the country. Government opposition was led by Wisconsin's Democratic officials, who provided cover for those demonstrating in Madison by fleeing the state for three weeks to prevent a vote on the governor's "Budget Repair" bill. Polling of Wisconsin residents and Americans found that a majority disagreed with government efforts to limit collective bargaining and reduce worker pay, and were opposed to the pension and healthcare cuts pushed by Walker, in addition to his efforts to prohibit the collection of required union dues.[30] Some conservatives cited polling that suggested most Americans agreed with Walker's actions, at least when polling questions were framed in terms of limiting collective bargaining as a means of "balancing budgets."[31] Such questions were lacking in seriousness, however, as there is no correlation between a state's position on collective bargaining (whether it is allowed or not for public employees) on the one hand, and the state's level of public debt on the other.[32] To include promises that the forced elimination of collective bargaining will somehow put states on the path to fiscal health, then, is a propaganda talking point of the American right. It is not a legitimate premise for polling the public, as it improperly biases questions in favor of the political agenda of anti-unionists.

Public protests in Wisconsin against Scott Walker's anti-labor agenda represented a milestone for workers. Major regional and national unions became involved in the struggle, including the American Federation of State, County and Municipal Employees (AFSCME), the Service Employees International Union (SEIU), the Wisconsin Professional Police Association (WPPA), the Wisconsin Education Association Council (WEAC), and the Professional Fire Fighters of Wisconsin (PFFW). Wisconsinites were beginning to join the rest of the world in opposing austerity measures that were designed to limit worker benefits in a time of economic instability. The protests in Madison on any given day appeared equal in turnout to all Tea Party rallies combined during mid-April 2010. Available data for total turnout for the Tea Party's April 15, 2010, Tax Day rallies suggested that perhaps 100,000 to 200,000 people demonstrated nationwide.[33] Protests in Madison easily saw 100,000 people turnout on some days during the second half of February 2011. Aggregate turnout for February exceeded hundreds of thousands. On any given day in late February, one was likely to see at least tens of thousands of protesters in the state's capitol and in the halls of the capitol building, demonstrating against the policies of Scott Walker and state Republicans.

My analysis of the Tea Party extends to the protests in Wisconsin against Scott Walker, which I directly observed and took part in during the latter half of February 2011. Traveling to Madison numerous times in February, I witnessed and participated in the labor revolt firsthand, speaking with those on the front lines of this struggle. The feeling throughout the protests was widespread that the Tea Party did *not* represent the interests of Wisconsinites, and that their support for Scott Walker represented a betrayal of working-class interests. Tea Partiers, however, were mainly seen as an afterthought in the protests, primarily because their turnouts in Madison were nearly nonexistent. The lack of a sustained Tea Party presence was seen as evidence of the lack of vigor of the "movement" at a time when local and national Tea Party leaders were pleading with the "rank and file" to appear in large numbers to express their solidarity with Scott Walker.

Most important, the Wisconsin protests differed from Tea Party rallies I observed and studied as related to the context of a mass movement. The Wisconsin marches included many of the classic prerequisites of a movement, such as stable institutional (in this case union) support, mass protest turnouts, and active lobbying at demonstrations through leafleting, pamphleteering, and organizational presence. Unlike the Tea Party rallies, the Madison protests were not transparently operating as a springboard for a long list of aspiring political candidates seeking to launch their electoral campaigns. The stark differences in turnout between the Tea Partiers and labor protesters left little question as to what a real social movement looks like.

TEA PARTY MIA IN MADISON

In the days I attended rallies, I rarely encountered Tea Party protesters. Such protesters occasionally appeared in Madison to protest labor demonstrators, although they were dwarfed by a sea of Walker opponents.

On one day, February 19, Tea Partiers promised a "mass" turnout in support of Walker, but on-the-ground estimates suggested that no more than 500 to 1,000 Tea Partiers gathered to support Walker, compared to the approximate total of 70,000 who rallied in Madison, most all of whom were there to protest Walker.[34] A second Tea Party protest in Madison during mid-April was also overshadowed by a larger presence of anti-Walker protests, despite brandishing national conservative-Republican speakers such as Sarah Palin and Andrew Breitbart.[35] The Tea Party's meager numbers might have served as a sobering revelation for organizers, who could have used this opportunity to recognize the importance of institution building in galvanizing mass participation and sustained activism. The numerous union organizations that protested Walker employed their significant resources to communicate with rank-and-file union members and to coordinate the rallies occurring throughout late February. Union representatives were widely visible at rallies, conducting outreach with other demonstrators, Madison residents, and the mass media in order to communicate their messages. As demonstrated in this book, the Tea Party has virtually no support base with which to organize. As a result, the Tea Party simply cannot compete with union groups in mobilizing demonstrators.

My engagements with Tea Partiers throughout the Chicago area, some of whom claimed to have attended a rally in Madison, found that most refused to acknowledge the importance of institutional resources in mobilizing protests. They took every opportunity to condemn, rather than learn from, the unions organizing there.[36] Their attacks centered on claims that demonstrators were being paid off by, or unfairly receiving support from, the unions. "Real" protesters, Tea Partiers claimed, were rugged individualists who refused to accept support from, or rely on, larger institutions to succeed. This response certainly helped Tea Partiers feel better about being overshadowed by anti-Walker protesters, but it did little to inform them about how to build an effective mass movement. Condescending condemnations of the institution building necessary to create a movement fits comfortably with the neoliberal, Ayn Randian paradigm supported by Tea Partiers. This mindset conceives of activism as acceptable only at the individual rather than institutional level. It also dooms the group to permanent minority status. Tea Partier ignorance regarding the collective component of movement building prevents the group from constructing a mass support base.

MADISON ASTROTURFING

As with organizing in the Chicago area, rather than building mass-based institutions to sustain a movement, Tea Party organizers chose an alternative route for coordinating rallies in Madison. Their elite top-down approach, described in chapter 2, was repeated. The Tea Party's April 2011 Madison rally, which saw no more than a few thousand demonstrators, was organized by the group Americans for Prosperity, which is directly funded by the billionaire Koch brothers. The AFP centered the rally on a top-down, corporate-friendly message from Palin, which demonized union demonstrators for "thug tactics." Palin's characterization of the union rallies as composed of "violent rent-a-mobs" who "trash[ed] your Capitol and vandalize business" was widely refuted by those who actually attended the rallies, which were nonviolent and respectful toward local businesses and property.[37] Nonetheless, such rhetoric is commonplace among Republican elites, who uncritically disseminate pro-business, anti-labor propaganda.

A second group that spearheaded the Madison Tea Party protest was American Majority. The group is an elitist partisan creation of Ned Ryun, a former speechwriter for George W. Bush and the son of former Republican House representative Jim Ryun. The Ryun family shares a long history of Republican activism, with Ned Ryun's brother serving as the deputy director of the Republican National Committee in 2004 and also working for the Tea Party-affiliated American Majority. Other members and former members of the group include director Joseph Lehman, a former engineer at Dow Chemical; director Denis Calabrese, former chief of staff for Republican House majority leader and now FreedomWorks representative; Dick Armey; and president John Tsarpalas, the past director of the Illinois State Republican Party. American Majority receives most of its funding from Sam Adam's Alliance, a group that is supported by the Koch brothers.[38]

The effects of the Tea Party's elitist approach to Madison are apparent. Groups such as American Majority and Americans for Prosperity are more interested in garnering short-term benefits in the form of positive media coverage than they are in long-term goals such as building a grassroots conservative movement that empowers local members. Leaving organization of Tea Party rallies in their hands produced predictable consequences. Little to no sustained action on the part of Tea Partiers ever took place in Madison, as was clear to those who attended the anti-Walker

rallies. The fundamental difference between the two organizational struc-
tures was obvious. Union groups employed their resources to mobilize in
favor of the interests of their members by opposing pay and healthcare
cuts and resisting the curtailment of collective bargaining and union dues
collection. Astroturf Tea Party groups pursued a public relations strategy that heavily benefited their organizations while disempowering midwestern Tea Party supporters. In the context of these results, it becomes
increasingly difficult to defend the claim that the unions, rather than Tea
Party groups, were engaged in elitism.

THE POST-MIDTERM TEA PARTY:
ASSESSING MEDIA COVERAGE

The intimate relationship between right-wing media and the Tea Party has
existed since the onset of the so-called movement. These ties were effectively described by Tea Party Express founder Sal Russo, who explained
in mid-2011 that "there would not have been a Tea Party without Fox."[39]
Russo's statement cut to the core of the main thesis of this book—that the
Tea Party is essentially a mediated, top-down phenomenon. But the Tea
Party's support from the mass media extended far beyond Fox News. Fox
reporters and pundits were the most prominent cheerleaders for the
group, but sympathetic reporting was apparent throughout the mass
media. Liberal outlets such as MSNBC and the *New York Times* ran commentary that was critical of the group, but consistently disseminated the
image of the Tea Party as a grassroots rebellion against establishment politics in Washington. This pro-Tea Party bias was instrumental in solidify-
ing the public image of the group as a legitimate populist uprising.

Conservatives complain that the mass media are biased against the Tea
Party. In the case of the Madison protests, the right-wing Media Research
Center (MRC) complains that there was a journalistic "double standard"
at play. The national networks, MRC claimed, "repeatedly denounced
'incivility' from the Tea Party" while ignoring "nasty signs from union
protesters" in Wisconsin. The MRC highlighted the following three
examples from the mass media as evidence of bias:

- *CBS World News* anchor Diane Sawyer's 2010 description of "protesters roaming Washington, some of them increasingly emotional, yelling
  slurs and epithets."

- CBS News journalist Nancy Cordes's characterization of 2010 Tea Party protests as defined by "incivility."

- ABC News anchor Charles Gibson's 2009 report, which mentioned "protesters [who] brought pictures of President Obama with a Hitler-style mustache to a Town Hall meeting."[40]

There were many problems with the MRC narrative. For one, three anecdotes do not constitute evidence of a systematic media bias against the Tea Party. Second, it is not clear that the examples provided even constitute evidence of anti–Tea Party bias. "Bias" can only be demonstrated by documenting a pattern in reporting that is not confirmed by events. In the case of the Obama-Hitler references, such placards *did* appear at many Tea Party rallies, although they constituted a minority of all messages in print. Also left unmentioned by MRC is the fact that conflation of Obama and the Democrats with Hitler is standard practice at Fox News, the media mouthpiece of the Tea Party.[41] Obama-Hitler analogies may or may not be rejected by most Tea Partiers, as there is no polling data available on this question to provide an answer either way. It is not clear, however, that the mass media are being biased against the Tea Party simply by reporting the instances when Tea Partiers express such messages. As the most incendiary and polemic of all placards, attempts to link Obama and Hitler are alluring to journalists who look for novelty in protest stories. Coverage of outrageous messages helps draw in news audiences in a period when media are increasingly defined at every level through spectacle. Emphasis on the perverse is a regular part of reporting, whether it is in local crime stories, sensationalized murder trials, incessant celebrity gossip updates, or incendiary protests.

MRC's attacks on CBS News for covering racial slurs and "emotional" protesters at Tea Party rallies are also without merit. Self-designated Tea Partiers are more likely to say that they are angry at the government, as revealed in national polling.[42] This characterization, then, is technically accurate, rather than a statement of bias on the part of CBS. Furthermore, Tea Partiers have shouted racial slurs at rallies, and most of them display deeply racist attitudes toward Muslims, African Americans, and other minorities, as documented in national surveys.[43] Rather than becoming angry about some fictitious "media bias," MRC appears to be angry at the mass media for refusing to parrot uninformed claims that the Tea Party does not harbor racist or irate members. Discussions of Tea

Partiers' anger and racism may be embarrassing for conservatives, but they are not evidence of media bias.

MRC's claim that the mass media employ a "double standard" by ignoring extreme rhetoric at Wisconsin rallies while overemphasizing Tea Party extremists is empirically weak. MRC states that "none of the signs in the hands of liberal [Madison] protesters [such as those comparing Scott Walker to Hitler or Stalin] have drawn the slightest complaint from network journalists. MRC analysts examined all 53 ABC, CBS, and NBC morning and evening news stories, segments and anchor briefs on the Wisconsin protests from February 17 (when they first drew national coverage) through Monday, February 21. While eight of the 53 stories (15 percent) visually displayed one or more signs [described by the MRC as extremist], none elicited a single remark from the network correspondents." MRC's nonexistent empirical standard for evaluating bias in this case is worth highlighting. MRC provides no comparison point with which to evaluate media bias, refusing to analyze the number of times extreme signs appeared in reporting on the Tea Party within a comparable time period. As a result, the "15 percent" figure is left to float on its own, and it is unhelpful in any way in determining comparative media bias. National networks may or may not have focused more often on extreme signs at Tea Party rallies than those seen in Madison labor protests. One does not know for sure, however, since MRC did not bother to do the research needed to validate its own claim. Furthermore, even if reporting did emphasize extreme Tea Party signs more often, this would not necessarily constitute evidence of bias. One would also need to show that such signs did not appear more often in Tea Party rallies across the country than in the Madison demonstrations. MRC did not undertake such an analysis.

My content analysis of Tea Party and Madison protest coverage suggests that both protests received quite a bit of attention in reporting, although the Tea Party protest actually benefited from more sympathetic coverage. The large size and sustained turnout of protests in Madison made it difficult for journalists to ignore them. This study found that the level of attention a social movement obtains in media is heavily determined by the level of political support it receives from government officials. One would expect, then, to see consistent coverage of the Wisconsin protests in the news, considering the strong Democratic support for the demonstrations. This is precisely what I found when examining reporting. Table 7.1 displays the ratio of total stories on the Tea Party in com-

TABLE 7.1: Framing Social Movements: The Tea Party vs.
the Wisconsin Revolt
(April 15–28, 2010); (February 14–27, 2011)

News Outlet	Ratio of Total Stories on Tea Party v. Wisconsin Protests	% of Tea Party Stories Referring to It as a Movement	% of Wisconsin Protest Stories Referring to It as a Movement
NY Times	1.15:1	76%	3%
Wash. Post	1.4:1	77%	10%
MSNBC	1.15:1	35%	28%
Fox News	1:1.5	53%	11%
CNN	1:1.15	54%	1%
NBC	1:2	85%	0%
CBS	1:3.9	71%	7%
ABC	1:3	89%	4%

Source: LexisNexis

parison to those on the Madison protests. The periods analyzed include the two-week period following the April 15, 2010, Tea Party Tax Day rallies, and the two-week period coinciding with the February 2011 Madison protests. The data suggest that coverage of Madison did reach very high levels in comparison to the massive attention directed toward the Tea Party. The evidence for bias is mixed with regard to the level of attention directed toward both the Tea Party and Madison. In three of the news outlets, the *New York Times*, the *Washington Post*, and MSNBC, the Tea Party received more attention. However, Fox News, CNN, NBC, CBS, and ABC mentioned the Madison protests more often. One could interpret the results as a noticeable bias in favor of the Madison protests, although that supposed bias is called into question when looking more closely at reporting. As Table 7.1 suggests, reporters were radically more likely to refer to the Tea Party as a social "movement" in comparison to the Madison protests.[44]

The Tea Party may have received slightly less coverage during the two time periods, but that coverage was far more sympathetic. The more frequent references to the Tea Party as a movement amount to a sort of double bias in favor of the group, since the Tea Party is not really a social movement, compared to the union protests, which displayed many classic features of a bottom-up, grassroots rebellion. Furthermore, the Tea Party's total coverage greatly eclipsed that of the Madison protests when looking at coverage throughout 2011. The Tea Party received saturation coverage throughout the entire year, while the Madison protests received significant attention for less than a month. This labor conflict largely fell out of the headlines after February, as Scott Walker passed his anti-union legislation, and as the protests declined in strength. In short, there is little evidence here to suggest that media coverage is biased against the Tea Party. If anything, coverage of the group in 2011 was far more frequent, and much more sympathetic in tone.

It is true that the Madison protests fell out of the news because of their episodic nature. As the demonstrations weakened, journalists, understandably, saw less reason to pay attention to them. However, the main reason that the mass media favored the Tea Party over the Madison protests (with regard to the tone of reporting) concerns the relationship of both groups to the major political parties. The Madison protest was embraced by only a very small number of Democrats—those in Wisconsin—and for a very brief period of time. In contrast, the Tea Party is regularly embraced at the local, state, and national level among Republicans, and among conservative-leaning business interests. Such support ensures that the Tea Party receives regular, sympathetic coverage. This finding should not be surprising in a media system that determines the newsworthiness of a "movement" by the level of support it receives from the political system.

In this book I sought to provide a better understanding of how citizens interact with the political system in an increasingly mediated society. I examined the Tea Party and its effect on healthcare as my case study. The analysis I undertook concluded with a number of findings:

- Contrary to popular political and media portrayals, the Tea Party does not constitute a legitimate social movement on a par with other movements of the past and present. The comparison of the Tea Party to the Wisconsin labor revolt demonstrated the difference between genuine and "Astroturf" social movements.

- Despite its superficial characteristics, the Tea Party succeeded in captivating public opinion and pulling the political culture to the right, in large part due to the sympathetic actions of political elites, supportive business elites, and a compliant mass media. The Tea Party represents at its core a rebranding of the Republican Party, meant to dress it up as a grassroots rebellion and insurgency against "establishment" interests. It is a classic example, in the words of William Greider, of "rancid populism," Astroturf to the core and harmful in its effects on the public at large. Such "movements" have become incredibly effective in manufacturing public dissent against liberal and progressive policies.

- In a democratic society, indoctrination and propaganda are most effectively institutionalized through intangible hegemonic variables, rather than through materialist forces or brute force. Such intangible forces include the powers of partisanship, ideology, media consumption, and political attentiveness, although other variables could also be included. Factors more closely associated with material affluence, such as sex, income, education, and race, play an important part in influencing public opinion, although they are not as consistently powerful as intangible hegemonic variables.

- The rise of the Tea Party phenomenon represents an astounding concession from political elites that they are no longer able to effectively govern through traditional means. In an era of extreme public distrust in government and economic instability, the populist-sounding rhetoric of Republicans is simply not enough to convince the public to support an increasingly reactionary political-economic agenda. To ram through highly unpopular neoliberal austerity measures, they must construct false movements from the top down, which tenaciously campaign for "free market" pro-corporate policies in the name of implementing the "public will."

Notes

Introduction: Manufacturing Dissent in a Time of Political Distrust

1. William Dinan and David Miller, *A Century of Spin: How Public Relations Became the Cutting Edge of Corporate Power* (London: Pluto Press, 2008), 173.
2. For more on the privileged position of business, see Charles L. Lindblom, *Politics and Markets: The World's Political-Economic Systems* (New York: Basic Books, 1977).
3. American National Election Studies, "ANES Guide to Public Opinion and Electoral Behavior," *ANES*, 2010, www.electionstudies.org/nesguide/toptable/tab5a_2.htm.
4. Anthony Pratkanis and Elliot Aronson, *Age of Propaganda: The Everyday Use and Abuse of Persuasion* (New York: Owl Books, 1992), 11.
5. Edward Bernays, *Propaganda* (Brooklyn, NY: IG Publishing, 2005), 37; Walter Lippmann, *The Phantom Public* (New Brunswick, NJ: Transaction Publishers, 1993).
6. Bernays, *Propaganda*, 37.
7. Stuart Ewen, *PR! A Social History of Spin* (New York: Basic Books, 1996), 399.
8. Bernays, *Propaganda*, 109.
9. See Edward S. Herman and Noam Chomsky, *Manufacturing Dissent: The Political Economy of the Mass Media* (New York: Pantheon, 2002).
10. Erin Steuter and Deborah Wills, *At War with Metaphor: Media, Propaganda, and Racism in the War on Terror* (Lanham, MD: Lexington Books, 2008).
11. For more on these points, see my and Paul Street's lengthy discussion of the Tea Party's exoneration of Wall Street and its unwarranted paranoia about "Obama socialism" in Paul Street and Anthony DiMaggio, *Crashing the Tea Party: Mass Media and the Remaking of American Politics* (Boulder, CO: Paradigm Publishers, 2011).
12. Dinan and Miller, *A Century of Spin*. The reference to PR as the "cutting edge" of corporate power originally appears in the subtitle of Dinan and Miller's book.

13. Stuart Ewen, *Captains of Consciousness: Advertising and the Social Roots of the Consumer Culture* (New York: McGraw Hill, 1976), 33.
14. Ibid., 53–54.
15. Lee Artz, "Globalization, Media Hegemony, and Social Class," in *The Globalization of Corporate Media Hegemony,* ed. Lee Artz and Yahya R. Kamalipour (Albany: State University of New York Press, 2003), 11.
16. David Forgacs, ed., *The Antonio Gramsci Reader: Selected Writings 1916–1935* (New York: New York University Press, 2000), 422–23.
17. Lee Artz, "On the Material and the Dialectic: Toward a Class Analysis of Communication," *Marxism and Communication Studies: The Point Is to Change It,* ed. Lee Artz, Steve Macek, and Dana L. Cloud (New York: Peter Lang Publishers, 2006), 31.
18. Dinan and Miller, *A Century of Spin,* 1.
19. Fabiana Woodfin, "Lost in Translation: The Distortion of Egemonia," in Artz et al., *Marxism and Communication Studies,* 133; Tamara Goeddertz and Marwan M. Kraidy, "The 'Battle in Seattle': U.S. Prestige Press Framing of Resistance to Globalization," in Artz and Kamalipour, *The Globalization of Corporate Media Hegemony,* 80.
20. Woodfin, *Marxism and Communication Studies,* 133.
21. Daniel Little, "False Consciousness," University of Michigan-Dearborn, www-personal.umd.umich.edu/~delittle/iess%20false%20consciousness%20V2.htm.
22. See chap. 7 of Anthony DiMaggio, *When Media Goes to War: Hegemonic Discourse, Public Opinion, and the Limits of Dissent* (New York: Monthly Review Press, 2010).
23. Walter Lippmann, *Public Opinion* (New York: Free Press, 1997), 158.
24. Ewen, *PR!,* 108.
25. Ibid., 64.
26. Lippmann, *Public Opinion,* 157–58; Ewen, *PR!,* 155.
27. For one recent example, see Kurt Lang and Gladys Engel Lang, "Noam Chomsky and the Manufacture of Consent for American Foreign Policy," *Political Communication* 21/1 (January 2004): 93–101.
28. Lippmann, *Public Opinion,* 127; Lippmann, *The Phantom Public,* 51.
29. Lippmann, *Public Opinion,* 127.
30. Ibid., 158.
31. Lippmann, *The Phantom Public,* 13, 43, 139, 47–48, 139.
32. Lippmann, *Public Opinion,* 195.
33. Lippmann, *The Phantom Public,* 134–35.
34. For more on political contempt for public opinion, see Anthony DiMaggio, "The Politics of Cynicism: Obama, Afghanistan, and the 2012 Elections," *CounterPunch,* December 9, 2009, http://www.counterpunch.org/dimaggio12092009.html; DiMaggio, *When Media Goes to War*; Benjamin I. Page and Marshall M. Bouton, *The Foreign Policy Disconnect: What Americans Want from Our Leaders but Don't Get* (Chicago: University of Chicago Press, 2006); Richard Sobel, *The Impact of Public Opinion on U.S. Foreign Policy since Vietnam* (Oxford: Oxford University Press, 2001); Richard Sobel, ed., *Public Opinion in U.S. Foreign Policy: The Controversy over Contra Aid* (Lanham, MD: Rowman and Littlefield Publishers, 1993).

35. Lawrence R. Jacobs and Robert Y. Shapiro, *Politicians Don't Pander: Political Manipulation and the Loss of Democratic Responsiveness* (Chicago: University of Chicago Press, 2000), xv–xvi.

36. A more thorough discussion of the hegemonic role played by journalists as junior partners in the ruling class is explored at length in chapters 4 and 5 of DiMaggio, *When Media Goes to War.*

37. Edward S. Herman, *Triumph of the Market: Essays on Economics, Politics, and the Media* (Boston: South End Press, 1995), 168–69.

38. Ibid.,170.

39. Herman and Chomsky, *Manufacturing Consent*, 2.

40. For further discussion of the propaganda model in other critical research, see Jeffrey Klaehn, ed., *Filtering the News: Essays on Herman and Chomsky's Propaganda Model* (New York: Black Rose Books, 2005); Anthony R. DiMaggio, *Mass Media, Mass Propaganda: Examining American News in the "War on Terror"* (Lanham, MD: Lexington Books, 2008); DiMaggio, *When Media Goes to War*; David Edwards and David Cromwell, *Newspeak in the 21st Century* (London: Pluto Press, 2009); David Edwards and David Cromwell, *Guardians of Power: The Myth of the Liberal Media* (London: Pluto Press, 2006). For a discussion of mainstream scholars systematically ignoring the propaganda model, see Introduction, DiMaggio, *When Media Goes to War.*

41. In running regressions for the filters listed here, I include income and race variables for all models. For my variables covering Evangelism—white versus nonwhite Evangelicals and wealthier versus poorer Evangelicals—I only look at income and race for the Evangelical subset of survey respondents.

42. A multivariate-ordered logistic regression analysis of the July 2009 survey from the Pew Research Center finds that there is a statistically significant relationship between race, sex, religious fundamentalism (Evangelism), education, and political efficacy (voters vs. non-voters) on the one hand, and income on the other hand, after controlling for a variety of other independent variables, including media consumption (Fox News vs. non-Fox viewers), partisanship, ideology, age, religious denomination (Protestant vs. non-Protestant), and church attendance.

43. For a review of the growing power of business ideology in the educational process, see Henry Giroux, *The University in Chains: Confronting the Military Industrial Complex* (Boulder, CO.: Paradigm Publishers, 2007); Jennifer Washburn, *University Inc.: The Corporate Corruption of Higher Education* (New York: Basic Books, 2006); Frank Donoghue, *The Last Professors: The Corporate University and the Fate of the Humanities* (New York: Fordham University Press, 2008); Christopher Newfield, *Unmaking the Public University: The 40-Year Assault on the Middle Class* (Cambridge: Harvard University Press, 2008); Gaye Tuchman, *Wannabe U: Inside the Corporate University* (Chicago: University of Chicago Press, 2009); John K. Wilson, *Patriotic Correctness: Academic Freedom and Its Enemies* (Boulder, CO: Paradigm Publishers, 2008); Derek Bok, *Universities in the Marketplace: The Commercialization of Higher Education* (Princeton: Princeton University Press, 2004).

44. Nolan McCarty, Keith Rosenthal, and Henry Poole, *Polarized America: The Dance of Ideology and Unequal Riches* (Cambridge, MA: MIT Press, 2006).

45. A multivariate-ordered logistic regression analysis finds that there is no statistically significant relationship between partisanship, ideology, and Fox News consumption on the one hand, and income on the other hand, after controlling for a variety of other independent variables addressed in endnote 42.

46. Pew Research Center, "Socialism Not so Negative, Capitalism Not so Positive," May 4, 2010, http://pewresearch.org/pubs/1583/political-rhetoric-capitalism-socialism-militia-family-values-states-rights; Frank Newport, "Socialism Viewed Positively by 36 Percent of Americans," *Gallup.com*, February 4, 2010, www.gallup.com/poll/125645/socialism-viewed-positively-americans.aspx.

47. In analyzing the Pew data, I undertake a multivariate binary logistic regression analysis, controlling for the following variables: race, income, party, ideology, sex, education, religious denomination (Protestants vs. non-Protestants), Evangelism, political efficacy (registered voters vs. non-voters), age, and church attendance. I find that race, income, party, ideology, sex, education, and Evangelism (based on race) are all statistically significant predictors of opinions of either socialism and/or capitalism at the five percent level or lower. Statistical significance refers to the likelihood that a relationship exists between variables that is unlikely to be due to chance variation within the sample of people surveyed.

48. For more on the heavily PR-oriented nature of Obama's victory, see Paul Street, *The Empire's New Clothes: Barack Obama and the Real World of Power* (Boulder, CO.: Paradigm Publishers, 2010), 2–5.

49. William Greider, *Who Will Tell the People: The Betrayal of American Democracy* (New York: Touchstone, 1992), 270.

50. Ibid., 275.

51. For more on the problem of stagnating incomes and growing inequality, see: Jacob S. Hacker and Paul Pierson, *Winner-Take-All Politics: How Washington Made the Rich Richer and Turned Its Back on the Middle Class* (New York: Simon and Schuster, 2010).

1. Don't Call It a Movement

1. James Oliphant and Michael A. Memoli, "Election Surprises Show 'Tea Party' Strength," *Los Angeles Times*, 25 August 2010, www.latimes.com/news/nation-world/nation/la-na-primary-alaska-20100826,0,1966211.story.

2. Kate Zernike, "Shaping Tea Party Passion into Campaign Force," *New York Times*, 26 August 2010, www.nytimes.com/2010/08/26/us/politics/26freedom.html.

3. Kate Zernike, "For G.O.P., Tea Party Wields a Double-Edged Sword," *New York Times*, 6 September 2010, http://www.nytimes.com/2010/09/06/us/politics/06teaparty.html.

4. Liz Sidoti, "Is the Tea Party Becoming the New Grand Old Party?" *Associated Press*, 2 September 2010, http://news.yahoo.com/s/ap/us_tea_party_power.

5. Karen Tumulty, "Christine O'Donnell's Big Win in Delaware Sends Message to Republican Establishment," *Washington Post*, 15 September 2010, www.washingtonpost.com/wp-dyn/content/article/2010/09/15/AR2010091506986.html.

6.   Jane Mayer, "Covert Operations: The Billionaire Brothers Who Are Waging a War Against Obama," *The New Yorker*, 30 August 2010, http://www.newyorker.com/reporting/2010/08/30/100830fa_fact_mayer.

7.   P. J. Gladnick, "New Yorker Publishes Hit Piece Demonizing Koch Brothers for Thought Crime of Supporting Conservative Causes," News Busters/Media Research Center, 23 August 2010, http://newsbusters.org/blogs/p-j-gladnick/2010/08/23/new-yorker-publishes-hit-piece-demonizing-koch-brothers-thought-crime-#ixzz106SelEVq; Frank Rich, "The Billionaires Backing the Tea Party," *New York Times*, 29 August 2010, www.nytimes.com/2010/08/29/opinion/29rich.html; Calvin Trillin, "On Revelations of Where the Secret Funding for the Tea Party Comes From," *The Nation*, 2 September 2010, http://www.thenation.com/article/154451/revelations-where-secret-funding-tea-party-comes.

8.   Jeremy Scahill, "Media Matters with Robert McChesney," *Illinois Public Media*, 18 April 2010, http://will.illinois.edu/mediamatters/show/april-18th-2010/.

9.   Sidney Tarrow, *Power in Movement: Social Movements and Contentious Politics* (Cambridge: Cambridge University Press, 1998), 202.

10. Kate Zernike, *Boiling Mad: Inside Tea Party America* (New York: Times Books, 2010), 1.

11. For more on the growing ideological unity of American political parties, see David W. Rohde, *Parties and Leaders in the Postreform House* (Chicago: University of Chicago Press, 1991); and John H. Aldrich, *Why Parties? The Origin and Transformation of Political Parties in America* (Chicago: University of Chicago Press, 1995). For more on the growing conservatism of the Republican Party, see Keith Poole and Howard Rosenthal, *Ideology and Congress: A Political-Economic History of Roll Call Voting* (New Brunswick, NJ: Transaction Publishers, 2007); Jon R. Bond and Richard Fleischer, eds., *Polarized Politics: Congress and the President in a Partisan Era* (Washington, D.C.: CQ Press, 2000); Jacob S. Hacker and Paul Pierson, *Off Center: The Republican Revolution and the Erosion of American Democracy* (New Haven: Yale University Press, 2005); and Nolan M. McCarthy, Keith Poole, and Howard Rosenthal, *Polarized America: The Dance of Ideology and Unequal Riches* (Cambridge, MA.: MIT Press, 2008).

12. Jeffrey M. Berry, *The Interest Group Society* (New York: Longman, 1997); Christopher J. Bosso, *Environment, Inc.: From Grassroots to Beltway* (Lawrence: University Press of Kansas, 2005); Jack L. Walker, *Mobilizing Interest Groups in America: Patrons, Professions, and Social Movements* (Ann Arbor: University of Michigan Press, 2000); Doug McAdam, *Political Process and the Development of Black Insurgency, 1930–1970* (Chicago: University of Chicago Press, 1999), 114.

13. See Frank Baumgartner, Jeffrey M. Berry, Marie Hojnacki, David C. Kimball, and Beth L. Leech, *Lobbying and Policy Change: Who Wins, Who Loses, and Why* (Chicago: University of Chicago Press, 2009); and David Lowery and Holly Brasher, *Organized Interests and American Government* (New York: McGraw Hill, 2004).

14. For a discussion of business's privileged position, see Charles E. Lindblom, *Politics and Markets: The World's Political-Economic Systems* (New York: Basic

Books, 1977); and E. E. Schattsneider, *The Semi-Sovereign People: A Realist's View of Democracy in America* (Florence, KY: Wadsworth, 1988). For a discussion of the fractured competition between business and other elite interests, see Theodore J. Lowi, *The End of Liberalism Ideology: Policy, and the Crisis of Public Authority* (New York: W. W. Norton, 1969); Baumgartner et al., *Lobbying and Policy Change*; and John P. Heinz, Edward O. Lauman, Robert L. Nelson, and Robert H. Salisbury, *The Hollow Core: Private Interests in National Policy Making* (Cambridge, MA: Harvard University Press, 1997).

15.   For discussions on the rise of unregulated corporate power, the backlash against New Deal liberalism and anti-poverty policies, and the deliberate pro-business bias of the U.S. political system, see Kim Phillips-Fein, *Invisible Hands: The Businessmen's Crusade Against the New Deal* (New York: W. W. Norton, 2009); Robert Pollin, *Contours of Descent: U.S. Economic Fractures and the Landscape of Global Austerity* (London: Verso, 2005); Joel Bakan, *The Corporation: The Pathological Pursuit of Profit and Power* (New York: Free Press, 2004); Charles Derber, *Corporation Nation: How Corporations Are Taking Over Our Lives and What We Can Do About It* (New York: St. Martin's Griffin, 1998); Sheldon Danziger and Peter Gottschalk, *America Unequal* (Cambridge, MA: Harvard University Press, 1995); Herbert J. Gans, *The War Against the Poor: The Underclass and Antipoverty Policy* (New York: Basic Books, 1995); and Carl Boggs, *The End of Politics: Corporate Power and the Decline of the Public Sphere* (New York: Guilford Press, 2000).

16.   Heinz et al., *The Hollow Core*, 1997.

17.   Arthur F. Bentley, *The Process of Government: A Study of Social Pressures* (Cambridge, MA: Harvard University Press, 1965); David B. Truman, *The Governmental Process: Political Interests and Public Opinion* (Berkeley: Institute of Governmental Studies, 1951); Robert A. Dahl, *Who Governs? Democracy and Power in an American City* (New Haven: Yale University Press, 1961).

18.   For more on elite power, see G. William Domhoff, *Who Rules America? Power and Politics* (New York: McGraw Hill, 2002); G. William Domhoff, *The Power Elite and the State: How Policy Is Made in America* (Hawthorne, NY: Aldine de Gruyter, 1990); Floyd Hunter, *Community Power Structure: A Study of Decision Makers* (Chapel Hill: University of North Carolina Press, 1969). For a discussion of the faulty assumptions of equal participation among marginalized groups, see McAdam, *Political Process and the Development of Black Insurgency*.

19.   For more on the theory of a power elite, see C. Wright Mills, *The Power Elite* (Oxford: Oxford University Press, 2000). For more on theories of government dominance by multiple groups of elites, see Lowi, *The End of Liberalism*; and Mancur Olson, *The Logic of Collective Action: Public Goods and the Theory of Groups* (Cambridge, MA: Harvard University Press, 1971).

20.   For more on the dominance of organizing on the part of business groups and professional groups, see David Lowery and Holly Brasher, *Organized Interests and American Government* (New York: McGraw Hill, 2004); and Baumgartner et al., *Lobbying and Policy Change*, 2009. For more on the dominance of business money, see Thomas Ferguson, *Golden Rule: The Investment Theory of*

Party Competition and the Logic of Money-Driven Political Systems (Chicago: University of Chicago Press, 1995); Anthony J. Nownes, *Pressure and Power: Organized Interests in American Politics* (New York: Houghton Mifflin, 2001); and Darrell M. West and Burdett A. Loomis, *The Sound of Money: How Political Interests Get What They Want* (New York: W. W. Norton, 1998).

21. Frank R. Baumgartner and Beth L. Leech, *Basic Interests: The Importance of Groups in Politics and in Political Science* (Princeton: Princeton University Press, 1998), 92.

22. Andrew S. McFarland, *Neopluralism: The Evolution of Political Process Theory* (Lawrence: University Press of Kansas, 2004); and Arthur M. Schlesinger Jr., *The Cycles of American History* (New York: Houghton Mifflin, 1986).

23. Fein, *Invisible Hands*, 2009.

24. The rightward drift of the political system is explored in great detail in chapter 5 of Paul Street and Anthony DiMaggio, *Crashing the Tea Party: Mass Media and the Remaking of American Politics* (Boulder, CO: Paradigm Publishers, 2011).

25. McFarland, *Neopluralism*, 2004; Frank R. Baumgartner and Bryan D. Jones, *Agendas and Instability in American Politics* (Chicago: University of Chicago Press, 1993); Bryan D. Jones and Frank R. Baumgartner, *The Politics of Attention: How Government Prioritizes Problems* (Chicago: University of Chicago Press, 2005); Jeffrey M. Berry, *The New Liberalism: The Rising Power of Citizen Groups* (Washington, D.C.: Brookings Institution Press, 2000); and Walker, *Mobilizing Interest Groups in America*, 2000.

26. Public distrust of government reached 80 percent of the public as of early to mid 2010, as revealed in Derek Thompson, "80 Percent of Americans Don't Trust the Government," *The Atlantic*, 19 April 2010, www.theatlantic.com/business/archive/2010/04/80-percent-of-americans-dont-trust-the-government-heres-why/39148/. Public support for greater regulation of banks and other major financial institutions reached 61 percent by August 2010, and by May 2010, 50 percent said that "financial institutions and Wall Street have too much influence on the Obama administration." For more on both polls, see "USA Today/Gallup Poll," Pollingreport.com, 27–30 August 2010, www.pollingreport.com/business.htm; and "CBS News Poll," Pollingreport.com, 20–24 May 2010, www.pollingreport.com/business.htm.

27. Jacob S. Hacker and Paul Pierson, *Off Center: The Republican Revolution and the Erosion of American Democracy* (New Haven: Yale University Press, 2005), 129–30.

28. Matthew R. Kerbel, *Netroots: Online Progressives and the Transformation of American Politics* (Boulder, CO: Paradigm Publishers, 2009), 47–48.

29. Charles Tilly and Lesley J. Wood, *Social Movements, 1798–2008* (Boulder, CO: Paradigm Publishers, 2009), 3–4.

30. Donatella Della Porta and Mario Diani, *Social Movements: An Introduction,* 1st ed. (Malden, MA: Blackwell Publishing, 1999), 127; Porta and Diani, *Social Movements,* 2nd ed. (2006), 20–21.

31. Porta and Diani, *Social Movements* (2006), 21.

32. One prominent recent example of public support for social movements includes Americans' embrace of antiwar protestors. In 2003 at the onset of the

invasion of Iraq, 64 percent of Americans thought that "Americans who oppose the war should be able to hold protest marches and rallies," while only 27 percent said they thought these protests "hurt the war effort." For more on this, see "CBS News Poll," Pollingreport.com, March 26–27, 2003, http://www.pollingreport.com/iraq12.htm. When asked in 2005 about the antiwar protester Cindy Sheehan, 53 percent of Americans indicated that they "supported what Sheehan was doing" as she camped outside of George Bush's home in Texas, demanding to meet with him after her son was killed in Iraq. For more on this, see "ABC News/Washington Post Poll," Pollingreport.com, August 25–28, 2005, http://www.pollingreport.com/iraq12.htm.

33.   Henry A. Giroux, *The Terror of Neoliberalism: Authoritarianism and the Eclipse of Democracy* (Boulder, CO: Paradigm Publishers, 2004), xiii, xxiii, 105.

34.   Jason Hackworth, *The Neoliberal City: Governance, Ideology, and Development in American Urbanism* (Ithaca, NY: Cornell University, 2007), 11.

35.   A massive literature has developed around the theme that neoliberalism increases poverty and inequality. A sample: Ray Bush, *Poverty and Neoliberalism: Persistence and Reproduction in the Global South* (London: Pluto Press, 2007); Walden Bello, *Dark Victory: The United States, Structural Adjustment, and Global Poverty* (London: Pluto Press, 1994); Noam Chomsky, *Profit Over People: Neoliberalism and Global Order* (New York: Seven Stories Press, 1999); Catherine Caufield, *Masters of Illusion: The World Bank and the Poverty of Nations* (New York: Henry Holt, 1996); Kevin Danaher, ed., *Fifty Years Is Enough: The Case Against the World Bank and the International Monetary Fund* (Cambridge, MA: South End Press, 1994); John Rapley, *Globalization and Inequality: Neoliberalism's Downward Spiral* (Boulder, CO: Lynn Rienner, 2004); Richard Peet, *Unholy Trinity: The IMF, World Bank, and WTO* (London: Zed Books, 2003); John Pilger, *The New Rulers of the World* (London: Verso, 2002); Harold R. Kerbo, *World Poverty: Global Inequality and the Modern World System* (New York: McGraw Hill, 2006); Alfredo Saad-Filho and Deborah Johnston, *Neoliberalism: A Critical Reader* (London: Pluto Press, 2005).

36.   Ayn Rand, Nathaniel Brandan, Alan Greenspan, and Robert Hessen, *Capitalism: The Unknown Ideal* (New York: Signet, 1986), 271, 291.

37.   Ibid., 291–303.

38.   Ayn Rand, *The Virtue of Selfishness: A New Concept of Egoism, Centennial Edition* (New York: Signet, 1964), 103, 120, 119.

39.   Ibid., 147–57.

40.   Krissah Thompson and Dan Balz, "Rand Paul Comments About Civil Rights Stir Controversy," *Washington Post*, 21 May 2010, http://www.washington-post.com/wp-dyn/content/article/2010/05/20/AR2010052003500.html.

41.   Ayn Rand, *The Fountainhead* (New York: Plume, 2005), 600.

42.   Johann Hari, "The Last Person on Earth to Turn to Now Is Ayn Rand," Huffington Post, 10 March 2009, http://www.huffingtonpost.com/johann-hari/the-last-person-on-earth_b_173535.html.

43.   Boggs, *The End of Politics*, 103.

44.   Heidi Przybyla, "Tea Party Advocates Who Scorn Socialism Want a Government Job," *Bloomberg News*, March 25, 2010, www.bloomberg.com/apps/news?pid=newsarchive&sid=aLBZwxqgYgwI.

45. Zernike, *Boiling Mad*, 4–5.

46. Kate Zernike, "For G.O.P., Tea Party Wields a Double-Edged Sword," *New York Times*, 5 September 2010, http://www.nytimes.com/2010/09/06/us/politics/06teaparty.html.

47. Zernike, *Boiling Mad*, 5, 52, 96–97.

48. Will Bunch, *The Backlash: Right-Wing Radicals, High-Def Hucksters, and Paranoid Politics in the Age of Obama* (New York: Harper, 2010), xi–xii, 337–38.

49. Scott Rasmussen and Douglas Schoen, *Mad as Hell: How the Tea Party Movement Is Fundamentally Remaking Our Two-Party System* (New York: Harper, 2010), 3–5. More information on the discredited numbers Rasmussen and Schoen draw on from the Media Research Center is provided in chapter 5 of this book.

50. Ibid., 3–5, 240–41, 145–50.

51. There were no national estimates of Tea Party turnout in the April 15, 2010, Tax Day rallies. As a result, I was forced to come up with our own figure, by analyzing the Wikipedia list that aggregated all the local protests and provided numbers for each.

52. A compiled list of Tea Party events for the 2010 Tax Day protest is difficult to find. The only source available—which I consulted for my study—was a list provided by Wikipedia covering local towns that claimed significant turnouts. The list is available at: http://en.wikipedia.org/wiki/List_of_Tea_Party_protests,_2010.

53. The national Tea Party Patriots website provides information on local chapters, which I examined, in addition to links to individual chapter websites, which I also examined when assessing Chicago metropolitan Tea Party activism.

54. CNN, "CNN/Opinion Research Corporation Poll, April 9–11, 2010," Pollingreport.com, 2010, http://www.pollingreport.com/politics.htm.

55. My estimates are again drawn from the Wikipedia list of April 15, 2010, protests across the country.

56. Cynthia Dizikes, "Tea Partiers Rally, Plan for Bigger Role," *Chicago Tribune*, 15 April 2010, http://articles.chicagotribune.com/2010-04-15/news/ct-met-tax-day-tea-party-chicagoland-rall20100415_1_tea-party-rallies-tax-day.

57. Selim Algar and Jennifer Fermino, "NY Is Tea Party Country," *New York Post*, 16 April 2010, http://www.nypost.com/p/news/local/ny_is_tea_party_country_8RotVz2MdWvavncfcMJKxK.

58. Reid Forgrave, "Tea Party Rally Turnout Less than Hoped For," *Des Moines Register*, 15 April 2010, http://blogs.desmoinesregister.com/dmr/index.php/2010/04/15/tea-party-rally-turnout-less-than-hoped-for/; Kathleen Hennessey, "Tax Day 'Tea Parties' Draw Thousands across U.S.," *Los Angeles Times*, 15 April 2010, http://articles.latimes.com/2010/apr/16/nation/la-na-tea-party-protests16-2010apr16/2; "Tea Party Protests Descend on D.C. with New 'Contract From America,'" FoxNews.com, 15 April 2010, www.foxnews.com/politics/2010/04/15/tea-party-protesters-descend-dc-new-contract-america/.

59. The Morton Grove Tea Party took place in St. Paul Woods, Morton Grove, on September 12, 2010, and was heavily organized by local Tea Party chapters.

60. Dante Chinni, "The Tea Party: How Big Is It?" *Patchwork Nation/Christian Science Monitor*, 21 April 2010, http://patchworknation.org/content/tea-party-how-big-is-it-and-where-is-it-based/.

61. Stephanie Mencimer, "Tea Party 'LibertyXPO' Fail," *Mother Jones*, 10 September 2010, http://motherjones.com/mojo/2010/09/tea-party-liberty-xpo-fail; Evan McMorris-Santoro, "Vegas Hotel: The Tea Party Convention Is Cancelled," TalkingPointsMemo, 20 September 2010, http://tpmdc.talking-pointsmemo.com/2010/09/did-the-second-tea-party-unity-convention-crash-and-burn.php.

62. Evan McMorris-Santoro, "Tea Party's 9/12 Rally Looking Much, Much Smaller than Last Year's," Talking Points Memo,12 September 2010, http://tpmdc.talkingpointsmemo.com/2010/09/tea-partys-912-rally-looking-much-much-smaller-than-last-years.php.

63. Christina Bellantoni, "Tea Party Convention Postponed—Vegas in July Is Too Hot!" TalkingPointsMemo, 28 June 2010, http://tpmdc.talkingpointsmemo.com/2010/06/tea-party-convention-postponed.php; Evan McMorris-Santoro, "Vegas Hotel: The Tea Party Convention Is Canceled," TalkingPointsMemo, 20 September 2010, http://tpmdc.talkingpointsmemo.com/2010/09/did-the-second-tea-party-unity-convention-crash-and-burn.php.

64. Ed Pilkington, "Prejudice and Principle Brew as Tea Party Meet," *Guardian*, 6 February 2010, www.guardian.co.uk/world/2010/feb/05/tea-party-united-states.

65. Mencimer, "Tea Party 'LibertyXPO' Fail."

66. "Turnout Strong as Beck Rallies to Restore 'Honor' to the Nation," FoxNews.com, 28 August 2010, www.foxnews.com/politics/2010/ 08/28/thousands-expected-glenn-beck-rally-civil-rights-leaders-protest-event/.

67. Lee Fang, "The Tea Party Profiteers: How Republican Operatives Are Exploiting Economic Anxiety for Power, Cash," ThinkProgress, 2 February 2010, http://thinkprogress.org/2010/02/02/tea-party-profiteers/.

68. For an example of the obscurity of the 1776 Tea Party Patriots, see the Illinois website for the group: http://www.teaparty.org/illinoisteaparty.html.

69. The various subgroups of the Tea Party discussed in this chapter are acknowledged by others who have studied the phenomenon. For more, see Leonard Zeskind, "Excerpt from My Presentation to the NAACP National Convention," LeonardZeskind.com, 11 July 2010, http://www.leonardzeskind.com/index.php?option=com_content&view=article&id=81:excerpt-from-my-presentation-to-the-naacp-national-convention&catid=21:articles-op-eds-etc&Itemid=35.

70. "Tea Party Leader Says He's Done Talking about Race Controversy," CNN.com, 18 July 2010, http://articles.cnn.com/2010-07-18/politics/tea.party.imbroglio_1_national-tea-party-federation-naacp-resolution-racist-elements?_s=PM:POLITICS.

71. To learn more about Resistnet/Patriot Action Network and their local activism, visit their website: http://www.patriotactionnetwork.com

72. All of these statistics are derived from simple examinations of membership in Resistnet/Patriot Action Network for each precinct, as compared to the entire population of the major cities in those precincts.

73. I attended these meetings during the spring, summer, and fall of 2010.

74. For more, see chapter 6 in Paul Street and Anthony DiMaggio, *Crashing the Tea Party: Mass Media and the Remaking of American Politics* (Boulder, CO: Paradigm Publishers, 2011).

75. Lee Fang, "Right-Wing Harassment Strategy against Dems Detailed in Memo," ThinkProgress, 31 July 2009, http://thinkprogress.org/2009/07/ 31/recess-harassment-memo/; Steve Inskeep, "Is the Tea Party Really a Grassroots Movement?" *National Public Radio*, 17 September 2010, http://www.npr.org/templates/story/story.php?storyId=129926390; Stephanie Condon, "Freedom Works 'Apology' Takes Aim at Liberal Critics," CBS News.com, 12 August 2009, http://www.cbsnews.com/8301-503544_162-5237285-503544.html.

76. For the details on Dick Armey's voting record, see the *Washington Post*'s voting database at: http://projects.washingtonpost.com/congress/members/a000217/.

77. Media Matters for America, "CBS, Fox Reports on Town Hall Disruptions Ignore Conservative Strategy," 5 August 2009, http://mediamatters.org/research/200908050017.

78. Beau Hodai, "Secrets of the Tea Party: The Troubling History of Tea Party Leader Dick Armey," *In These Times*, 21 March 2010, http://www.inthese-times.com/article/5698/secrets_of_the_tea_party/; "Dick Armey Calls Medicare Tyranny," Politico, 16 August 2009, http://www.politico.com/blogs/politicolive/0809/Dick_Armey_calls_Medicare_tyranny.html.

79. For more information on Bachmann's campaign contributors, see her profile at the Center for Responsive Politics at www.opensecrets.org/politicians/industries.php?cycle=2010&cid=N00027493&type=I.

80. "Anti-Socialist Bachmann Got $250K in Federal Farm Subsidies," Politico, 22 December 2009, www.politico.com/blogs/glennthrush/1209/Antisocialist_Bachmann_got_250k_in_federal_farm_subsidies.html.

81. "Bachmann Responds to Democratic Attempts to Infiltrate Tea Party Movement," FoxNews.com, 11 August 2010, http://www.foxnews.com/on-air/hannity/transcript/bachmann-responds-democrats039-attempts-infiltrate-tea-party-movement.

82. Stephanie Condon, "Poll: Tea Party Supporters View Palin, Beck, and Bush Favorably," CBS News.com, 14 April 2010, http://www.cbsnews.com/8301-503544_162-20002534-503544.html.

83. For more on McCain and Palin's campaign contributions and her support for oil drilling, see their 2008 presidential profile and donors at the Center for Responsive Politics at http://www.opensecrets.org/pres08/indus.php?cycle=2008&cid=n00006424; and see Massie Ritsch, "The Money behind Palin," Center for Responsive Politics, 29 August 2008, www.opensecrets.org/news/2008/08/the-money-behind-palin-1.html.

84. David Corn, "Sarah Palin: Wall Street Bailout Hypocrite," *Mother Jones*, November 18, 2010, http://motherjones.com/politics/2010/11/sarah-palin-wall-street-bailout-tarp.

85. Matt Gertz, "More on the Fox-Pushed Tea Party Express Scam," Media Matters for America, 14 April 2010, http://mediamatters.org/blog/201004140045; Kenneth P. Vogel, "G.O.P. Operatives Crash the Tea Party,"

Politico, 14 April 2010, http://dyn.politico.com/printstory.cfm?uuid=FA90462A-18FE-70B2-A8C4C7D0CC493FF2.

86. Zachary Roth, "Tea Party Dilemma: To GOP or Not to GOP," TalkingPointsMemo, 22 January 2010, http://tpmmuckraker.talking-pointsmemo.com/2010/01/tea_party_dilemma_to_gop_or_not_to_gop.php.

87. To see the Tea Party's Contract From America, visit http://www.thecontract.org/the-contract-from-america/.

88. Jane Hamsher, "Corporate Lobbyists Raising Money for Tea Parties," FiredogLake.com, 13 April 2009, http://firedoglake.com/2009/04/13/corporate-lobyists-raising-money-for-tea-parties/.

89. Zachary Roth, "Tea Party Leader Was Involved with G.O.P.-Tied Political Firm," TalkingPointsMemo, 2 March 2010, http://tpmmuckraker.talking-pointsmemo.com/2010/03/tea_party_leader_was_involved_with_political_firm.php.

90. Bob Williams and Kevin Bogardus, "Koch's Low Profile Belies Political Power," Center for Public Integrity, 15 July 2004, http://projects.publicintegrity.org/oil//report.aspx?aid=347. For more information on Koch Industries campaign contributions to Republicans, see the data at the Center for Responsive Politics at http://www.opensecrets.org/industries/indus.php?ind=e01#.

91. Michael Scherer, "It's Tea Time: A Conservative Revolt Is Shaking Up the Republican Party Nationwide," *Time*, 27 September, 2010, 27–28.

92. "South Dakota Congressional Races in 2010," Center for Responsive Politics, 2010, http://www.opensecrets.org/races/election.php?state=SD; "Incumbent Advantage," Center for Responsive Politics, 2010, http://www.opensecrets.org/overview/incumbs.php?cycle=2010&Type=A&Party=S.

93. "Total Raised and Spent: New Jersey Congressional Race District 06," Center for Responsive Politics, www.opensecrets.org/races/summary.php?id=NJ06&cycle=2010.

94. "Total Raised and Spent: 2010 Race: Delaware Senate," Center for Responsive Politics, 2010, www.opensecrets.org/races/summary.php?id=DES2&cycle=2010.

95. "Total Raised and Spent: 2010 Race: Utah Senate," Center for Responsive Politics, 2010, www.opensecrets.org/races/summary.php?id=UTS2&cycle=2010; "Robert F. Bennett," Center for Responsive Politics, 2010, http://www.opensecrets.org/politicians/summary.php?type=C&cid=N00006347&newMem=N&cycle=2010.

96. "Total Raised and Spent: 2010 Race: Alaska Senate," Center for Responsive Politics, 2010, www.opensecrets.org/races/summary.php?id=AKS2&cycle=2010; "Lisa Murkowski," Center for Responsive Politics, 2010, http://www.opensecrets.org/politicians/summary.php?cid=n00026050.

97. "2009 Congressional Voting Record," Americans for Democratic Action, Spring 2010, http://www.adaction.org/media/votingrecords/2009.pdf.

98. Ibid.

99. Jeffrey M. Jones, "Debt, Government Power among Tea Party Supporters' Top Concerns," Gallup, 5 July 2010, http://www.gallup.com/poll/141119/debt-gov-power-among-tea-party-supporters-top-concerns.aspx.

100. Lisa Lerer, "Poll: Tea Party Economic Gloom Fuels Republican Momentum,"

Bloomberg News, 13 October 2010, http://www.bloomberg.com/news/2010-10-14/tea-party-s-economic-gloom-fuels-republican-election-momentum-poll-says.html.

101. John M. O'Hara, *A New American Tea Party: The Counterrevolution against Bailouts, Handouts, Reckless Spending, and More Taxes* (Hoboken, NJ: Wiley, 2010), 81, 100; Rasmussen and Schoen, *Mad as Hell*, 280.

102. See chapter 4 of Gary C. Jacobson and Samuel Kernell, *Strategy and Choice in Congressional Elections* (New Haven: Yale University Press, 1983); Edward R. Tufte, "Determinants of the Outcomes of Congressional Midterm Elections," *American Political Science Review* 69 (1975): 812–26.

103. Zernike, *Boiling Mad*, 39.

104. The numbers provided here that address Tea Party Caucus campaign contributions were compiled by examining the individual profiles of Tea Party members at the Center for Responsive Politics website.

105. "Business-Labor Ideology Split in PAC and Individual Donations and Parties," Center for Responsive Politics, 2010, www.opensecrets.org/overview/blio.php.

106. Again, figures for each candidate's reliance on business PACs were compiled by examining candidates' individual profiles at the Center for Responsive Politics website.

107. Andrew Kreighbaum, "Tea Party Caucus Members Bankrolled by Health Professionals, Retirees, and Oil Interests," Center for Responsive Politics, July 30, 2010, http://www.opensecrets.org/news/2010/07/members-of-tea-party-caucus-major-r.html.

108. For a discussion of the origins of the housing crisis, financialization of the economy, and economic deregulation as the impetus for the 2008 economic collapse, see Richard Bitner, *Confessions of a Subprime Lender: An Insider's Tale of Greed, Fraud, and Ignorance* (Hoboken, NJ: 2008); Dean Baker, *False Profits: Recovering from the Bubble Economy* (Sausalito, CA: PoliPointPress, 2010); Dean Baker, *Plunder and Blunder: The Rise and Fall of the Bubble Economy* (Sausalito, CA: PoliPointPress, 2009); Danny Schechter, *Plunder: Investigating Our Economic Calamity and the Subprime Scandal* (New York: Cosimo, 2010); Les Leopold, *The Looting of America: How Wall Street's Game of Fantasy Finance Destroyed Our Jobs, Pensions, and Prosperity* (White River Junction, VT: Chelsea Green Publishing, 2009); Graham Turner, *The Credit Crunch: Housing Bubbles, Globalisation, and the Worldwide Economic Crisis* (London: Pluto, 2008); and Joseph E. Stiglitz, *Freefall: America, Free Markets, and the Sinking of the World Economy* (New York: W. W. Norton, 2010). For a discussion of the larger economic forces under capitalism driving the modern crisis, see John Bellamy Foster and Fred Magdoff, *The Great Financial Crisis: Causes and Consequences* (New York: Monthly Review Press, 2009); Fred Magdoff and Michael D. Yates, *The ABCs of the Economic Crisis: What Working People Need to Know* (New York: Monthly Review Press, 2009).

109. Felicia Sonmez and Paul Farhi, "Christine O'Donnell Fights Back at Values Voter Summit," *Washington Post*, 18 September 2010, http://www.washingtonpost.com/wp-dyn/content/article/2010/09/17/AR2010091706766.html; Damian Paletta, "Castle's Defeat: The TARP Curse?" *Wall Street Journal*, 14

September 2010, http://blogs.wsj.com/washwire/2010/09/14/castles-defeat-the-tarp-curse/.

110. Amanda Terkel, "Joe Miller Gains Attention as Alaska's Tea Party Insurgent," Huffington Post, 23 August 2010, www.huffingtonpost.com/2010/08/23/joe-miller-alaska-senate_n_691796.html; Alexandra Gutierrez, "Sarah Palin's Tea Party," Slate.com, 25 August 2010, http://www.slate.com/id/2265056/; Paletta, "Castle's Defeat," 2010.

111. Amy Gardner, "Tea Party Wins Victory in Utah as Incumbent GOP Senator Loses His Bid for Nomination," *Washington Post*, 9 May 2010, www.washing-tonpost.com/wp-dyn/content/article/2010/05/08/AR2010050803430.html.

112. For a thorough discussion, see Street and DiMaggio, *Crashing the Tea Party*.

113. I conducted a multivariate binary logistic regression analysis for every candidate running in the 2010 midterms, including as independent variables each candidate's status as a Democrat/non-Democrat, as a Republican/non-Republican, as a third partier/non-third partier, as a Tea Party/non–Tea Party candidate, while also including variables measuring candidates' levels of campaign contributions and whether they were incumbents/non-incumbents. My dependent variable measured whether each candidate won or lost their respective races. After controlling for all of these factors, I find that only two variables are statistically significant—that is, the observed relationship is not likely due to chance—and that is in the level of campaign contributions and incumbency. In other words, being an incumbent, or having larger levels of campaign contributions, were statistically more likely to contribute to an electoral victory or defeat, whereas being a Democrat, Republican, Tea Partier, or third partier were no more likely to contribute to a win or loss. The incumbency variable is statistically significant at the .01 percent level, and the campaign contributions variable is significant at the 1 percent level.

114. "House Vote on Passage: H.R. 4577, Consolidated Appropriations Act, 2001," GovTrack.us, 14 June 2000, www.govtrack.us/congress/vote.xpd?vote=h2000-273.

115. "House Vote on Conference Report: S. 900, Gramm-Leach-Bliley Act," GovTrack.us, 4 November 1999, www.govtrack.us/congress/vote.xpd?vote=h1999-570.

2. The Tea Party Does Not Exist

Both authors of this chapter were responsible for the observation of the Tea Party, particularly as related to rallies, PR events, and other public meetings. Paul Street was responsible for human-subject-related data gathering, as related to interviewing Tea Partiers and attending weekly meetings of specific chapters.

1. Dante Chinni, "Tea Party Mapped: How Big Is It and Where Is It Based?" *PBS NewsHour*, April 21, 2010, http://www.pbs.org/newshour/rundown/2010/04/tea-party-how-big-is-it-and-where-is-it-based.html.

2. We have been involved in the social movements discussed here at a variety of levels, including through activism and observation of local Midwest chapters (those throughout Chicago and central Illinois), and involvement in national organizing through Washington-based protests taking place throughout the 2000 to 2010 period.

3. For a more detailed discussion, see Anthony DiMaggio, "A Post-Election Retrospective: Tackling Neoliberal Doomsday Propaganda," *Z Magazine*, November 14, 2010, www.zcommunications.org/a-post-election-retrospective-by-anthony-dimaggio.

4. Stephanie Condon, "What's Obama Doing to Your Taxes?" CBS News, April 15, 2010, www.cbsnews.com/8301-503544_162-20002548-503544.html

5. Socialism, as widely understood on the left, refers to either government or worker ownership of the means of production. Neither of these conditions was fulfilled during the early years of the Obama administration. Contrary to right-wing depictions of the GM bailout as "socialism," reporting of the event demonstrated that the initiative was a simple example of corporate welfare and taxpayer-funded bailout of the American business elite. These points are described in more detail in chapter 5 of Paul Street and Anthony DiMaggio, *Crashing the Tea Party: Mass Media and the Campaign to Remake American Politics* (Boulder, CO: Paradigm Publishers, 2011).

6. Heidi Przybyla, "Tea Party Advocates Who Scorn Socialism Want a Government Job," Bloomberg News, March 26, 2010, www.bloomberg.com/apps/news?pid=newsarchive&sid=aLBZwxqgYgwI.

7. "National Survey of Tea Party Supporters," CBS–*New York Times* poll, April 5–12, 2010, http://documents.nytimes.com/new-york-timescbs-news-poll-national-survey-of-tea-party-supporters.

8. For all of the polling data in this paragraph, see ibid.

9. John Harwood, "53 Percent in U.S. Say Free Trade Hurts Nation," CNBC, September 28, 2010, http://www.cnbc.com/id/39407846/53_in_US_Say_Free_Trade_Hurts_Nation_NBC_WSJ_Poll.

10. CBS–*New York Times*, "National Survey of Tea Party Supporters," April 5–12, 2010.

11. Ibid.

12. "Polling the Tea Party," CBS–*New York Times*, April 14, 2010, www.nytimes.com/interactive/2010/04/14/us/politics/20100414-tea-party-poll-graphic.html.

13. To view Palin's entire speech, see www.youtube.com/watch?v=E7gVp3diPbI.

14. Jennifer Parker, "Palin in Spotlight: 'Average Hockey Mom' Slams Obama's 'Change' Mantra," ABCnews.com, 3 September 2008, http://abcnews.go.com/Politics/Conventions/story?id=5718030.

15. Dick Armey, "Dick Armey and the Tea Party Movement: A New Majority?" *Washington Post*, February 8, 2010, http://www.washingtonpost.com/wp-dyn/content/discussion/2010/02/05/DI2010020503095.html.

16. Ibid.

17. CBS–*New York Times*, "Polling the Tea Party," April 14, 2010 .

18. John O'Hara, *A New American Tea Party: The Counterrevolution against Bailouts, Reckless Spending, and More Taxes* (Hoboken, NJ: Wiley, 2010).

19. Ibid., 249–50.

20. Ibid., 250.

21. Anthony DiMaggio, "The More You Watch, the Less You Know," CounterPunch, July 29, 2009, http://www.counterpunch.org/dimaggio07292009.html; Anthony DiMaggio, "Boons for Business," MR Zine, March 25, 2010, http://mrzine.month-lyreview.org/2010/dimaggio250310.html; Anthony DiMaggio, "The Empathy

Problem," *Z Magazine*, March 18, 2010, http://www.zcommunications.org/the-empathy-problem-poverty-privilege-and-health-care-reform-by-anthony-dimaggio; Anthony DiMaggio, "A Distorted Debate," *Z Magazine*, July 21, 2009, http://zcommunications.org/a-distorted-debate-by-anthony-dimaggio.

22. Reed Abelson, "In healthcare Overhaul, Boons for Hospitals, Drug Makers," *New York Times*, March 21, 2010, http://www.nytimes.com/2010/03/22/business/22bizhealth.html.

23. Frances Fox Piven and Richard A. Cloward, *Poor People's Movements: Why They Succeed, How They Fail* (New York, Vintage, 1978), xv, 36.

24. All of the national protests of left-leaning groups we attended over the years were characterized by a strong presence of national and regional but especially local groups, which were most evident in tabling activities and leaflets/pamphlets handed out by these groups.

25. Jeffrey S. Juris, *Networking Futures: The Movements against Corporate Globalization* (Durham, NC: Duke University Press, 2008), xxv, 31–38.

26. Ibid., 31.

27. Freedom Works, "9–12 Taxpayer March on Washington D.C.—2010," Freedom Works, http://www.freedomworks.org/912-taxpayer-march-on-washington-2010; Zernike, *Boiling Mad*, 2010, 35.

28. Quinnipiac, "Tea Party Could Hurt GOP in Congressional Races," Quinnipiac, March 24, 2010 www.quinnipiac.edu/x1295.xml?ReleaseID=1436; "CNN-Opinion Poll Research," CNN, 17 February 2010, http://i2.cdn.urner.com/cnn/2010/ images/02/17/rel4b.pdf; Pew Research Center, "Midterm Election Challenges for Both Parties," February 2010, http://people-press.org/dataarchive/. Information from the Pew Research Center on Tea Party partisanship is drawn from the February 2010 Pew Research poll, which is available for download at the Pew Center's website under the "data sets" subsection.

29. Rasmussen and Schoen, *Mad as Hell*, 4–15; Zernike, *Boiling Mad*, 5.

30. Zernike, *Boiling Mad*, 41–43.

31. "CNN–Opinion Poll Research," 17 February 2010.

32. Chinni, "Tea Party Mapped."

33. Andrew S. McFarland, *Boycotts and Dixie Chicks: Creative Political Participation at Home and Abroad* (Boulder, CO: Paradigm Publishers, 2010).

3. The Counter-Revolution Will Be Televised

1. Anderson Cooper, *Anderson Cooper 360 Degrees*, CNN, November 3, 2010.

2. For a further exploration, see Paul Street and Anthony DiMaggio, *Crashing the Tea Party: Mass Media and the Remaking of American Politics* (Boulder, CO.: Paradigm Publishers, 2011).

3. In chapter 6 I discuss in more detail how public opinion supported specific provisions of Democratic policies in terms of the stimulus and healthcare reform. This support belies alleged public opposition to the Obama administration's agenda.

4. Chris Matthews, *Hardball with Chris Matthews*, MSNBC, November 3, 2010.

5. See the postscript of Street and DiMaggio, *Crashing the Tea Party*.

6.   Kate Zernike, "Tea Party Comes to Power on an Unclear Mandate," *New York Times*, November 2, 2010, www.nytimes.com/2010/11/03/us/politics/03repubs.html.

7.   Katie Couric, *CBS Evening News*, November 3, 2010; see also the postscript of: Street and DiMaggio, *Crashing the Tea Party*.

8.   Dan Balz, "Republicans Ride the Tea Party Tiger," *Washington Post*, September 15, 2010, www.washingtonpost.com/wp-dyn/content/article/2010/09/15/AR2010091503387.html.

9.   Andrea Mitchell, *NBC Today*, November 3, 2010; Ross Douthat, "The Tea Party Giveth . . . " *New York Times*, November 3, 2010, http://douthat.blogs.nytimes.com/2010/11/03/the-tea-party-giveth/.

10.   "After the Election Victories, Tea Party Activists Look Ahead to 2012," Fox News, November 5, 2010, http://www.foxnews.com/politics/2010/11/05/election-victories-tea-party-activists-look-ahead/.

11.   Howard Zinn, *A People's History of the United States* (New York: Perennial, 1999), 629.

12.   Edward S. Herman and David Peterson, *The Politics of Genocide* (New York: Monthly Review Press, 2010); Edward S. Herman and Noam Chomsky, *Manufacturing Consent: The Political Economy of the Mass Media* (New York: Pantheon, 1988); Noam Chomsky and Edward S. Herman, *The Washington Connection and Third World Fascism: The Political Economy of Human Rights*, vol. 1 (Boston: South End Press, 1979); Noam Chomsky and Edward S. Herman, *After the Cataclysm: Postwar Indochina and the Reconstruction of Imperial Ideology: The Political Economy of Human Rights*, vol. 2 (Boston, South End Press, 1979).

13.   Maxwell McCombs, *Setting the Agenda: The Mass Media and Public Opinion* (Cambridge: Polity Press, 2006); James W. Dearing and Everett M. Rogers, *Agenda Setting* (Thousand Oaks, CA: Sage, 1996); David L. Protess and Maxwell McCombs, eds., *Agenda Setting: Readings on Media, Public Opinion, and Policymaking* (Mahwah, NJ: Lawrence Erlbaum Associates, 1991). For more on framing, see Robert M. Entman, *Projections of Power: Framing News, Public Opinion, and U.S. Foreign Policy* (Chicago: University of Chicago Press, 2004); Karen S. Johnson-Cartee, *News Narratives and News Framing: Constructing Political Reality* (Lanham, MD.: Rowman and Littlefield, 2004); Pippa Norris, Montague Kern, and Marion Just, eds., *Framing Terrorism: The News Media, the Government, and the Public* (London: Routledge, 2003); Diana Kendall, *Framing Class: Media Representations of Wealth and Poverty in America* (Lanham, MD.: Rowman and Littlefield, 2005); Nicholas J. G. Winter, *Dangerous Frames: How Ideas about Race and Gender Shape Public Opinion* (Chicago: University of Chicago Press, 2008); Karen Callaghan and Frauke Schnell, eds., *Framing American Politics* (Pittsburgh: University of Pittsburgh Press, 2005); Shanto Iyengar and Donald R. Kinder, *News that Matters: Television and American Opinion* (Chicago: University of Chicago Press, 1987); Shanto Iyengar, *Is Anyone Responsible? How Television Frames Political Issues* (Chicago: University of Chicago Press, 1991). For more on how the media influence how people think about issues, see Iyengar, *Is Anyone Responsible?*. For more on how the media influence people's political opin-

ions, see Anthony R. DiMaggio, *When Media Goes to War: Hegemonic Discourse, Public Opinion, and the Limits of Dissent* (New York: Monthly Review Press, 2010); and chapter 6 of this book.

14. Kathleen Parker, "The Tea Party's Allegiance to No One," *Washington Post*, May 5, 2010, www.washingtonpost.com/wp-dyn/content/article/2010/05/04/AR2010050404051.html.

15. Charles Krauthammer, "What Scott Brown's Win Means for the Democrats," *Washington Post*, January 22, 2010, http://www.washingtonpost.com/wp-dyn/content/article/2010/01/21/AR2010012103500.html.

16. David Brooks, "The Government War," *New York Times*, April 22, 2010, http://www.nytimes.com/2010/04/23/opinion/23brooks.html.

17. Peggy Noonan, "Try a Little Tenderness," *Wall Street Journal*, July 30, 2010, http://online.wsj.com/article/SB10001424052748703578104575397671235195094.html.

18. Editorial, "Bubba's Blame Game," *New York Post*, April 20, 2010, http://www.nypost.com/p/news/opinion/editorials/bubba_blame_game_0YY4L31zGcbTUceySRR75L.

19. Editorial, "Crashing the Tea Party," *Washington Times*, April 14, 2010, http://www.washingtontimes.com/news/2010/apr/14/crashing-the-tea-party/.

20. "Report: 'Fair and Balanced' Fox News Aggressively Promotes 'Tea Party' Protests," Media Matters for America, April 8, 2009, http://mediamatters.org/reports/200904080025.

21. John Halpin, James Heidbreder, Mark Lloyd, Paul Woodhull, Ben Scott, Josh Silver, and S. Derek Turner, "The Structural Imbalance of Political Talk Radio," Center for American Progress, June 20, 2007, http://www.americanprogress.org/issues/2007/06/talk_radio.html; Pew Research Center, "Americans Spending More Time Following the News," 12 September 2010, http://pewresearch.org/pubs/1725/where-people-get-news-print-online-readership-cable-news-viewers.

22. Rush Limbaugh, "Bill Clinton Links Talk Radio, Tea Parties to Non-Existent Terrorism," April 16, 2010, www.rushlimbaugh.com/home/daily/site_041610/content/01125108.guest.html.

23. "Limbaugh: Tea Party Is 'The First Time' that 'Everyday Citizens' Have 'Risen Up' Since the Civil War," Media Matters for America, April 19, 2010, http://mediamatters.org/mmtv/201004190043.

24. Sean Hannity, *Hannity*, Fox News, on April 16, 2010; April 9, 2010; April 12, 2010; April 7, 2010; April 8, 2010; and Rich Lowry, *Hannity*, Fox News, April 2, 2010.

25. Bill O'Reilly, *The O'Reilly Factor*, Fox News, April 16, 2010 and February 16, 2010.

26. CBS–*New York Times*, "Polling the Tea Party," *New York Times*, April 14, 2010, www.nytimes.com/interactive/2010/04/14/us/politics/20100414-tea-party-poll-graphic.html.

27. Glenn Beck, "Tea Party at Critical Stage," GlennBeck.com, July 26, 2010, www.glennbeck.com/content/articles/article/198/43454/. Emphasis added.

28. All statistics in this chapter that pertain to the volume of stories and the number of television programs on the Tea Party are based upon keyword searches in the LexisNexis academic database.

29. Scott Rasmussen and Douglas Schoen, *Mad as Hell: How the Tea Party Movement Is Fundamentally Remaking Our Two-Party System* (New York: Harper, 2010), 132.

30. For methodological clarity, stories are defined in this study for television outlets as any individual programs mentioning the Tea Party. For print news, stories are defined to include any articles in newspapers, such as national and metropolitan news stories, op-eds, editorials, letters, and business stories.

31. Naftali Bendavid, "Tea Party Activists Complicate Republican Comeback Strategy," *Wall Street Journal*, October 16, 2009, http://online.wsj.com/article/SB125564976279388879.html.

32. "Tea Party Movement," *New York Times*, May 21, 2010, http://topics.nytimes.com/top/reference/timestopics/subjects/t/tea_party_movement/index.html; Kate Zernike, "Disputes Among Tea Party Groups Are Taking a Toll on February Convention," *New York Times*, January 26, 2010; Kate Zernike, "Convention Is Trying to Harness Tea Party Spirit," *New York Times*, February 6, 2010.

33. Marc A. Thiessen, "Will a Tea Partier Save Harry Reid's Job?" *Washington Post*, March 30, 2010, http://www.washingtonpost.com/wp-dyn/content/article/2010/03/29/AR2010032901333.html; Philip Rucker, "Fractious First Tea Party Convention Gets Underway," *Washington Post*, February 5, 2010. Emphasis added.

34. Jon Meacham, "How the Tea Party Could Help All of Us," *Newsweek*, February 15, 2010, 4.

35. David Von Drehle, "Why the Tea Party Movement Matters," *Time*, February 18, 2010, www.time.com/time/politics/article/0,8599,1964903,00.html.

36. Paul Bedard, "Media Cheers Obama, Ignores Tea Party Movement," *U.S. News and World Report*, April 13, 2010, http://politics.usnews.com/news/washington-whispers/articles/2010/04/13/media-cheers-obama-ignores-tea-party-movement.html.

37. Rich Noyes, "MRC Special Report: How the Media Have Dismissed and Disparaged the Tea Party Movement," Media Research Center, April 13, 2010, http://newsbusters.org/?q=blogs/rich-noyes/2010/04/13/mrc-special-report-how-media-have-dismissed-and-disparaged-tea-party-mov.

38. Katie Couric, *CBS Evening News*, April 14, 2010; Brian Williams, *NBC Nightly News*, April 15, 2010; Diane Sawyer, *ABC World News*, April 15, 2010.

39. The criteria for concluding that these protests were part of social movements is described in more detail in chapter 4. Data for the turnouts at the protests discussed in Table 5.1 was drawn from the following sources: John Vidal, "Farmer Commits Suicide at Protests," *Guardian*, September 11, 2003, www.guardian.co.uk/world/2003/sep/11/wto.johnvidal; National Org- anization of Women, "March for Women's Lives Est. 1 Million," 2004, http://march.now.org/; "Abortion Activists on the March," BBC News, April 26, 2004, http://news.bbc.co.uk/2/hi/americas/3657527.stm; Robin Toner, "At a Distance, Bush Joins Abortion Protest," *New York Times*, January 23, 2003, http://www.nytimes.com/2003/01/23/us/at-a-distance-bush-joins-abortion-protest.html; "Seattle Protests," Z Media, 30 November 1999, http://www.zmedia.org/WTO/N30.htm; "Millions Join Anti-War Protests," BBC News, February 27, 2003, http://news.bbc.co.uk/2/hi/europe/2765215.stm.

40. The key words used for each social movement when examining media coverage are "women's rights" and "movement," "anti-corporate globalization" and "movement," "anti-war" and "movement," "anti-abortion" or "pro-life" and "movement," and "Tea Party" and "movement." My examination of the coverage of each social movement includes two-week periods for each, covering the weeks before and after each protest, and covering all national stories, op-eds, editorials, and letters for the news outlets in question. There is good reason to believe that the protests discussed in Table 5.1 represent larger social movements. The antiwar movement drew hundreds of thousands from 2003 through at least 2005, and tens of thousands afterward; the pro-life movement claims tens of thousands to hundreds of thousands of protesters over a number of years, and has been organized as part of local church-based initiatives in recent decades; the anti-corporate globalization movement began in 1999, and continued in this sample through 2003, in numerous protests around the globe. My involvement in the antiwar, women's rights, and anti-corporate globalization protests entailed (among other activities) attending rallies from 2002 through 2007, which drew tens of thousands to hundreds of thousands. These protests were organized at the local level in communities I lived in, many of which advocated ideological positions far outside what was considered acceptable by either the Democratic or Republican parties, with the exception of the March for Women's Lives, which was primarily motivated by protection of reproductive rights and abortion rights.

41. Julie Hollar, "Tea Party vs. U.S. Social Forum," *Extra!* September 2010, http://www.fair.org/index.php?page=4143.

42. For more on the comparatively heavy coverage of the Nashville Tea Party convention in comparison to left convention organizing, see: www.fair.org/index.php?page=4143.

43. Kate Zernike, "Tea Party Convention: An Event Falls Through," *New York Times*, September 25, 2010; Amy Gardner, "'Tea Party' Faces Challenge of No Leader, Single Goal," *Washington Post*, September 22, 2010.

44. Philip Rucker, "Nikki Haley Surged before Palin Endorsement, GOP Says," *Washington Post*, 2010, http://voices.washingtonpost.com/44/2010/06/gop-says-nikki-haley-surged-be.html.

45. Associated Press, "Lincoln Survives, Cal GOP Chooses Whitman, Fiorina," *Guardian*, 9 June 2010, www.guardian.co.uk/world/feedarticle/9118434.

46. Jeff Zeleny, "GOP Leaders Say Delaware Upset Damages Senate Hopes," *New York Times*, September 14, 2010, www.nytimes.com/2010/09/15/us/politics/15elect.html; Karen Tumulty, "'Tea Party' Win in Del. Is Message to the GOP," *Washington Post*, 16 September 2010; Matt DeLong, "Christine O'Donnell in 1999: 'I Dabbled in Witchcraft,'" *Washington Post*, September 2010, http://voices.washingtonpost.com/44/2010/09/christine-odonnell-i-dabbled-i.html.

47. Kate Zernike, "Tea Party Convention Is Canceled," *New York Times*, September 24, 2010, http://thecaucus.blogs.nytimes.com/2010/09/24/tea-party-convention-is-canceled/.

48. United Press International, "Few Tea Party Victories in Primaries," June 9, 2010, http://www.upi.com/Top_News/US/2010/06/09/Few-tea-party-victories-in-primaries/UPI-42321276089271/.

49. David Corn, "Is the Tea Party Losing Its Strength?" Politics Daily, June 9, 2010, http://www.politicsdaily.com/2010/06/09/tea-party-losing-its-strength/.

50. Krissah Thompson and Dan Balz, "Rand Paul Comments About Civil Rights Stir Controversy," *Washington Post*, May 21, 2010, www.washingtonpost.com/wp-dyn/content/article/2010/05/20/AR2010052003500.html; Rick Klein, "Sharon Angle: 'I'm a Mainstream American'; Harry Reid 'Responsible' for Economic Mess," *ABC News*, September 8, 2010, http://blogs.abcnews.com/thenote/2010/09/angle-im-a-mainstream-american-reid-responsible-for-economic-mess.html.

51. Joan Walsh, "Rachel Maddow Demolishes Rand Paul," Salon.com, May 19, 2010, www.salon.com/news/opinion/joan_walsh/politics/2010/05/19/rachel_maddow_demolishes_rand_paul.

52. Linda Feldmann, "Rand Paul: Civil Rights Act Brouhaha Clouds Senate Campaign," *Christian Science Monitor*, May 20, 2010, www.csmonitor.com/USA/Politics/The-Vote/2010/0520/Rand-Paul-Civil-Rights-Act-brouhaha-clouds-Senate-campaign.

53. Joe Strupp, "How Did the Press Miss Rand Paul's Civil Rights Views Earlier?" Media Matters for America, May 21, 2010, http://mediamatters.org/strupp/201005210013.

54. Sam Stein, "Palin: Maddow Was 'Prejudiced' in Her Rand Paul Interview," Huffington Post, May 23, 2010, www.huffingtonpost.com/2010/05/23/palin-on-maddow-rand-paul_n_586353.html.

55. James Taranto, "Rand Paul and Civil Rights," *Wall Street Journal*, May 20, 2010, http://online.wsj.com/article/.

56. Greg Sargent, "Sunday Roundup," *Washington Post*, May 2010, http://voices.washingtonpost.com/plum-line/2010/05/sunday_roundup_1.html.

57. "John Stossel's Continued Advocacy for a Right to Discriminate," Media Matters for America, May 26, 2010, http://mediamatters.org/research/201005260059.

58. Maureen Dowd, "Hail the Conquering Professor," *New York Times*, March 24, 2010; Bob Herbert, "An Absence of Class," *New York Times*, March 23, 2010; Frank Rich, "The Rage Is Not About healthcare," *New York Times*, March 28, 2010.

59. Bob Herbert, "'A Different Creature,'" *New York Times*, April 13, 2010, 25.

60. In the aftermath of the April 15 Tea Party Tax Day rallies I was unable to find any editorials through a LexisNexis search of the *New York Times* and *Washington Post* that directly weighed in on the opinions of each paper's editors on the Tea Party as a "movement" or a social phenomenon.

61. Editorial, "Far Over the Line," *New York Times*, June 18, 2010, http://www.nytimes.com/2010/06/19/opinion/19sat3.html.

62. Editorial, "Limits of Libertarianism," *New York Times*, May 21, 2010, http://www.nytimes.com/2010/05/22/opinion/22sat4.html.

63. Paul Krugman, "Sex & Drugs & the Spill," *New York Times*, May 10, 2010; Charles Blow, "Trying to Outrun Race," *New York Times*, May 8, 2010.

64. Frank Rich, "The Great Tea Party Rip-Off," *New York Times*, January 16, 2010, http://www.nytimes.com/2010/01/17/opinion/17rich.html.

65. Thomas Friedman, "Tea Party with a Difference," *New York Times*, April 25, 2010.

66. Editorial, "Lawmakers Head Warily for Home," *New York Times*, March 27, 2010.

67. Charles M. Blow, "Whose Country Is It?" *New York Times*, March 27, 2010.

68. Editorial, "A Teachable Moment," *Washington Post*, January 20, 2010.

69. Editorial, "Tuesday's Lessons," *Washington Post*, November 5, 2009; Editorial, "The Beck Effect," *Washington Post*, January 3, 2010.

70. E. J. Dionne Jr., "Populism of Privilege," *Washington Post*, April 19, 2010.

71. Eugene Robinson, "Suspicious Minds," *Washington Post*, 20 April 2010; Eugene Robinson, "Where the Rhetoric of Rage Can Lead," *Washington Post*, March 30, 2010.

72. Colbert I. King, "The Tea Party Faithful Holler Back," *Washington Post*, April 10, 2010; Colbert I. King, "Faces We've Seen Before: The Deeper Roots of Tea Party Rage," *Washington Post*, March 27, 2010.

73. Rachel Maddow, *The Rachel Maddow Show*, MSNBC, August 5, 2009.

74. Ed Schultz, *The Ed Show*, MSNBC, August 19, 2009.

75. Keith Olbermann, *Countdown*, MSNBC, August 20, 2009.

76. Katrina Vanden Heuvel, "Could Progressives Find Allies in the Tea Party?" *Washington Post*, April 14, 2010, http://www.washingtonpost.com/wp-dyn/content/article/2010/04/13/AR2010041302492.html.

77. Medea Benjamin, "Peace Activists Extend an Olive Branch to Tea Party to Talk about War," Huffington Post, April 13, 2010, www.huffingtonpost.com/medea-benjamin/peace-activists-extend-an_b_535772.html.

78. Chuck Collins, "How to Talk to a Tea Party Activist," *The Nation*, April 14, 2010, www.thenation.com/article/how-talk-tea-party-activist.

79. John Nichols, "Bad Brew: What's Become of Tea Party Activism," *The Nation*, April 14, 2010, http://www.thenation.com/blog/bad-brew-whats-become-tea-party-populism?page=full.

80. Alexander Cockburn, "The Tea Party: A Mutiny America Did Not Expect," The First Post, May 24, 2010, www.thefirstpost.co.uk/63721,news-comment,news-politics,the-tea-party-a-mutiny-america-did-not-expect#ixzz0tULjaPVD.

81. David Rovics, "Breaking Ranks: Tea Parties, Espresso Snobs, Freedom and Equality," *CounterPunch*, April 15, 2010, www.counterpunch.org/rovics04152010.html.

82. For a discussion of Chomsky and the Tea Party, see Paul Street and Anthony DiMaggio, *Crashing the Tea Party: Mass Media and the Remaking of American Politics* (Boulder, CO: Paradigm Publishers, 2011). For an academic discussion of the harmful effects of neoliberalism and "free markets" for the masses and poor, see Doug Henwood, *After the New Economy: The Binge…and the Hangover that Won't Go Away* (New York: New Press, 2005); James K. Gailbrath, *The Predator State: How Conservatives Abandoned the Free Market and Why Liberals Should Too* (New York: Free Press, 2008); Paul Krugman, *The Return of Depression Economics and the Crisis of 2008* (New York: W. W. Norton, 2009); Joseph E. Stiglitz, *Globalization and Its Discontents* (New York: W. W. Norton, 2003); Joseph E. Stiglitz, *Freefall: America, Free Markets, and the Sinking of the World Economy* (New York: W. W. Norton, 2010).

83. Leslie Savan, "Feeling Randy," *The Nation*, May 19, 2010, http://www.thenation.com/blog/feeling-randy; Glen Ford, "White Nationalism on the March,"

Black Agenda Report, April 14, 2010, www.blackagendareport.com/?q=content/white-nationalism-march.

84.   Ron Jacobs, "Revolution Is Not a Tea Party," *CounterPunch*, January 20, 2010, http://www.counterpunch.org/jacobs01202010.html.

85.   Adele M. Stan, "The Tea Party Is Dangerous: Dispelling 7 Myths That Help Us Avoid Reality About the New Right-Wing Politics," Alternet, July 1, 2010, http://www.alternet.org/news/147307/the_tea_party_is_dangerous%3A_dispelling_7_myths_that_help_us_avoid_reality_about_the_new_right-wing_politics/.

86.   Since most of these websites do not contain archives for past articles, I instead followed them regularly during the spring and summer of 2010 as I compiled articles on the Tea Party. Google searches of "Tea Party" plus each website's name helped fill in any holes after compiling the sample.

4. Mediated Populism

1.   Andrew Kohut, "Majority of Respondents Don't Trust Washington," National Public Radio, April 19, 2010, www.npr.org/templates/story/story.php?storyId=126101559.

2.   Paul Krugman, "Stimulus Too Small, Second Package Likely," Huffington Post, February 17, 2009, http://www.huffingtonpost.com/2009/02/17/paul-krugman-stimulus-too_n_167721.html; Dean Baker, "Barack Obama's Big Stimulus," *Guardian*, January 19, 2009, http://www.guardian.co.uk/commentisfree/cifamerica/2009/jan/19/barack-obama-economic-stimulus.

3.   Dan Levy, "U.S. Home Foreclosures Climb 44 Percent to Record in May," *Business Week*, June 10, 2010, http://www.businessweek.com/news/2010-06-10/u-s-home-foreclosures-climb-44-to-record-in-may-update1-.html; Frank James, "Nearly One in Four U.S. Homes with Mortgages Underwater," National Public Radio, November 24, 2009, http://www.npr.org/blogs/thetwo-way/2009/11/one_in_four_us_homes_underwate.html.

4.   Kate Zernike and Megan Thee-Brenan, "Poll Finds Tea Party Backers Wealthier and More Educated," *New York Times*, April 14, 2010, http://www.nytimes.com/2010/04/15/us/politics/15poll.html.

5.   Steven Kull, "Big Government Is Not the Issue," World Public Opinion, 19 August 2010, http://www.worldpublicopinion.org/pipa/articles/brunitedstatescanadara/665.php?nid=&id=&pnt=665&lb=.

6.   Ibid.

7.   For a listing of all the polls described, see the Pollingreport.com polling aggregator http://www.pollingreport.com/politics.htm.

8.   "CNN/Opinion Research Corporation Poll," Pollingreport.com, November 11–14, 2010, http://www.pollingreport.com/politics.htm.

9.   "Fox News/Opinion Dynamics Poll," Pollingreport.com, February 2–3, 2010, http://www.pollingreport.com/politics.htm.

10.   "Tea Party 48%, Obama 44%," Rasmussen Reports, April 5, 2010, http://www.rasmussenreports.com/public_content/politics/general_politics/april_2010/tea_party_48_obama_44.

11.   "Most Say Tea Party Has a Better Understanding of Issues than Congress,"
      Rasmussen Reports, March 28, 2010, http://www.rasmussenreports.com/pub-
      lic_content/politics/general_politics/march_2010/most_say_tea_party_has_b
      etter_understanding_of_issues_than_congress.

12.   The general study of social consructionism is often traced back to a number of
      works, including Peter L. Berger and Thomas Luckmann, *The Social
      Construction of Reality: A Treatise in the Sociology of Knowledge* (New York:
      Anchor Books, 1966); and John Searle, *The Construction of Social Reality*
      (New York: Free Press, 1995). The study of social constructionism in relation
      to public opinion surveys is covered in works including Justin Lewis,
      *Constructing Public Opinion: How Political Elites Do What They Like and Why
      We Seem to Go Along with It* (New York: Columbia University Press, 2001);
      Benjamin Ginsberg, *The Captive Public: How Mass Opinion Promotes State
      Power* (New York: Basic Books, 1986); Herbert I. Schiller, *The Mind Managers*
      (Boston: Beacon Press, 1973); and Anthony R. DiMaggio, *When Media Goes to
      War: Hegemonic Discourse, Public Opinion, and the Limits of Dissent* (New
      York: Monthly Review Press, 2010).

13.   One could draw upon many examples of biased survey designs, but some
      examples are instructive. One Rasmussen survey, for example, finds that "just
      9 percent [of Americans] want no limits on what the federal government can
      do." The question wording here is automatically set up to overestimate the
      impression that the public opposes the central government. After all, there are
      relatively few Americans (as the survey results show) who say that the govern-
      ment should have "no limits" on its behavior. One might just as well have asked
      the public if they believe the government should be allowed to prohibit free-
      dom, considering that such loaded question wording would also produce the
      finding that the public is overwhelmingly "conservative" in that it is opposed to
      expansive federal government power. A second example of Rasmussen's social
      construction of public opinion, in relation to the Tea Party, is their survey of
      whether Tea Party supporters see themselves as Republican. In the book *Mad
      as Hell*, Rasmussen and Schoen point out that less than half of supporters self-
      identify as Republican (159), supposedly an indication that the Tea Party is not
      a partisan affair. However, a closer probing of public opinion (at a time when a
      growing number of people do not want to openly be associated with either
      party, but who cling to partisan rhetoric nonetheless), partisanship tends to be
      underestimated by such questions. Fox News viewers are notorious in this
      regard, consistently claiming they are independent of party, and yet consistent-
      ly demonizing Democrats along the lines of the rhetoric forwarded by the
      Republican Party. To count these individuals as independent of party under
      these circumstances would be unwarranted. Closer polling of the Tea Party,
      with more precise question wording, finds that the vast majority of them
      (between three-quarters to more than 80 percent) either see themselves as
      Republican or Republican-leaning, or indicate that they prefer to vote
      Republican. In short, the way in which questions are asked makes a major dif-
      ference in the results, and Rasmussen's polling questions are often blatantly
      biased to overestimate conservatism in some instances, and artificially conceal
      it in others.

14. A review of Rasmussen reports finds that they regularly frame the public as conservative across most political issues. A sample of such conservative Rasmussen reports released during the writing of this book include: "52% Favor Sacrificing Freedom of Speech to Protect Children From Indecency," "Most Americans Not Willing to Pay Higher Taxes for Public Employees, Entitlement Programs," "Americans Not Sure on Financial Reform Bill, but Don't Think Some Banks Are Too Big to Fail," "60% in Florida Favor Arizona-Like Immigration Law in Their State," "54% in Illinois Say No to Abolishing Death Penalty," "77% Think U.S. Nuclear Weapons Arsenal Is Important to National Security," "Most Oppose Citizenship for Children of Illegal Immigrants," "55% Favor Repeal of Healthcare Law," "Just 9% Want No Limits on What Federal Government Can Do," "54% Oppose Health Insurance Requirement in New Health Law," "64% Support Offshore Oil Drilling, 55% Favor Deepwater Drilling," "57% Say Healthcare Plan Bad for the Country, 59% Favor Repeal." These findings are very different from the findings of experts in the study of public opinion, who find that the public—at least in relation to social welfare and entitlement programs and foreign policy—is far more to the left, or at least not as consistently conservative, as argued by Rasmussen. For examples of public opinion scholarship, see Benjamin I. Page and Lawrence R. Jacobs, *Class War? What Americans Really Think about Economic Inequality* (Chicago: University of Chicago, 2009); Benjamin I. Page and Marshall M. Bouton, *The Foreign Policy Disconnect: What Americans Want from Our Leaders but Don't Get* (Chicago: University of Chicago, 2006); Michael Corbett, *American Public Opinion* (New York: Longman, 1991); Robert S. Erikson and Kent L. Tedin, *American Public Opinion* (New York: Longman, 2003); Martin Gilens, *Why Americans Hate Welfare: Race, Media, and the Politics of Antipoverty Policy* (Chicago: University of Chicago Press, 1999); Steven Kull and I. M. Drestler, *Misreading the Public: The Myth of New Isolationism* (Washington, D.C.: Brookings Institution, 1999); Jacob S. Hacker and Paul Pierson, *Off Center: The Republican Revolution and the Erosion of American Democracy* (New Haven: Yale University Press, 2005); Larry M. Bartels, *Unequal Democracy: The Political Economy of the New Gilded Age* (Princeton: Princeton University Press, 2008); Morris P. Fiorina, *Culture War? The Myth of a Polarized America* (New York: Longman, 2006); Samuel Kernell, Gary C. Jacobson, and Thad Kousser, *The Logic of American Politics* (Washington, D.C.: CQ Press, 2009); Anthony R. DiMaggio, *When Media Goes to War: Hegemonic Discourse, Public Opinion, and the Limits of Dissent* (New York: Monthly Review Press, 2010); Anthony R. DiMaggio, *Mass Media, Mass Propaganda: Examining American News in the "War on Terror"* (Lanham, MD: Lexington Books, 2010).

15. Scott Rasmussen, *In Search of Self-Governance* (CreateSpace, 2010).

16. Polling Report, "Pew Research Center," Pollingreport.com, September 16–19, 2010, http://www.pollingreport.com/politics.htm.

17. Benjamin I. Page, and Robert Y. Shapiro, *The Rational Public: Fifty Years in Trends in Americans' Policy Preferences* (Chicago: University of Chicago Press, 1992), xi.

18. Pew Research Center, "November 2010 Post-Election Survey," November 4–7, 2010, http://people-press.org/reports/questionnaires/673.pdf.

19. The public opinion data from figure 4.1 was drawn from the Pew Research Center's question database for the period from March through November 2010.

20. Ibid.

21. Jon Cohen and Philip Rucker, "Poll Finds Most Americans Are Unhappy with Government," *Washington Post*, February 11, 2010, http://www.washington-post.com/wp-dyn/content/article/2010/02/10/AR2010021004708.html.

22. Pew Research Center, "Inviting Centrists to the Tea Party," February 1, 2010, http://pewresearch.org/pubs/1482/tea-party-movement-appeal-independents-split-republicans; "ABC-*Washington Post* Poll, Pollingreport.com, April 22–25, 2010, http://www.pollingreport.com/politics.htm.

23. Pew Research Center, "Distrust, Discontent, Anger and Partisan Rancor," April 18, 2010, http://people-press.org/report/?pageid=1703.

24. Liz Halloran, "Pew Poll: Trust in Government Hits Near Historic Low," National Public Radio, April 18, 2010, www.npr.org/templates/story/story.php?storyId=126047343.

25. Ibid.; Derek Thompson, "80 Percent of Americans Don't Trust the Government, Here's Why," *The Atlantic*, April 19, 2010, http://www.theat-lantic.com/business/archive/2010/04/80-percent-of-americans-dont-trust-the-government-heres-why/39148/.

26. American National Election Studies, "The ANES Guide to Public Opinion and Electoral Behavior," 2010, http://www.electionstudies.org/nesguide/topt-able/tab5a_2.htm; "Poll: GOP, Dems Approval Ratings Stay Low," United Press International, June 1, 2010, www.upi.com/Top_News/US/2010/06/01/Poll-GOP-Dems-approval -ratings-stay-low/UPI-81381275415546/.

27. Gary C. Jacobson and Samuel Kernell, *Strategy and Choice in Congressional Elections* (New Haven: Yale University Press, 1983).

28. "General Election: Obama vs. McCain," Real Clear Politics, November 2008, http://www.realclearpolitics.com/epolls/2008/president/us/general_elec-tion_mccain_vs_obama-225.html.

29. "President Obama: Job Ratings," Pollingreport.com, September 2010, http://www.pollingreport.com/obama_job.htm

30. As a concept, retrospective voting is widely discussed by political scientists. For some examples, see Morris Fiorina, *Retrospective Voting in American National Elections* (New Haven: Yale University Press, 1981); R. Douglas Arnold, *The Logic of Congressional Action* (New Haven: Yale University Press, 1990); Richard Nadeau and Michael S. Lewis-Beck, "National Economic Voting in U.S. Presidential Elections," in *Controversies in Voting Behavior,* ed. Richard G. Niemi and Herbert F. Weisberg (Washington, D.C.: CQ Press, 2001), 200–220; Gary C. Jacobson and Samuel Kernell, *Strategy and Choice in Congressional Elections* (New Haven: Yale University Press, 1981).

31. See chapter 7 of Street and DiMaggio, *Crashing the Tea Party*.

32. "Exit Poll for House Race," CBSnews.com, November 2, 2010, www.cbsnews.com/election2010/exit.shtml?state=US&jurisdiction=0&race=H&tag=contentBody;electionCenterHome; Frank James, "Pew Exit Poll," National

Public Radio, November 2, 2010, www.npr.org/blogs/itsallpolitics/2010/11/ 02/131021153/pew-exit-poll-shows-surge-of-angry-conservatives.

33. Pew Research Center, "Mixed Reactions to Republican Midterm Win," November 11, 2010, http://people-press.org/reports/pdf/675.pdf.

34. "Poll: Tea Party Movement Fails to Make Any Impression on 4 Out of 10," *CNN News*, February 5, 2010, www.cnn.com/2010/POLITICS/02/05/ poll.tea.party/index.html.

35. CBS-*New York Times* poll, "National Survey of Tea Party Supporters," April 5–12, 2010.

36. Ibid.

37. Ibid.

38. This point is made in greater detail in chapter 6.

39. CBS–New York Times, "National Survey of Tea Party Supporters," 2010.

40. Frank Newport, "Socialism Viewed Positively by 36 Percent of Americans," Gallup, February 4, 2010, http://www.gallup.com/poll/125645/socialism-viewed-positively-americans.aspx

41. CBS-*New York Times* poll, "National Survey of Tea Party Supporters," April 15, 2010.

42. "Bloomberg Poll," *Pollingreport.com*, March 19–22, 2010, www.pollingreport.com/social.htm.

43. CNN–Opinion Research Poll, October 3–5, 2008, Pollingreport.com, www.pollingreport.com/social.htm; Frank Newport, "Public Opinion on Privatizing Social Security Still Fluid," Gallup.com, January 26, 2005, www.gallup.com/poll/14737/public-opinion-privatizing-social-security-still-fluid.aspx#2.

44. CNN, "Poll: Tea Party Movement Fails to Make Any Impression on 4 Out of 10"; Pew Research Center, "Distrust, Discontent, Anger and Partisan Rancor."

45. Susan Davis, "WSJ/NBC News Poll: Tea Party Tops Democrats and Republicans," *Wall Street Journal*, December 16, 2009, http://blogs.wsj.com/washwire/2009/12/16/wsjnbc-news-poll-tea-party-tops-democrats-and-republicans/.

46. CBS-*New York Times* poll, "National Survey of Tea Party Supporters," April 5–12, 2010.

47. Pew Research Center, "Distrust, Discontent, Anger and Partisan Rancor."

48. "Fox News/Opinion Dynamics Poll," Pollingreport.com, February 2–3, 2010, http://www.pollingreport.com/politics.htm.

49. Pew Research Center, "The Vote for Congress: GOP Fares Better with Whites, Men, Independents, and Seniors," http://pewresearch.org/pubs/1693/2010-congressional-horse-race-voting-blocks-swing-voters-partisan-engagement-gap.

50. Pew Research Center, "Independents Oppose Party in Power. . . . Again," September 23, 2010, http://people-press.org/report/658/.

51. Jeffrey M. Jones, "GOP Losses Span Nearly All Demographic Groups," Gallup.com, May 18, 2009 http://www.gallup.com/poll/118528/gop-losses-span-nearly-demographic-groups.aspx.

52. Scott Rasmussen and Douglas Schoen, *Mad as Hell: How the Tea Party Movement Is Fundamentally Remaking Our Two-Party System* (New York: Harper, 2010), 164.

53. Susan Page and Naomi Jagoda, "What Is the Tea Party? A Growing State of Mind," *USA Today*, July 8, 2010, http://www.usatoday.com/news/politics/2010-07-01-tea-party_N.htm.

54. Pew Research Center, "Republicans Faring Better with Men, Whites, Independents, and Seniors," August 10, 2010, http://people-press.org/report/643/.

55. Pew Research Center, "Distrust, Discontent, Anger and Partisan Rancor."

56. Pew Research Center, "The Vote for Congress."

57. Jones, "GOP Losses Span Nearly All Demographic Groups."

58. Pew Research Center, "Republicans Faring Better with Men, Whites, Independents, and Seniors."

59. For more on exit polling and the power of the Tea Party to influence voting, see chapter 7 of Street and DiMaggio, *Crashing the Tea Party*.

60. Thomas Frank, *What's the Matter with Kansas?: How Conservatives Won the Heart of America* (New York: Holt, 2005).

61. Larry Bartels, *Unequal Democracy: The Political Economy of the New Gilded Age* (Princeton: Princeton University Press, 2008), 90.

62. Andrew Gelman, *Red State, Blue State: Rich State, Poor State: Why Americans Vote the Way They Do* (Princeton: Princeton University Press, 2008), 53.

63. Bartels, *Unequal Democracy*, 78.

64. Ibid., 80–89.

65. Pew Research Center, "February 2010 Political Survey," February 12, 2010, http://people-press.org/dataarchive/.

66. Conducting a multivariate-ordered logistic regression analysis for survey questions covering support for the Tea Party in February and March 2010 (drawn from the Pew Research Center's surveys), I find a statistically significant relationship between Evangelism, party, education, ideology, and race as independent variables, and opinions of the Tea Party as a dependent variable. All the above variables are statistically significant at the 5 percent level or lower. This does not mean that other variables retain no statistically significant relationship with support for the Tea Party, but simply that no such relationships were evident in February or March surveys. Unfortunately, I only had access to survey data on the Tea Party through March (since the Pew Research Center only makes data available six months after its initial release), and this book was completed in November of 2010. Statistically significant relationships between church attendance, income, voter status, age, Evangelism, and sex on the one hand and opinions of the Tea Party on the other may very well exist in surveys from April through November 2010, although such an analysis is beyond the scope of this study. A relationship also exists in the regression analyses I ran between education and opinions of the Tea Party, in which the highly educated are more likely to oppose the group. This relationship is significant at the 5 percent level.

67. For more on the data I analyzed, see Quinnipiac University, "Democrats on Top in Ohio Senate," March 31, 2010, www.quinnipiac.edu/x1284.xml?What=tea party&strArea=;&strTime=120&ReleaseID=1440#Question011; Quinnipiac University, "Obama's Bounce Goes Flat," April 21, 2010, www.quinnipiac.edu/x1284.xml?What=tea party&strArea=;&strTime=120&ReleaseID=1447#Question011.

68. For more on the remarkably stable nature of public opinion, see Benjamin I. Page and Robert Y. Shapiro, *The Rational Public: Fifty Years of Trends in Americans' Policy Preferences* (Chicago: University of Chicago Press, 1993); see

also Anthony R. DiMaggio, *When Media Goes to War: Hegemonic Discourse, Public Opinion, and the Limits of Dissent* (New York: Monthly Review Press, 2010).

69.   Pew Research Center, "Distrust, Discontent, Anger and Partisan Rancor."

70.   Pew Research Center, "Pew Weekly News Interest Index," April 2009, http://people-press.org/questions/?qid=1732508&pid=51&ccid=51#top.

71.   Pew Research Center, "healthcare Still Top Story, but Many Track Volcano," April 22, 2010, http://people-press.org/report/607./

72.   CBS–*New York Times* poll, "National Survey of Tea Party Supporters," April 15, 2010.

73.   Pew Research Center, "Awareness of the Tea Party Movement Increasing," April 22, 2010, http://people-press.org/reports/pdf/607.pdf.

74.   Pew Research Center, "Distrust, Discontent, Anger and Partisan Rancor."

75.   The results of my multivariate-ordered logistic regression analysis demonstrate that the relationship between consumption of Washington-related news and approval of the Tea Party is statistically significant at the 1 percent level. By statistical significance, I am referring to an observed relationship between two variables that is unlikely to be the result of chance variation within the population of observed values.

76.   The relationship discussed is significant, after controlling for many other demographic variables, including: age, party, ideology, income, voter status (registered/un-registered), sex, age, race, Evangelism (born again vs. not-born again), church attendance, religious affiliation (Protestant vs. non-Protestant), and education.

77.   The results of my multivariate-ordered logistic regression analysis demonstrate that the relationship between attention to the national debate and reporting on the Tea Party and support for the group is highly statistically significant at the .01 percent level. The relationship remains, even after controlling for all the demographic variables listed in this study.

5. The Plot to Kill Grandma

1.   Scholars and public opinion researchers document the regular pressures exerted upon journalists by businesses and advertisers, and found that those pressures play a significant role in influencing reporting in favor of pro-business views. For a sample of this research, see Robert W. McChesney, *The Problem of the Media: U.S. Communication Politics in the 21st Century* (New York: Monthly Review Press, 2004), 83; Dean Alger, *Megamedia: How Giant Corporations Dominate Mass Media, Distort Competition, and Endanger Democracy* (Lanham, MD: Rowman and Littlefield, 1998), 163–64; David Croteau and William Hoynes, *The Business of Media: Corporate Media and the Public Interest* (Thousand Oaks, CA: Pine Forge Press, 2001), 179–80; Pew Research Center, "Self-Censorship: How Often and Why," April 30, 2000, http://people-press.org/report/39/.

2.   By discussing uniformity on the right, I am not suggesting that there are no other reactionary ideologies outside of those promoted by the Republican Party and its servants in right-wing media. Other variations of right-wing ide-

ology do exist, but none that are anywhere near as widely disseminated, or as dominant as the reactionary ideology promoted by Fox News–Republican alliance. Conservative ideologies—such as paleoconservatism and libertarianism (among other strains of right-wing thought) have largely been drowned out by the corporate right, and have been made, for all intents and purposes, irrelevant in terms of appealing to a mass audience throughout the United States.

3.   For more on the media's indexing of official sources, see these academic works: Jonathan Mermin, *Debating War and Peace: Media Coverage of U.S. Intervention in the Post-Vietnam Era* (Princeton: Princeton University Press, 1999); Daniel C. Hallin, *The "Uncensored War": The Media and Vietnam* (Oxford: Oxford University Press, 1986); W. Lance Bennett, Regina G. Lawrence, and Steven Livingston, *When the Press Fails: Political Power and the News Media from Iraq to Katrina* (Chicago: University of Chicago Press, 2007); Anthony R. DiMaggio, *When Media Goes to War: Hegemonic Discourse, Public Opinion, and the Limits of Dissent* (New York: Monthly Review Press, 2010).

4.   For more, see Paul Street and Anthony DiMaggio, *Crashing the Tea Party: Mass Media and the Remaking of American Politics* (Boulder, CO: Paradigm Publishers, 2011).

5.   Reed Abelson, "In Healthcare Overhaul, Boons for Hospitals and Drug Makers," *New York Times*, March 21, 2010, www.nytimes.com/2010/03/22/business/22bizhealth.html.

6.   "Top of the Ticket," *Los Angeles Times*, March 22, 2010, http://latimesblogs.latimes.com/washington/2010/03/obama-boehner-steele-kaine-healthcare-text.html; Sarah Palin, "Obama and the Bureaucratization of Healthcare," *Wall Street Journal*, September 8, 2009, http://online.wsj.com/article/SB10001424052970203440104574400581157986024.html.

7.   Daniel Gross, "What 'Government Takeover'?" Slate.com, March 9, 2010, http://www.slate.com/id/2247393/. For Bachmann's website, see http://michelebachmann.townhall.com/blog.

8.   Jake Tapper, "Spread the Wealth?" ABC News, October 14, 2008, http://blogs.abcnews.com/politicalpunch/2008/10/spread-the-weal.html.

9.   John McCain, "McCain Says Obama Wants Socialism," *Los Angeles Times*, October 19, 2008, http://articles.latimes.com/2008/oct/19/nation/na-campaign19.

10.   Associated Press, "McCain and Obama Spar over Tax Cuts," MSNBC.com, October 18, 2008, www.msnbc.msn.com/id/27250527/.

11.   This ignorance, with regard to confusing Democrats' increasingly centrist policies with "socialism," is explored in greater detail in chapter 5 of Street and DiMaggio, *Crashing the Tea Party*.

12.   Sarah Palin, "Statement on the Current Health Care Debate," Facebook, August 7, 2009, www.facebook.com/note.php?note_id=113851103434.

13.   Jim Rutenberg and Jackie Calmes, "False 'Death Panel' Rumor Has Some Familiar Roots," *New York Times*, August 13, 2009, www.nytimes.com/2009/08/14/health/policy/14panel.html.

14.   Rush Limbaugh, "Palin Is Dead Right on Death Panels," August 13, 2009, http://www.rushlimbaugh.com/home/daily/site_081309/content/01125108.guest.html.

15. Glenn Beck, *Glenn Beck*, Fox News, August 12, 2009; Bill O'Reilly and Laura Ingraham, *The O'Reilly Factor*, Fox News, August 14, 2009; Sean Hannity, *Hannity*, Fox News, August 13, 2009.

16. Media Matters for America, "After Repeated Debunkings of 'Death Panels,' Conservative Media Backtrack to 'De Facto Death Panels,'" August 19, 2009, http://mediamatters.org/research/200908190053.

17. Rachel Maddow, *The Rachel Maddow Show*, MSNBC News, August 10, 2009; Ed Schultz, *The Ed Show*, MSNBC News, August 10, 2009; Keith Olbermann, *Countdown*, MSNBC News, August 11, 2009.

18. The public option was eclipsed by coverage of death panels in August, as demonstrated in Figures 5.2 and 5.3.

19. Chris Wallace, *Fox News Sunday*, Fox News, August 16, 2009.

20. Media Matters for America, "CBS, Fox Reports on Town Hall Disruptions Ignore Conservative Strategy," August 5, 2009, http://mediamatters.org/research/200908050017; Sean Hannity, "Health Care Uprising; Taxing the Middle Class," Fox News, August 3, 2009; Glenn Beck, *Glenn Beck*, Fox News, September 25, 2009.

21. Greta Van Susteren, On the Record with Greta Van Susteren, Fox News, August 11, 2009.

22. Laura Ingraham, "Town Hall Protester Roughed Up By SEIU Members," Fox News, August 10, 2009.

23. David M. Herszenhorn and Sheryl Gay Stolberg, "Health Plan Opponents Make Their Voices Heard," *New York Times*, August 4, 2009. Emphasis added.

24. Dan Eggen and Philip Rucker, "Loose Network of Activists Drives Reform Opposition," *Washington Post*, August 16, 2009; Ben Pershing, "Armey's Army Marches against Obama," *Washington Post*, September 27, 2009.

25. Joe Klein, "Obama's Appeal: A Test of National Character," *Time*, September 10, 2009, www.time.com/time/politics/article/0,8599,1921451,00.html.

26. Samuel Kernell, *Going Public: New Strategies of Presidential Leadership* (Washington, D.C.: CQ Press, 2007).

27. For more information on these speeches, visit the White House website at http://www.whitehouse.gov.

28. Ed Schultz, *The Ed Show*, MSNBC News, October 30, 2009; Keith Olbermann, *Countdown*, MSNBC News, November 9, 2009; Rachel Maddow, *The Rachel Maddow Show*, MSNBC News, November 18, 2009.

29. Editorial, "A Public Plan for Health Insurance?" *New York Times*, April 6, 2009, http://www.nytimes.com/2009/04/07/opinion/07tue1.html.

30. Editorial, "No Longer an Option," *Washington Post*, August 20, 2009, www.washingtonpost.com/wp-dyn/content/article/2009/08/19/AR2009 081903449.html; Editorial, "A Chance to Change," *Washington Post*, March 24, 2010.

31. For more information on these plans, see Lori Robertson, "Still on the Table?" *Newsweek*, February 25, 2010, www.newsweek.com/2010/02/24/still-on-the-table.html.

32. For nearly all the analysis of healthcare frames in this chapter, I counted the stories that appeared in all the sections of the papers/television channels in question, and counted the stories that appeared on "healthcare," in conjunction

with other key words in question (such as the "public option," "single payer" care, etc.). Tabulations of stories covering "healthcare" and its "cost" were one exception, as I only included articles referencing the key words "cost" or "costs" that appeared within 50 words of "healthcare."

33. Pew Research Center's Project for Excellence in Journalism, "State of the News Media: 2011," Stateofthemedia.org, http://stateofthemedia.org/2011/overview-2/.

34. Ibid.

35. Steven Reinberg, "U.S. Health Care Ranks Low among Developed Nations: Report," *BusinessWeek*, June 23, 2010, www.businessweek.com/lifestyle/content/healthday/640404.html; Editorial, "World's Best Medical Care?" *New York Times*, August 12, 2007, http://www.nytimes.com/2007/08/12/opinion/12sun1.html; Will Dunham, "France Best, U.S. Worst in Preventable Death Ranking" Reuters, January 8, 2008, www.reuters.com/article/idUSN0765165020080108; Nicholas Bakalar, "Inefficiency Hurts U.S. Longevity in Rankings," *New York Times*, November 29, 2010, http://www.nytimes.com/2010/11/30/health/30life.html.

36. ABC News, "CBO: Health Care Bill Will Cost $115 Billion More than Previously Assessed," May 12, 2010, http://blogs.abcnews.com/politicalpunch/2010/05/cbo-health-care-bill-will-cost-115-billion-more-than-previously-assessed.html.

37. For a discussion of the false attacks on Obama for being "radical," see the insightful analysis of Obama by Paul Street in his *Barack Obama and the Future of American Politics* (Boulder, CO: Paradigm Publishers, 2009); Paul Street, *The Empire's New Clothes: Barack Obama and the Real World of Power* (Boulder, CO: Paradigm Publishers, 2010). For more on Obama, also see Tariq Ali, *The Obama Syndrome: Surrender at Home, War Abroad* (London: Verso, 2010).

38. Karl Marx and Friedrich Engels, *The Communist Manifesto* (New York: Washington Square Press, 1964), 81, 93–94.

39. ABC News, "CBO: Health Care Bill Will Cost $115 Billion More than Previously Assessed," May 12, 2010, http://blogs.abcnews.com/politicalpunch/2010/05/cbo-health-care-bill-will-cost-115-billion-more-than-previously-assessed.html.

40. Hans-Georg Gadamer, *Truth and Method* (London: Continuum, 2004); Jürgen Habermas, *The Theory of Communicative Action: Reason and the Rationalization of Society* (Boston: Beacon, 1984); Jürgen Habermas, *The Structural Transformation of the Public Sphere: An Inquiry into a Category of Bourgeois Society* (Cambridge, MA: MIT Press, 1991); Richard Rorty, *Philosophy and the Mirror of Nature* (Princeton: Princeton University Press, 1979).

41. Richard Wolf, "Number of Uninsured Americans Rises to 50.7 Million," *USA Today*, September 17, 2010, http://www.usatoday.com/news/nation/2010-09-17-uninsured17_ST_N.htm; Stan Dorn, "Uninsured and Dying Because of It," Urban Institute, January 8, 2008, http://www.urban.org/publications/411588.html; Susan Heavey, "Study Links 45,000 U.S. Deaths to Lack of Insurance," Reuters, September 17, 2009, www.reuters.com/article/idUSTRE58G6W520090917.

42. Kaiser Family Foundation, "Health Care Costs: A Primer," March 2009, http://www.kff.org/insurance/upload/7670_02.pdf; Sylvia Hall, "Rising Health Care Costs Leave Businesses Realing," Medill Reports, October 14, 2010, http://news.medill.northwestern.edu/chicago/news.aspx?id=170436.

43. Media Matters for America, "Limbaugh Again Says Obama Health Care Logo 'Looks Damn Like the Nazi Logo,'" August 7, 2009, http://mediamatters. org/mmtv/200908070029; Rush Limbaugh, "Barney Frank Loses It at Town Hall," Rushlimbaugh.com, August 19, 2009, www.rushlimbaugh.com/home/ daily/site_081909/content/01125106.guest.html.

44. Glenn Beck, *Glenn Beck*, Fox News, August 6, 2009.

45. Ibid., March 1, 2010.

46. Even on the most general level, a Google search of "Obama" and "Hitler" reveals dozens of pictures from protests around the country against healthcare reform.

47. Erin Steuter and Deborah Wills, *At War with Metaphor: Media, Propaganda, and Racism in the War on Terror* (Lanham, MD: Lexington Books, 2008), 18.

48. Geoffrey Baym, *From Cronkite to Colbert: The Evolution of Broadcast News* (Boulder, CO: Paradigm Publishers, 2010), 138, 126, 128.

49. All of the right-wing pundits discussed in this chapter frame their commentaries as "the truth," brought to their audiences through unbiased means with no reliance upon political spin and official propaganda. A few examples: Fox News claims to be "fair and balanced," and Bill O'Reilly promises viewers they are entering the "No Spin Zone." Rush Limbaugh's common radio theme is that the "state-controlled media ends here."

50. For the large literature claiming the media is liberal, see David H. Weaver and G. Cleveland Wilhoit, *The American Journalist in the 1990s: U.S. News People at the End of an Era* (Mahwah, NJ: Lawrence Erlbaum Associates, 1996); S. Robert Lichter, Stanley Rothman, and Linda S. Lichter, *The Media Elite: America's New Powerbrokers* (New York: Hastings House, 1990); Bernard Goldberg, *A Slobbering Love Affair: The True (and Pathetic) Story of the Torrid Romance between Barack Obama and the Mainstream Media* (New York: Regnery, 2009); Bernard Goldberg, *Bias: A CBS Insider Exposes How the Media Distort the News* (New York: Perennial, 2003); John Gibson, *How the Left Swiftboated America: The Liberal Media Conspiracy to Make You Think George Bush Was the Worst President in History* (New York: HarperCollins, 2009); L. Brent Bozell III, *Weapons of Mass Distortion: The Coming Meltdown of the Liberal Media* (New York: Three Rivers Press, 2005).

51. For more on challenges to the liberal media argument, see Eric Alterman, *What Liberal Media? The Truth about Bias in the News* (New York: Basic Books, 2003); Trudy Lieberman, *Slanting the Story: The Forces that Shape the News* (New York: New Press, 2000); and Maria Elizabeth Grabe and Erik Page Bucy, *Image Bite Politics: News and the Visual Framing of Elections* (Oxford: Oxford University Press, 2009). Other studies challenge the idea that the media is a liberal watchdog against government abuse, and highlight that media often have a conservative bias, but are, more than anything else, characterized by a pro-business bias in the news. For more on these studies, see David Edwards and David Cromwell, *Guardians of Power: The Myth of the Liberal Media* (London:

Pluto Press, 2006); David Edwards and David Cromwell, *Newspeak in the 21st Century* (London: Pluto Press, 2009); Edward Herman, *The Myth of the Liberal Media: An Edward Herman Reader* (New York: Peter Lang, 1999); Robert W. McChesney, *The Problem of the Media: U.S. Communication Politics in the 21st Century* (New York: Monthly Review Press, 2004).

52.   Some scholars fail to find a consistent liberal or conservative bias. For an example, see Tawnya J. Adkins Covert and Philo C. Wasburn, *Media Bias? A Comparative Study of Time, Newsweek, The National Review, and the Progressive Coverage of Domestic Social Issues, 1975–2000* (Lanham, MD: Lexington, 2009); and W. Lance Bennett, *News: The Politics of Illusion* (New York: Longman, 2001).

53.   David Domke, *God Willing? Political Fundamentalism in the White House, the "War on Terror," and the Echoing Press* (London: Pluto Press, 2004).

54.   Robert W. McChesney, *Rich Media, Poor Democracy: Communication Politics in Dubious Times* (New York: New Press, 1999); Robert W. McChesney, *The Problem of the Media*, 83; Dean Alger, *Megamedia: How Giant Corporations Dominate Mass Media, Distort Competition, and Endanger Democracy* (Lanham, MD: Rowman and Littlefield, 1998), 163–64; David Croteau and William Hoynes, *The Business of Media: Corporate Media and the Public Interest* (Thousand Oaks, CA: Pine Forge Press, 2001), 179–80; Pew Research Center, "Self-Censorship: How Often and Why," 30 April 2000, http://people-press.org/report/39/.

55.   Michael Parenti, *Inventing Reality: The Politics of News Media* (New York: St. Martin's Press, 1993), 33–35.

56.   Vincent Mosco, "Revisiting the Political Economy of Communication," in *Marxism and Communication Studies: The Point Is to Change It*, ed. Lee Artz, Steve Macek, and Dana L. Cloud (New York: Peter Lang, 2006).

57.   Herbert J. Gans, *Deciding What's News: A Study of CBS Evening News, NBC Nightly News, Newsweek, and Time* (New York: Vintage Books, 1980); William J. Puette, *Through Jaundiced Eyes: How the Media View Organized Labor* (Ithaca, NY: ILR Press, 1992); Jerry Rollings, "Mass Communication and the American Worker," in *The Critical Communications Review: Labor, the Working Class, and the Media*, vol. 1, ed. Vincent Mosco and Janet Wasko (Norwood, NJ: Ablex Publishing, 1983); Michael Parenti, *Inventing Reality*, 1993; Michael Parenti, *Make-Believe Media: The Politics of Entertainment* (New York: St. Martin's Press, 1992); Christopher R. Martin, *Framed! Labor and Corporate Media* (Ithaca, NY: ILR Press, 2004).

58.   Henry A. Giroux and Susan Searls Giroux, "Corporate Culture versus Public Education and Democracy: A Call for Critical Pedagogy," in Artz, Macek, Cloud, *Marxism and Communication Studies*, 204.

59.   "CBS–*New York Times* Poll," November 13–16, 2009, December 4–8, 2009, Pollingreport.com, http://www.pollingreport.com/health4.htm; Kevin Sack and Marjorie Connelly, "In Poll, Wide Support for Government-Run Health," *New York Times*, June 20, 2009, http://www.nytimes.com/2009/06/21/health/policy/21poll.html.

60.   Gary Langer, "Health Care Pains," ABC News, October 20, 2003, http://abcnews.go.com/sections/living/us/healthcare031020_poll.html; Ruy Teixeira,

"Public Opinion Snapshot: Universal Health Care Momentum Swells," Center for American Progress, March 23, 2007, www.americanprogress.org/issues/2007/03/opinion_health_care.html; Sack and Connelly, "In Poll, Wide Support for Government-Run Health."

61.   Todd Gitlin, *The Whole World Is Watching* (Berkeley: University of California Press, 1980); Andrew Rojecki, *Silencing the Opposition: Antinuclear Movements and the Media in the Cold War* (Urbana: University of Illinois Press, 1999); Robert M. Entman, *Projections of Power: Framing News, Public Opinion, and U.S. Foreign Policy* (Chicago: University of Chicago Press, 2004); DiMaggio, *When Media Goes to War*; Jules Boykoff, *The Suppression of Dissent: How the State and Mass Media Squelch American Social Movements* (London: Routledge, 2006); David Croteau and William Hoynes, *By Invitation Only: How the Media Limit Political Debate* (Monroe, ME: Common Courage Press, 1994), 105–37.

62.   For more information on the general success of interest groups in receiving coverage, see Jeffrey Berry, *The New Liberalism: The Rising Power of Citizen Groups* (Washington, D.C.: Brookings Institution Press, 2000). For more information on the potential of progressive groups to receive positive media coverage, see Deepa Kumar, *Outside the Box: Corporate Media, Globalization, and the UPS Strike* (Urbana: University of Illinois, 2007).

63.   For more on this pattern, see Rojecki's *Silencing the Opposition*.

64.   Matt Bai, "For GOP, Sorting Out Candidates Gets Messy," *New York Times*, June 9, 2010, www.nytimes.com/2010/06/10/us/politics/10bai.html.

6. Manufacturing Dissent

1.   Program on International Policy Attitudes (PIPA), "Voters Say Election Full of Misleading and False Information," December 9, 2010, http://www.worldpublicopinion.org/pipa/articles/brunitedstatescanadara/671.php?nid=&id=&pnt=671&lb=.

2.   Ibid.

3.   Kaiser Family Foundation, *Poverty in America*, National Public Radio, 2010, http://www.npr.org/programs/specials/poll/poverty/.

4.   Pew Research Center, "Earmarks Could Help Candidates in the Midterm; Palin and Tea Party Connections Could Hurt," Pew Research Center, August 4, 2010, http://people-press.org/report/642/.

5.   Data for the Pew Research Center July 2009 poll is publicly available via http://people-press.org/dataarchive/.

6.   In deciding whether the various demographic groups in this study were delineated by higher and lower levels of privileged, I examined their relationship at the bivariate level with income in the July 2009 Pew survey. The groups I included in this study were distinguished by greater and lesser affluence, as measured by income. I compared each group to others in order to determine each one's influence on policy attitudes. This was done by using bivariate-ordered logistic regression, while the relationships between each variable and income were significant at the 5 percent level or lower. I followed a similar pro-

cedure for determining whether groups were more or less susceptible to pro-business, hegemonic messages. The variables I include in this category—party, ideology, and Fox News consumption—are all significantly associated with conservative, pro-business ideology. The ideology variable, according to common sense, is distinguished by greater and lesser support for conservative viewpoints. The Fox News and party variables, however, are significantly associated with the ideology variable at the .01 percent level.

7. "Statistical significance" refers to the probability that a relationship was achieved due to chance variation within the sample, or whether that relationship reflects a meaningful association between the variables in question. Every statistical regression run in this chapter controls for a variety of other independent variables, including all of those listed in my list, in addition to controls for age and level of church attendance.

8. I conducted a number of binary logistic multivariate regressions and ordered multivariate logistic regression analyses with regard to opinions of Obama and healthcare. The relationship between being insured and opposing the government on healthcare is significant at the 5 percent level.

9. The relationship between opposition to the public option and being insured is significant at the 1 percent level. The relationship between distrust of government in handling healthcare and being insured is significant at the 5 percent level.

10. The relationship between earning a higher income and distrusting the government in handling healthcare is significant at the 1 percent level. The relationship between earning higher income and opposing taxes on the wealthy to pay for healthcare is significant at the 5 percent level.

11. The relationship between race and trust of government to deal with healthcare reform is significant at the 1 percent level. The relationship between race and opinions of Obama's job approval is significant at the .01 percent level, for race and opinions of Obama's handling of the economy at the 1 percent level, for race and opinions of Obama's handling of healthcare at the 1 percent level, and for race and opinions of Obama's handling of the deficit at the .01 percent level.

12. William Julius Wilson, *The Truly Disadvantaged: The Inner City, the Underclass, and Public Policy* (Chicago: University of Chicago Press, 1987); Melvin L. Oliver and Thomas M. Shapiro, *Black Wealth/White Wealth: A New Perspective on Racial Inequality* (London: Routledge, 1995).

13. Kathleen Hall Jamieson and James Cappella, *Echo Chamber: Rush Limbaugh and the Conservative Media Establishment* (Oxford: Oxford University Press, 2008), 91–104.

14. Ibid., 214–36.

15. Across the 13 questions examined, consumption of Fox News is associated with increased opposition to Obama and Democratic healthcare reform for all variables at the 5 percent level or lower.

16. The relationship between Fox News consumption and opposition to the government on healthcare reform is significant at the .01 percent level.

17. Anthony R. DiMaggio, "You Are What You Watch: Ideology, Polarization, and Partisan Media Consumption," paper presented at the American Association on Public Opinion Research Conference, Chicago, 2010.

18. Jamieson and Cappella, *Echo Chamber*, 2008.

19. Jacob S. Hacker and Paul Pierson, *Off Center: The Republican Revolution and the Erosion of American Democracy* (New Haven: Yale University Press, 2005), 73.

20. Media Matters for America, "Fox Passes Off GOP Press Release as Its Own Research, Typo and All," February 10, 2009, http://mediamatters.org/research/ 200902100019; Media Matters for America, "'Foxfact[s]' About GOP Budget Nearly Identical to GOP Rep. Ryan's Op-Ed," April 1, 2009, http://mediamatters. org/research/200904010017?f=h_latest.

21. Hacker and Pierson, *Off Center*, 180.

22. Hall and Jamieson, *Echo Chamber*, 163-76.

23. Polling data on media consumer habits related to Fox News, CNN, and MSNBC from 2004 through 2009 is publicly available in the Pew Research Center database: http://people-press.org/dataarchive/.

24. Hall and Jamieson, *Echo Chamber*, 245.

25. The relationships between partisanship and opinions of Obama and Democratic healthcare reform are significant for all questions at the 5 percent level or lower.

26. Chris Hedges, *American Fascists: The Christian Right and the War on America* (New York: Free Press, 2006), 18-20.

27. The relationship between income and opinions of government healthcare reform proposals among Evangelicals is significant at the 5 percent level. The relationship between income and Obama's handling of the deficit is significant at the 5 percent level.

28. The relationship between race among Evangelicals and opinions of a government healthcare plan are significant at the 5 percent level.

29. All of these relationships are significant at the 5 percent level or lower.

30. Alton L. Abramowitz, *The Disappearing Center: Engaged Citizens, Polarization, and American Democracy* (New Haven: Yale University Press, 2010); Matthew Levendusky, *The Partisan Sort: How Liberals Became Democrats and Conservatives Became Republicans* (Chicago: University of Chicago Press, 2009).

31. All relationships for ideology and opinions of Obama and healthcare reform are significant at the 5 percent level or lower.

32. Abramowitz, *The Disappearing Center*.

33. All of these relationships are significant at the 5 percent level or lower.

34. John R. Zaller, *The Nature and Origins of Mass Opinion* (Cambridge: Cambridge University Press, 1992); Adam J. Berinsky, *In Time of War: Understanding American Public Opinion from World War II to Iraq* (Chicago: University of Chicago Press, 2009); Anthony R DiMaggio, *When Media Goes to War: Hegemonic Discourse, Public Opinion, and the Limits of Dissent* (New York: Monthly Review Press, 2009).

35. All of these relationships are significant at the 5 percent level or lower.

36. Data for the Pew Research Center October 2009 poll is publicly available at http://people-press.org/dataarchive/.

37. "Fox News/Opinion Dynamics Poll," PollingReport.com, March 16-17, 2010, http://www.pollingreport.com/health2.htm; "CBS News Poll," PollingReport.com, March 29-April 1, 2010, www.pollingreport.com/health2.htm.

38. Hacker and Pierson, *Off Center*, 70-71.

39. Pew Research Center, "Media Less Influential in Views on Health Care, Economy,tThan on Other Issues," September 30, 2009, http://people-press.org/report/548/.

40. Pew Research Center, "Health Care Debate Tops Public Interest, Coverage," 31 March 2010, http://people-press.org/report/601/healthcare.

41. Ibid..

42. Pew Research Center, "Top Stories of 2009: Economy, Obama, and Health Care," December 29, 2009, http://people-press.org/report/575//.

43. Ibid.; Pew Research Center, "Many Fault Media Coverage of Health Care Debate," August 6, 2009, http://pewresearch.org/pubs/1304/health-care-media-coverage-birther-controversy; Pew Research Center, "Health Care Dominates Interest and Coverage," March 17, 2010, http://people-press.org/report/597/healthcare.

44. Pew Research Center, "Top Stories of 2009: Economy, Obama, and Health Care."

45. The relationships between media consumption and opposition to healthcare are found after controlling for various demographic variables, including: sex, race, income, education, ideology, partisanship, age, religious status (Protestant vs. Non-Protestant), church attendance, marital status, voter registration status, and religion (Evangelical vs. Non-Evangelical). The relationship discussed is statistically significant, after controlling for these variables, at the 5 percent level and lower depending on the month in question for the relationship.

46. Pew Research Center, "Most Continue to Say He Brings 'New Approach' to Politics," September 17, 2009, http://people-press.org/reports/pdf/545.pdf.

47. Polling information was drawn from seven different time series, from the Associated Press, CNN, ABC-*Washington Post, USA Today*-Gallup, Pew Research Center, Quinnipiac, Fox News, and is available at the polling aggregator PollingReport.com, http://www.pollingreport.com/politics.htm.

48. Pew Research Center, "Health Care Finale: Heavy Coverage, Huge Interest," 23 March 2010, http://people-press.org/report/600/healthcare; Pew Research Center, "News about the Economy Less Dire, More Hopeful," August 12, 2009, http://people-press.org/report/535/.

49. Samuel Kernell, *Going Public: New Strategies in Presidential Leadership* (Washington, D.C.: CQ Press, 2007).

50. CBS News, "Poll: Obama's Speech Buoyed Public Support," September 11, 2009, http://www.cbsnews.com/8301-503544_162-5302288-503544.html.

51. "Newsweek Poll, February 17-18, 2010," PollingReport.com, 2010, http://www.pollingreport.com/health3.htm; Kaiser Family Foundation, "Kaiser Health Tracking Poll, February 11–16, 2010," PollingReport.com, http://www.pollingreport.com/health3.htm.

52. "NBC News/*Wall Street Journal* Poll," PollingReport.com, March 11–14, 2010, www.pollingreport.com/health3.htm; "Pew Research Center Poll," PollingReport.com, March 10–14, 2010, www.pollingreport.com/health3.htm.

53. Attention to the Tea Party remains significantly correlated with opinions of government healthcare reform at the 5 percent level, after running a multivariate binary logistic regression analysis controlling for all the other independent variables discussed in this chapter.

54.   Lydia Saad, "Tea Partiers are Fairly Mainstream in Their Demographics," Gallup.com, April 5, 2010, www.gallup.com/poll/127181/tea-partiers-fairly-mainstream-demographics.aspx.

55.   Steven Kull, "Big Government is Not the Issue," WorldPublicOpinion.org, August 19, 2010, http://www.worldpublicopinion.org/pipa/articles/brunited-statescanadara/665.php?nid=&id=&pnt=665&lb=brusc.

56.   Lawrence R. Jacobs and Robert Y. Shapiro, *Politicians Don't Pander: Political Manipulation and the Loss of Democratic Responsiveness* (Chicago: University of Chicago Press, 2000), xv, 101.

57.   Ibid., 102–5.

58.   Ibid., 102.

59.   Brandice Canes-Wrone, *Who Leads Whom? Presidents, Policy, and the Public* (Chicago: University of Chicago Press, 2006), 186–87.

60.   Marc J. Hetherington, *Why Trust Matters: Declining Political Trust and the Demise of American Liberalism* (Princeton: Princeton University Press, 2005), 3, 139, 54.

61.   Ibid., 139.

62.   Dana Blanton, "Fox News Poll: 55 Percent Oppose Health Care Reform," FoxNews.com, March 18, 2010, www.foxnews.com/politics/2010/03/18/fox-news-poll-oppose-health-care-reform/.

63.   Martin Gilens, *Why Americans Hate Welfare: Race, Media, and the Politics of Antipoverty Policy* (Chicago: University of Chicago Press, 2000), 195.

64.   Ibid., 216.

65.   Benjamin I. Page and Robert Y. Shapiro, *Class War? What Americans Really Think about Economic Inequality* (Chicago: University of Chicago Press, 2009).

66.   Denny Braun, *The Rich Get Richer: The Rise of Income Inequality in the United States and the World* (Chicago: Nelson Hall Publishers, 1997), 209.

67.   George Orwell, *1984* (New York: Penguin, 1949).

68.   Pew Research Center, "Health Care Proposals Remain Hard to Follow," September 8, 2009, http://people-press.org/report/541/.

69.   Pew Research Center, "More Hearing Good News about Gulf Spill," August 11, 2010, http://people-press.org/report/644/; Pew Research Center, "Mixed Reaction to Leak of Afghan Documents," August 3, 2010, http://people-press.org/report/641/; Pew Research Center, "Public Sees Economic News Turning More Negative," July 8, 2010, http://people-press.org/report/631/; Pew Research Center, "Haiti, Snowstorms, Economy Vie for Public's Attention," February 17, 2010, http://people-press.org/report/590/; Pew Research Center, "Press Gets Good Marks for Covering Economic Troubles," February 11, 2010, http://people-press.org/report/588/; Pew Research Center, "Public Stays with Health Care, Media Focuses on Terror," January 13, 2010, http://people-press.org/report/577/.

70.   Pew Research Center, "Many Say Coverage of the Poor and Minorities is too Negative," August 19, 2010, http://people-press.org/report/646/.

71.   Pew Research Center, "Many Still Critical of Press Handling of Health Care," March 23, 2010, http://people-press.org/reports/pdf/600.pdf .

72.   Pew Research Center, "Health Care Proposals Remain Hard to Follow."

73.   Pew Research Center, "Most Plan to Watch Obama Health Care Speech," September 8, 2009, http://people-press.org/reports/pdf/541.pdf.

74. The data on public confusion regarding healthcare was obtained by contacting Pew directly, as the datasets were not made available publicly on the organization's website.

75. Danny Schechter, *The More You Watch the Less You Know* (New York: Seven Stories Press, 1999).

76. Anthony DiMaggio, "War of the Words: How Town Hall Crashers Are Transforming Public Opinion," Common Dreams, August 22, 2009, www.commondreams.org/view/2009/08/22-7.

77. For a discussion of public ignorance regarding civics IQ test questions, see Michael X. Delli Carpini and Scott Keeter, *What Americans Know about Politics and Why It Matters* (New Haven: Yale University Press, 1996); and John R. Zaller, "Elite Leadership of Mass Opinion: New Evidence from the Gulf War," in *Taken by Storm: The Media, Public Opinion, and U.S. Foreign Policy in the Gulf War*, ed. W. Lance Bennett and David L. Paletz (Chicago: University of Chicago Press, 1994). For a discussion of the lack of consistent ideology among many Americans and the reliance of more politically attentive citizens on elites to form their opinions, see John R. Zaller, *The Nature and Origins of Mass Opinion* (Cambridge: Cambridge University Press, 1992); Adam J. Berinsky, *In Time of War: Understanding American Public Opinion from World War II to Iraq* (Chicago: University of Chicago Press, 2009); Scott L. Althaus, *Collective Preferences in Democratic Politics: Opinion Surveys and the Will of the People* (Cambridge: Cambridge University Press, 2003); Angus Campbell, Philip E. Converse, Warren E. Miller, and Donald E. Stokes, *The American Voter: Unabridged Edition* (Chicago: University of Chicago Press, 1960); Philip E. Converse, "The Nature of Belief Systems in Mass Publics," in *Ideology and Discontent*, ed. David E. Apter (New York: Free Press, 1964).

78. For a discussion of the rational public theory in the literature on public opinion, see Arthur Lupia and Matthew D. McCubbins, *The Democratic Dilemma: Can Citizens Learn What They Need to Know?* (Cambridge: Cambridge University Press, 1998); Benjamin I. Page and Robert Y. Shapiro, *The Rational Public* (Chicago: University of Chicago Press, 1992); Samuel L. Popkin, *The Reasoning Voter: Communication and Persuasion in Presidential Campaigns* (Chicago: University of Chicago Press, 1994); James A. Stimson, *Public Opinion in America: Moods, Cycles, and Swings* (Boulder, CO: Westview Press, 1999); William A. Gamson, *Talking Politics* (Cambridge: Cambridge University Press, 1992); Doris A. Graber, *Processing Politics: Learning from Television in the Internet Age* (Chicago: University of Chicago Press, 2001); John Mueller, *Policy and Opinion in the Gulf War* (Chicago: University of Chicago Press, 1994); and Christopher Gelpi, Peter D. Feaver, and Jason Reifler, *Paying the Human Costs of War: American Public Opinion and Casualties in Military Conflicts* (Princeton: Princeton University Press, 2009).

Conclusion: The Post-Midterm Tea Party
and the Wisconsin Revolt

1. Marc Lacey, "Tea Party Groups Issue Warning to the GOP," *New York Times*, February 26, 2011, www.nytimes.com/2011/02/27/us/politics/27teaparty.html.

2. Robin Abcarian, "Tea Party Activists Rally at National Policy Conference," *Los Angeles Times*, February 26, 2011, http://articles.latimes.com/2011/feb/26/nation/la-na-tea-party-20110227.

3. Paul West, "Conference to Serve as Preview of 'Tea Party' Influence in 2012," February 10, 2011, http://articles.latimes.com/2011/feb/10/nation/la-na-cpac-20110210.

4. Felicia Sonmez, "PATRIOT Act Extension Passes House, One Week after Unexpected Defeat," *Washington Post*, February 14, 2011, http://voices.washingtonpost.com/44/2011/02/patriot-act-extension-passes-h.html.

5. David Brooks, "The Mother of All No-Brainers," *New York Times*, July 4, 2011, http://www.nytimes.com/2011/07/05/opinion/05brooks.html.

6. Stephen Stromberg, "After Health Care Reform Repeal, Tea Party Disappointment," *Washington Post*, January 19, 2011, http://voices.washingtonpost.com/postpartisan/2011/01/health-care_reform_repeal_and.html.

7. For a discussion of this rhetorical threat, see these columns, one from a conservative and the other from a liberal, warning about the dangers of Republican threats of debt default: Brooks, "The Mother of All No-Brainers," July 4, 2011; Paul Krugman, "Debt Limit Stakes," *New York Times*, June 28, 2011, http://krugman.blogs.nytimes.com/2011/06/28/debt-limit-stakes/.

8. Monica Davey, "Palin Speaks at Tea Party Rally in Madison," *New York Times*, April 16, 2011, www.nytimes.com/2011/04/17/us/politics/17palin.html; Monica Davey and G. Sulzberger, "Dueling Protests in a Capital as Nothing Much Gets Done," *New York Times*, February 19, 2011, www.nytimes.com/2011/02/20/us/politics/20wisconsin.html.

9. Davey, "Palin Speaks at Tea Party Rally in Madison."

10. For an indication of the earnings of the top 1 percent, see this 2007 *New York Times* story, which estimates such earnings are on average about $350,000: David Cay Johnston, "Income Gap Is Widening, Data Shows," *New York Times*, March 29, 2007, www.nytimes.com/2007/03/29/business/29tax.html. Many of the Tea Party leaders discussed here exceed this figure, while others earn a bit less, though within the same ballpark.

11. Adele M. Stan, "5 Professional Tea Partiers: Who's Sucking the Most Money from the Movement" Alternet, May 12, 2011, http://www.alternet.org/tea-party/150902/5_professional_tea_partiers%3A_who's_sucking_the_most_money_from_the_movement/?page=1.

12. U.S. Social Forum, "Funder Delegation to the US Social Forum: Detroit," *U.S. Social Forum*, June 21–25, 2010, www.fntg.org/test/fntg/docs/FNTGUSSF DelegationReport-OnlineVersion.pdf; Liz Ford, "World Social Forum Activists Buoyed by Fall of Egypt and Tunisia Regimes," *Guardian*, February 14, 2011, www.guardian.co.uk/global-development/2011/feb/14/world-social-forum-ends-activists-buoyed.

13. For more on the headlining of the 2011 Phoenix Tea Party convention, see Marc Lacey, "Tea Party Groups Issue Warning to the GOP," *New York Times*, February 26, 2011, http://www.nytimes.com/2011/02/27/us/politics/27tea-party.html; Robin Abcarian, "Tea Party Activists Rally at National Policy Conference," *Los Angeles Times*, February 26, 2011, http://articles.latimes.com/2011/feb/26/nation/la-na-tea-party-20110227; CNN, "Herman

Cain Wins Tea Party Presidential Live Straw Poll at Phoenix Summit," February 27, 2011, http://politicalticker.blogs.cnn.com/2011/02/27/herman-cain-wins-tea-party-presidential-live-straw-poll-at-phoenix-summit/; Associated Press, "Tea Party Supporters Pack Convention to Scope Out 2012 Candidates," Foxnews.com, February 26, 2011, http://www.foxnews.com/politics/2011/02/26/tea-party-supporters-pack-convention-scope-2012-candidates/. For more on the media's fixation on the Tea Party convention rather than the World Social Forum, see Julie Hollar, "Tea Party vs. U.S. Social Forum," *Extra!* September 2010, http://www.fair.org/index.php?page=4143.

14.   Stephanie Mencimer, "Will Palin Announce Presidential Bid at Tea Party Conference?" *Mother Jones*, February 11, 2011, http://motherjones.com/mojo/2011/02/tea-party-patriots-sarah-palin-phoenix.

15.   An analysis of the Thomas legislative database in mid-July 2011 (the database collects basic information on all legislation considered in Congress) finds hundreds of bills that were considered in the House of Representatives in the 112th Congress. This analysis, however, is primarily concerned with bills of major significance that receive major coverage in the mass media and heated discussion among political officials. The scholars discussed in n. 27 have already examined the entire universe of Tea Party votes through mid-2011 and found no substantive difference between Tea Party and non–Tea Party Republicans on political-economic issues. My analysis, then, is mainly concerned with exploring the lack of such differences on highly salient, high-stakes legislation.

16.   For the House voting record on the PATRIOT Act, see Office of the Clerk, "Final Vote Results for U.S. Roll Call 36: H.R. 514," U.S. House of Representatives, February 14, 2011, http://clerk.house.gov/evs/2011/ roll036.xml.

17.   U.S. Senate, "On Passage of the Bill H.R. 514 as Amended," Roll Call Votes, February 15, 2011, www.senate.gov/legislative/LIS/roll_call_lists/roll_call_vote_cfm.cfm?congress=112&session=1&vote=00019#position.

18.   U.S. Congress, "House Vote on Passage: H.R. 2: Repealing the Job Killing Health Care Law Act," Govtrack.us, January 19, 2011, www.govtrack.us/congress/vote.xpd?vote=h2011-14.

19.   David M. Herszenhorn, "Senate Democrats to Allow Early Vote on Health Care Repeal," *New York Times*, February 1, 2011, www.nytimes.com/2011/02/02/health/policy/02cong.html.

20.   "Republicans Introduce Balanced Budget Amendment," Republican.Senate.gov, March 31, 2011, http://republican.senate.gov/public/ index.cfm?FuseAction=blogs.view&blog_id=17898fbe-7b7c-4638-8bda-b39f6c6da787.

21.   For a list of all co-sponsors, see Library of Congress, "Bill Summary & Status: 112th Congress: H.J. Res. 2 Cosponsors," in Thomas database, January 5, 2011, http://thomas.loc.gov/cgi-bin/bdquery/z?d112:HJ00002:@@@P|/bss/.

22.   James Oliphant, "Democrats Seek to Pin Downgrade on 'Tea Party,'" *Los Angeles Times*, August 8, 2011, http://www.latimes.com/news/politics/la-pn-dems-downgrade-20110808,0,1362570.story; Theo Emery, "Kerry Calls Lower Credit Rating a 'Tea Party Downgrade,'" *Boston Globe*, August 8, 2011, http://www.boston.com/Boston/politicalintelligence/2011/08/kerry-calls-lower-credit-rating-tea-party-downgrade/7yh1wRgUqtKT5SZfOktH3K/index.html.

23. S. A. Miller, "Biden: Tea Party Stands for 'Terrorist,'" *New York Post*, August 2, 2011, http://www.nypost.com/p/news/national/biden_tea_stands_for_terrorist_WEL1JQbZ4aTL594RL6vZEL.

24. Alexander Bolton, "McConnell Has Senate Tea Party Problem," The Hill, July 2, 2011, http://thehill.com/homenews/senate/169505-mcconnell-has-his-own-tea-party-problem.

25. Philip Rucker, "Sen. Mike Lee: A Political Insider Refashions Himself as a Tea Party Revolutionary," *Washington Post*, February 5, 2011, http://www.washingtonpost.com/wp-dyn/content/article/2011/02/04/AR2011020406719.html.

26. See the following figures: "Party Polarization 1879–2010: Distance between the Parties' First Dimension," "Senate 1879–2010: Party Means on a Liberal Conservative Dimension," and "House 1879–2010: Party Means on a Liberal Conservative Dimension," at http://polarizedamerica.com/.

27. DW Nominate is a measurement of polarization in Congress. It is a dataset, based on the voting records of individual members of Congress. It is maintained by a number of congressional scholars, such as Keith Poole, Howard Rosenthal, and Nolan McCarthy, and is widely respected as one of the most authoritative (perhaps the most authoritative) measure of congressional polarization, as based on a recording of all votes cast over more than 100 years.

28. "Scaling Members of Congress Who Have Signed the 'Cut, Cap, and Balance' Pledge," Voteview Blog, July 7, 2011, http://voteview.spia.uga.edu/blog/.

29. "Scaling Members with Optimal Classification," Voteview Blog, http://voteview.spia.uga.edu/blog/?p=1585.

30. For a discussion of public opinion on these issues, see Anthony DiMaggio, "Masters of Spin: Rightwing Manipulation of the Wisconsin Revolt," *CounterPunch*, February 25–26, 2011, www.counterpunch.org/dimaggio0225 2011.html.

31. Discussion of polls that allege public opposition to worker and union rights appear in the following articles: Bruce Drake, "Polls Conflict on Public View of Bargaining Rights for Government Workers," Politics Daily, March 2, 2011, http://www.politicsdaily.com/2011/03/02/polls-conflict-on-publics-view-of-bargaining-rights-for-governm/; Scott Rasmussen, "What You Can Learn about Wisconsin Dispute from Differences in Poll Questions," Rasmussen Reports, March 17, 2011, www.rasmussenreports.com/public_content/political_commentary/commentary_by_scott_rasmussen/what_you_can_learn_about_wisconsin_dispute_from_differences_in_poll_questions; Stephen F. Hayes, "Americans' Message to States: Cut, Don't Tax and Borrow," NPR.org, March 17, 2011, http://www.npr.org/2011/03/17/134621387/weekly-standard-the-false-claims-on-wisconsin; Lydia Saad, "Americans' Message to States: Cut, Don't Tax and Borrow," Gallup.com, March 9, 2011, www.gallup.com/poll/146525/Americans-Message-States-Cut-Dont-Tax-Borrow.aspx.

32. Anthony DiMaggio, "The Great Budget Repair Swindle," *Z Magazine*, March 4, 2011, http://www.zcommunications.org/the-great-budget-repair-swindle-by-anthony-dimaggio.

33. Again, see chapter 1 of this book.

34. For these estimates, see Paul Street and Janet Razbadouski, "It's Not about $, It's about Rights," *Z Magazine*, February 24, 2011, http://www.zcommunica-

tions.org/it-s-not-about-it-s-about-rights-by-paul-street; Patricia Barden, "Wisconsin Protests, Saturday February 19, 2011," PR Watch, February 19, 2011, http://www.prwatch.org/news/2011/02/10091/wisconsin-protests-saturday-february-19-2011; Associated Press, "Madison Protests Hit Largest Numbers on Saturday," Huffington Post, February 19, 2011, http://www.huffingtonpost.com/2011/02/19/madison-protests_n_825616.html.

35.   Associated Press, "Labor Crowd Surrounds Palin's Tea Party Rally," CBSNews.com, April 16, 2011, http://www.cbsnews.com/stories/2011/04/16/politics/main20054601.shtml.

36.   For one example, see Chicago Tea Party Lexington Green and Steve Stevlic's condemnations of Wisconsin unions for organizing opposition to Walker as an affront to individual liberty and personal responsibility: Lexington Green, "Madison Tea Party Rally Ground Report," Chicago Tea Party, February 21, 2011, www.teaparty-chicago.org/posts/madison-tea-party-rally-on-the-ground-report; Bruce Wolf and Dan Proft, "Wisconsin Protest Interview with Steve Stevlic," WLS 890AM, www.wlsam.com/Article.asp?id=2115187&spid=37837.

37.   Colby Robertson and Julia Fello, "Palin Speaks at Wisconsin Tea Party Rally," ABC 27 Madison-WKOW.com, www.wkow.com/Global/story.asp?S=14458850.

38.   For a full background on the Sam Adam's Alliance, see Stephanie Mencimer, "Wisconsin: Tea Partiers, Breitbart Coming to Fight Unions," *Mother Jones*, February 18, 2011, http://motherjones.com/mojo/2011/02/wisconsin-tea-partiers-breitbart-fight-unions.

39.   Media Matters for America, "Tea Party Confessions: 'There Would Not Have Been a Tea Party without Fox,' May 23, 2011, http://mediamatters.org/research/201105230011.

40.   Rich Noyes and Scott Whitlock, "Wisconsin Unions vs. the Tea Party: A Classic Double Standard," Media Research Center, February 22, 2011, www.mrc.org/realitycheck/realitycheck/2011/20110222015522.aspx.

41.   See chapter 5 of this book.

42.   Brian Montopoli, "Tea Party Supporters: Who They Are and What They Believe," CBSNews.com, April 14, 2010, http://www.cbsnews.com/8301-503544_162-20002529-503544.html.

43.   See Paul Street and Anthony DiMaggio, *Crashing the Tea Party: Mass Media and the Campaign to Remake American Politics* (Boulder, CO: Paradigm Publishers, 2011).

44.   My examination of Tea Party stories including any references to the words "Tea Party" throughout the period in question. I included in my list of Madison protest stories any that mentioned "Scott Walker" or "Wisconsin" within 50 words of a reference to "demonstration," "demonstrators," "protest," or "protesters/protestors." Stories covering the Tea Party as a movement had to include the words "Tea Party" appearing within 50 words of a reference to "movement." Stories covering the Madison protests as a mass movement had to include the words "Scott Walker" or "Wisconsin" appearing within 50 words of a reference to "demonstrators," to a "demonstration," to "protest," or "protesters/protestors," which then appeared within 50 words of a reference to the "movement."

Index